ARMED FORCES

Edward Steichen. Sailors sleeping on the flight deck of the USS *Lexington*. Courtesy: National Archives and Records Administration. Photo no. 80-G-471182

ARMED FORCES

Masculinity and Sexuality in the American War Film

ROBERT EBERWEIN

RUTGERS UNIVERSITY PRESS
NEW BRUNSWICK, NEW JERSEY, AND LONDON

Library of Congress Cataloging-in-Publication Data

Eberwein, Robert T., 1940–
Armed forces : masculinity and sexuality in the American war film / Robert Eberwein.
   p. cm.
  Includes bibliographical references and index.
  ISBN-13: 978–0-8135–4079–5 (hardcover : alk. paper)
  ISBN-13: 978–0-8135–4080–1 (pbk. : alk. paper)
  1. War films—United States—History and criticism. 2. Male friendship in motion pictures. 3. Masculinity in motion pictures. I. Title.
  PN1995.9.W3E24 2007
  791.43′658—dc22

                                  2006032571

A British Cataloging-in-Publication record for this book is available from the British Library.

Manufactured in the United States of America

For Dolores Burdick

CONTENTS

ACKNOWLEDGMENTS

I am indebted to a number of individuals. First, at the Margaret Herrick Library, Academy of Motion Picture Arts and Sciences, I am especially grateful to Barbara Hall for her thoughtful and invaluable suggestions that helped in my investigation of Production Code Administration files; Val Almendarez's masterful cataloging of Lester Cowan's papers; and Kristine Krueger's expeditious response for information. Joshua Hirsch at the Archive Research and Study Center at the University of California at Los Angeles coordinated my viewing of several hard-to-find films. Others who helped in various ways are Patricia King Hanson at the American Film Institute; Dorinda Hartman at the Wisconsin Center for Film and Theater Research; Jennifer Ormson at the Library of Congress; Holly Reed at the Still Picture Branch of the National Archives and Records Administration; and Rachelle G. Weissenburger, administrator, the Edison Papers, Rutgers University.

Peter Lehman provided wise advice, sustained support, and encouragement for my earlier exploration of this topic, which first appeared in his anthology *Masculinity: Bodies, Movies, Culture* (Routledge, 2001). Material from that essay appears in several chapters of this book. Some of the commentary on *The Deer Hunter* was published earlier in the *Journal of Popular Film and Television*.

Krin Gabbard and Bill Luhr helped my thinking about parts of this book. Tom Doherty continues to be a genial authority and a major source of information for all students of the war film. Thanks to Jeanine Basinger, Steven Cohan, Kathryn Kalinac, and Charles Musser for their assistance. Thanks also to Douglas Cunningham, Joseph DeMent, Susan Hawkins, Tim Moran, Amos Williams, and former students James Pettinato, Dennis Peterson, and Stephanie Howse.

Several kind people at Photofest, Inc. merit special notice for their diligent assistance in helping me locate photographs: Eliza Brown, Derek Davidson, Andrew McGovern, and Buddy Weiss. Special thanks to Ronald Mandelbaum for his patience. Marina Beedle at Hite Over-Night has been very helpful.

At Oakland University, I'm fortunate in having access to the Kresge Library and its supportive and consistently helpful faculty and staff: Linda Hildebrand, Marilyn Jereau, Kristine Kondic, Mildred Merz, and Dan Ring. Patricia Clark and Dante Rance in Interlibrary Loans found everything I needed. Those in Classroom Support and Instructional Technical Services have helped tremendously: George Preisinger, assistant vice president; Linda Barc; Matthew Mangold; and Steve Sapilewski. Thanks to John A. Coughlin in E-Learning and Instructional Support.

I'm especially grateful to Andrea Eis, chair of Art and Art History, and Brian Murphy, professor emeritus of English, who have been a joy to work with as colleagues teaching film and as friends offering valued assistance. I have received generous support for my scholarship from former and current deans of the College of Liberal Arts and Sciences David Downing and Ronald Sudol, and chairs of the Department of English Bruce Mann and Kevin Grimm. Rosemary Aiello, administrative secretary, has helped in more ways than she knows. Dana Pierce, technological wizard extraordinaire, made it possible to handle the vagaries of the computer.

Robert Burchfield of Doghouse Editing and Research Services offered helpful recommendations. I'm also very grateful to four individuals at Rutgers University Press. I appreciate the helpful work of Anne Hegeman on the book's production and the suggestions of Alicia Nadkarni, editorial assistant and copublications coordinator. Yet once more, Marilyn Campbell, pre-press director, provided sharp advice and guidance. Any expression of thanks for Leslie Mitchner, editor in chief, will be inadequate. This book wouldn't exist if it weren't for her encouragement and superb editorial judgment. If there were a Nobel Prize for editing, she would get it.

Last—thanks to Jane, for tolerating all the noise and providing a war-free zone.

ARMED FORCES

DEFINITIONS

First—the cover and frontispiece of this book. They show a photograph taken by Edward Steichen in 1943, somewhere in the Pacific. We see three exhausted sailors on the USS *Lexington*. They support one another: one's head rests on another's stomach; that man's head and arms rest on a third man. It takes a while to sort out the placement of their arms, particularly in the middle of the photograph, where three arms form a complex triangle, completed by the head of the sailor who is touching his cap. There's also a fourth sailor, not part of the group of men lying down; he seems to rubbing his head. It isn't exactly clear how much we can infer about them, other than they must know each other sufficiently well enough to permit and share this physical intimacy. Curiously, even though the photograph shows someone looking, it is the viewer of the photograph rather than the fourth sailor who observes the tableau. We can't know if his glance away from them indicates indifference or distraction. The composition of the photograph puts the burden of interpretation on the external rather than the internal viewer. The weary subjects of the photograph cannot analyze their own representation. But we are incapable of ignoring such an extraordinary moment of supportive bonding and, unlike the fourth sailor, feel compelled to attempt to understand its meaning and significance. Even though there is physical intimacy, the contact is not sexualized in any way. In fact, the more one looks at the photograph, the more aware one becomes of the vulnerability and isolation of all the men, resting or awake. At this moment of relief, no one has a weapon.

Next—a quotation. "Don't fight. Don't fight. You love each other. Yes?" A random sample of cinephiles as to its source would likely produce several responses saying that (except for the syntax) it sounds as if it occurs at the moment when Tess Millay (Joanne Dru) scolds Tom Dunson (John Wayne) and Matt Garth (Montgomery Clift) at the end of Howard Hawks's western *Red River* (1948). To stop the men from fighting, Tess shoots a bullet at them and shouts: "Stop it!

Stop this fighting! Any fool with half a mind would know you love each other!"
But those who guessed this film would be wrong. No audiences have ever heard
this line of dialogue spoken. It first appears as an intertitle in Raoul Walsh's
World War I film *What Price Glory* (1926) when Charmaine (Dolores Del Rio)
says it to Sergeant Quirt (Edmund Lowe) and Captain Flagg (Victor McLaglen),
tough, brawling best friends who have been rivals for her love.

It's an important moment for the war film and cinematic history. Although
rivalry between friends for the same woman is a narrative commonplace, to my

What Price Glory. Publicity still. Courtesy: Photofest. © 20th Century Fox, 1926.

knowledge this is the first time that any character identifies this particular kind of complexity in the relationship between two men in a war film (or any other kind, for that matter). In this case, a woman given a voice to analyze how the men feel about each other articulates what neither man is capable of saying for himself, much less understanding.[1] Charmaine clearly realizes the love of Quirt and Flagg is not erotic, in contrast to their sexual desire for her and hers for them. In effect, she is saying: "You courageous soldiers share a love that is different in kind from what each of us has separately as a couple."

Steichen's photograph shows men in an intimate physical relationship that is not erotic. As soon as one understands its signification—these are exhausted buddies supporting each other—one realizes the interpretive challenges involved with analysis of something that denies at one level of signification what it apparently shows at another. In the case of *What Price Glory*, neither Charmaine nor its creators intend any suggestion about homosexuality because it simply isn't relevant. Men, even the combative, violent, excessively masculine heroes of this film, are capable of feeling affection. Nonetheless, Charmaine's comment unintentionally introduces the issue of male sexuality. The counterpart of their intense sexual love for her is the comparably strong nonsexual love each has for the other. In effect, to have the woman in question say "your love is *not* sexual" is to acknowledge the possibility of its alternative. The moment one begins to clarify something as "is not," the repressed of the term surfaces, albeit ever so slightly.

The photograph and *What Price Glory* introduce the aims I have in this book: to distinguish nonerotic love and affection between comrades in war films from both homosexual and heterosexual love, and to explore the complex relationship between masculinity and sexuality. Although a number of fine studies of the war film and masculinity have addressed these issues, none has made them the principal focus.[2]

Speaking of the male bonding in *Red River*, Donald Spoto offers a particularly trenchant suggestion that applies to *What Price Glory* and many other works to be examined here:

> For Hawks, the male bonding is a metasexual affinity. It points at the radical personal incompleteness his characters feel within themselves, an emptiness that may be filled in some respects by a woman, but in other respects only by another man. It is, finally, one of the highest forms of spiritual love, and is quite another thing than a homosexual relationship, as it's quite another thing than a heterosexual relationship. It's the kind of affinity, in the final analysis, toward which all other beautiful and true commitments tend.[3]

Spoto is essentially describing such bonding as liminal—neither heterosexual nor homosexual.[4] As will be clear, I think adopting this kind of conception can help significantly in sorting through the complexities of relationships in war films.

PROBLEMS OF GENRE

The fact I begin this introduction by referring to a western immediately raises the issue of what's unique about the war film. If the narrative situation involving the nonsexual love between men can move between genres, why devote a book to masculinity and sexuality in one genre exclusively? Jeanine Basinger titles one of her chapters in *The World War II Combat Film* "Problems of Genre"—with good reason. In it she identifies a number of narrative elements in the prison film *Brute Force* (Jules Dassin, 1947) that employ the conventions of the war film: "There is a group of representative men from diversified backgrounds and nationalities"; "They are without female companionship"; "They dream and talk of home, and of their former lives before they were forced into this group or situation"; "They look at a 'pin-up' and fantasize about women"; "They all die by gunfire, trying to achieve their objective."[5] Her discussion of this and another film leads to her observation that "the basic combat genre story can be relocated to another equally well established genre without changing the original generic definition. In other words, what defines one genre can appear in another without damaging either."[6]

Rick Altman's helpful definition of generic elements is relevant: "We can as a whole distinguish between generic definitions that depend on a list of common traits, attitudes, characters, shots, locations, sets, and the like—thus stressing the semantic elements that make up the genre—and definitions that play up instead certain constitutive relationships between undesignated and variable place-holders—relationships that might be called the genre's fundamental syntax. The semantic approach thus stresses the genre's building blocks, while the syntactic view privileges the structures into which they are arranged."[7] He uses this terminology to address the same kind of issue raised by Basinger and observes that the war films "*All Through the Night* (Vincent Sherman, 1942), *Sherlock Holmes and the Voice of Terror* (John Rawlins, 1942), or the serial *Don Winslow of the Navy* (1943) simply transfer to a new set of semantic elements the righteous cops-punish-criminals syntax that the gangster genre of the early 30s had turned to starting with *G-Men* (William Keighley, 1935)."[8]

Steve Neale surveys various examples of definitions of the war film, pointing out that some of the lack of consistency "may stem from an awareness of the extent to which generic overlap can occur, of the extent to which a service comedy like *The Wackiest Ship in the Army* ([Richard Murphy,] 1960) can culminate in scenes of serious combat, or the extent to which a 'combat film' like *Battle Cry* ([Raoul Walsh,] 1955) can include scenes of personal drama."[9]

But even though conventions can move between genres, and while there may be generic overlap, as Neale, Basinger, and Altman demonstrate, the issues of masculinity and sexuality in the war film are, as I understand them, distinctive because of the spectatorial stakes. In no other genre does the audience's relationship to characters (cowboys, gangsters, detectives, insurance salesmen) have quite the same history or significance as it does to soldiers. Beginning in 1898, with the appearance of various kinds of films about the Spanish-American War, audiences were able to watch actual and fictionalized soldiers in a context with a unique gendered logic that extends to the present. The fictionalized characters in narratives are assumed to be like the real soldiers in documentary-like newsreels in regard to assumptions about masculinity.

Basinger's insight about the "reality" of war pertains to this issue: "There is a strong link between the Western and the combat film. . . . Both also have historical roots, and both undergo the evolutionary process, reflecting changing ideology. . . . Westerns are based on myths, even though there was a real West. World War II films are based on reality, even though there is a myth. This has to do with the development of film. We never saw the real West of the 1870s captured on moving film for us, but we did have the real World War II on film. This changes a viewer's relationship to filmed narratives."[10] Precisely. Since 1898, films about war (even earlier ones) have been shown to audiences who "know" the reality of war, directly as combatants or, more likely, as viewers who have experienced depictions of masculinity in wars through films.

There is, though, another kind of knowledge of war inherently present in our experience of war films and our relationship to the soldiers. Barbara Ehrenreich's theory about the origins of war posits a number of elements, one being that, as humans, we are programmed to respond to dangers:

> We can say . . . that human beings inherit certain patterned responses to threats and that the threat which originally selected for these processes was probably that of predation. It seems likely, then, that the primordial experience of predation at least *colors* our emotional responses to situations other than predation itself—the sight of violence or bloodshed occasioned by our fellow humans, for example. This does not mean that we "remember," in any Jungian or mystical sense, the alarm felt by our distant ancestors when a leopard pounced on one of their comrades and began to rip him apart; only that there was an evolutionary advantage to the ability to feel this alarm, and that this ability has been passed along to us. . . . Thus, even in our relatively predator-free modern environment, the sight of bloodshed can trigger the fight-or-flight response, or at least a mild version of it: Our hearts beat faster, we breathe more rapidly; our skin may blanch and viscera contract. We pay attention.[11]

And masculinity is the chief element in war, which is, she suggests, "one of the most rigidly 'gendered' activities known to humankind."[12] In fact, war "is an activity that has often served to *define* manhood itself—which is exactly what we would expect if war in fact originated as substitute occupation for underemployed male hunter-defenders."[13] She believes "there is no compelling biological or 'natural' reason why men have so exclusively starred in the drama of war. Men make wars for many reasons, but one of the most recurring ones is to establish that they are, in fact, 'real men.' Warfare and aggressive masculinity have been, in other words, mutually reinforcing cultural enterprises."[14]

While Ehrenreich does not posit a "Jungian or mystical sense" for this phenomenon, it is nonetheless rooted in human experience. Appearing in the late nineteenth century as the United States began the Spanish-American War, the first war films displayed the kind of "aggressive masculinity" Ehrenreich sees supporting warfare, even as they entered into a context in which contemporaries were worried about a crisis in masculinity. That is, the war film originates in a gendered context that valorizes masculinity at a time of war. While certain narrative elements can move from it to other genres, its roots in a particular connection to reality and to the original viewer's relationship to the reality depicted in the films are unique.

TERMINOLOGY

Some of the most useful definitions of masculinity and sexuality I have found display a resistance to strict dichotomies similar to that informing Spoto's refusal to conceive of male bonding as homosexual or heterosexual. For example, explaining the various models for understanding and defining masculinity, R. W. Connell describes four main approaches: *essentialist* (taking "one feature that defines the core of the masculine"); *positivist* ("a simple definition of masculinity: what men actually are"); *normative* ("offer[s] a standard; masculinity is what men ought to be"); and *semiotic* ("a system of symbolic difference" in which masculinity is "defined as not-femininity").[15] Connell rejects any kind of narrowly conceived definition of masculinity: "Rather than attempting to define masculinity as an object (a natural character type, a behavioural average, a norm) we need to focus on the processes and relationships through which men and women conduct gendered lives. 'Masculinity,' to the extent the term can be defined at all, is simultaneously a place in gender relations, the practices through which men and women engage in that place in gender, and the effects of these practices in bodily experience, personality and culture."[16]

In addition to conceiving of masculinity as "a configuration of gender practice" and "necessarily a social construction," Connell makes an important distinction: "Masculinity *refers* to male bodies (sometimes directly, sometimes symbolically and indirectly), but it is not *determined* by male biology. It is, thus, perfectly logical to talk about masculine women or masculinity in women's lives, as well as masculinity in men's lives."[17]

A comparable caution in regard to applying either/or definitions appears in certain explanations of sexuality. For example, acknowledging the lack of agreement on the specific meanings of "sex, gender, and sexuality," Stevi Jackson and Sue Scott use the term "gender" to cover all aspects of what it means to be a woman or man and to refer to the social and cultural distinctions between women and men. "Sexuality" is then reserved for aspects of personal and social life which have erotic significance. In this sense, the concept of "sexuality" remains somewhat fluid, in part because what is deemed erotic, and hence sexual in this sense, is not fixed. . . . In using this rather slippery term, we wish to convey the idea that sexuality is not limited to "sex acts," but involves our sexual feelings and relationships, the ways we are or are not defined as sexual by others, and the ways in which we define ourselves.[18]

Joseph Bristow offers another measured response:

Sexuality is surely connected with sex. But if we find ourselves pressed to define what is meant by sex, then the situation becomes somewhat more complicated. . . . A sign with various connotations, sex refers not only to sexual activity (*to have sex*), it also marks the distinction between male and female anatomy (*to have a sex*). So it would perhaps be wise to think twice about the ways in which sexuality might be implicated in these distinct frameworks of understanding. Is sexuality supposed to designate sexual desire? Or does it refer instead to one's sexed being? If we find ourselves answering yes to both enquiries, then sexuality would appear to embrace ideas about pleasure *and* physiology, fantasy *and* anatomy. On reflection, then, sexuality emerges as a term that points to both internal and external phenomena, to both the realm of the psyche and the material world.

In a comment that recalls Connell's description of masculinity as "a place in gender relations," Bristow thinks that, "given the equivocal meaning of sex, one might suggest that sexuality occupies a place where sexed bodies (in all their shapes and sizes) and sexual desires (in all their multifariousness) intersect only to separate."[19]

While it may seem to complicate their meanings even more, such a spatialization of the concepts offers a potentially rich model for understanding their relevance in the narrative spaces of war films: representations of masculinity and sexuality in films occur not only in a narrative space visible on the screen but also in a liminal cultural-sexual space. Like the eye-fooling figure-ground figures, these spaces constantly shift their particular venues and our relation to them: at once a part of a particular narrative being presented and, simultaneously, an overdetermined site where all the complicated interrelationships between males and females come into play.

MASCULINITY, MODERNITY, AND THE FIRST WAR FILMS

War films appeared at a crucial moment in both American military and social history. The United States had begun its international expansion by engaging in the Spanish-American War, which began in April 1898. Judith A. Allen, K. A. Cuordileone, and Kristen Whissel provide helpful commentary about this period in terms of a number of developments. Allen suggests that the late 1890s were troubled by a "crisis in masculinity" and identifies the perceived "foes" as

> decadence—the spread of "unmanly" urban subcultures, including those of visible homosexuality; a literary vogue for sadism that rejected middle-class masculine values, the economic depression imperiling breadwinner status; white-collar work and other changes in patterns of male work; woman suffrage advocacy; female political activism, including pacifism; the New Woman, riding bicycles, deferring marriage, reducing childbearing, undertaking higher education and paid work; and a general blurring of carefully constructed dichotomous gender distinctions.[20]

Cuordileone suggests that this concern about a crisis in masculinity needs to be seen in conjunction with another phenomenon, modernity: "Concerns about male softness are surely as old as man himself, expressions of a 'crisis' in masculinity a recurrent feature of modernity. In particular, the late-nineteenth-century and early-twentieth-century American society saw a surge of anxiety about manhood, as bureaucratization, urbanization, commercialization, and social reform undermined older sources of masculine identity."[21]

Whissel connects the advent of the war to both modernity and the invention of motion pictures: "The rise of US overseas imperialism marks an unmistakable point of convergence between modernity's circulatory patterns and early cinematic forms of representation. Not only did the Spanish-American War coincide with the rise of the moving pictures, it is also inseparable from the American experience of modernity."[22]

"Convergence" is the key word here, since any consideration of masculinity and sexuality necessarily has to acknowledge a complex network of related elements. One cannot talk about a crisis in masculinity without relating it to the cultural episteme as well as to technology. This is of particular importance to keep in mind since the earliest war films of 1898 and 1899 don't offer even the slightest indication of a crisis in masculinity. There were three types of films. "Actualities" presented "actual" events pertaining to the war; anticipating later newsreels, they offered home-front viewers a kind of documentary perspective on the conflict. "Re-enactments" were fictionalized works that staged events, many with historical aspects such as those involving the Rough Riders. Narrative films interwove elements of the war with fictional stories.[23] All three kinds of films about the Spanish-American War focus on the valor, heroism, masculine power, and attributes being displayed in defense of the American public from the external threat posed by Spain. None of the films I have seen or read about depict anything that could be taken as illustrating what was understood at the time to be an internal threat: the crisis in masculinity.

Since the films capitalized on the widespread support and enthusiasm for the war, it would be inaccurate and disingenuous to read them as intentionally conscious responses to the crisis in masculinity, even though it's certainly possible to speculate that the depictions of heroic males engaged in military actions might have served as a means to assuage fears about the crisis described by Allen and Cuordileone. And we know that the hegemonic predominance of a genre at particular moments in a culture's experience of itself bears noting, as occurs obviously enough with the role played by the gangster film in the 1930s in relation to the Depression.

Certainly there are films that directly demonstrate the response of the time to various kinds of anxieties. Steven Cohan and Susan Jeffords have both shown how films appear to respond to various crises in masculinity in other periods. Cohan writes about a postwar crisis in masculinity and 1950s films, identifying its causes in the "restoration of gender relations," the impact of the Kinsey report, "an emerging upper middle class," and "Cold War politics": "Taken together, they all point to an even more profound, and, at the same time, less discernible transformation in the culture's understanding of the masculine gender in relation to male sexuality."[24] Jeffords explains how literature and films about the Vietnam War "can be used as an emblem for . . . the 'remasculinization' of American culture, the large-scale renegotiation and regeneration of the interests, values, and projects of patriarchy . . . taking place in U.S. social relations."[25] As I offer perspectives on masculinity and sexuality in war films, I will follow the example of such critics, who cautiously relate films to the concerns and anxieties within the cultures producing them.

THE FILMS

One of the first actualities to appear at the time of the crisis in masculinity preceded the formal declaration of war. *Burial of the "Maine" Victims* (Edison Manufacturing Co., 1898) records the funeral ceremony in Key West on 27 March 1898. Shot with a fixed camera, the one-minute–fifty-second film shows servicemen followed by hearses and mourners. Other actualities recorded life at training camps: *Blanket Tossing a New Recruit* (Thomas A. Edison, 1898), which depicts the enthusiastic horseplay of young men; *Soldiers Washing Dishes* (Thomas A. Edison, 1898), a view of their routine activities; and *9th Infantry Boys' Morning Wash* (Edison Manufacturing Co., 1898), a glimpse of them collectively sprucing up. *Wounded Soldiers Embarking in Row Boats* (American Mutoscope and Biograph, 1898) was a much more serious actuality focusing on the results of combat. (No actual combat scenes were photographed.)

Rather than actually recording an event, re-enactments, the second kind of film, such as *U.S. Infantry Supported by Rough Riders at El Caney* (James H. White, 1899; Thomas A. Edison), offered a staged version of a particular occurrence, in this case one involving the troops of Colonel Theodore Roosevelt. It opens on a road in a forest clearing. Soon foot soldiers carrying the American flag appear, fire their guns, and move on, backed by two cavalry soldiers. In what seems to be the same space, the scene is repeated, this time with more cavalry support. Then horsemen impersonating the Rough Riders enter boisterously. A second re-enactment directed by White about Roosevelt's soldiers, *Skirmish of Rough Riders* (Thomas A. Edison, 1899), appeared the same year.

These joined a number of actualities about the already famous leader. One shows him walking down the steps of the Treasury Building, *Theodore Roosevelt* (American Mutoscope Co., 1898). Several present him and/or his troop and staff. *Roosevelt's Rough Riders* (American Mutoscope and Biograph Co., 1898) displays what the Biograph catalog describes as "a charge full of cowboy enthusiasm by Troop 'I,' the famous regiment at Tampa, before its departure for the front."[26] Some of the other actualities include *Roosevelt's Rough Riders Embarking for Santiago* (Thomas A. Edison, 1898), *Roosevelt's Rough Riders at Drill* (American Mutoscope and Biograph Co., 1898), *Theodore Roosevelt and Officers of His Staff* (American Mutoscope and Biograph Co., 1898), and *Governor Roosevelt and His Staff* (American Mutoscope and Biograph Co., 1899).

Roosevelt's appearance in both actualities and re-enactments demonstrates his national importance and influence as a soldier and spokesman for war, masculinity, and manly valor. Before the war began, he had argued for his values in various widely known addresses and commentaries, and continued to present stridently aggressive statements about war and manhood after its conclusion. For example, in "The Manly Virtues and Practical Politics" (1897), he stated: "Another thing that must not be forgotten by the man desirous of doing good political work is the need of the rougher, manlier virtues, and above all the virtue of personal courage, physical as well as moral."[27] In "The Strenuous Life," Roosevelt asserted: "We do not admire the man of timid peace. We admire the man who embodies victorious effort; the man who never wrongs his neighbor, who is prompt to help a friend, but who has those virile qualities necessary to win in the stern strife of actual life."[28] He inveighed against "men who fear the strenuous life" and "believe in that cloistered life which saps the hardy virtues of a nation, as it saps the individual."[29]

Roosevelt's importance and his role in the Spanish-American War in relation to developing conceptions of manhood have been discussed by a number of scholars. Gail Bederman and Kristen L. Hoganson demonstrate his impact on the establishment of a particular conception of masculinity in the American consciousness.[30] Michael S. Kimmel observes that "the fin de siècle mission to thwart feminization and revirilize boyhood—and by extension—manhood—reached its symbolic apotheosis in Theodore Roosevelt."[31] Mary W. Blanchard sees Roosevelt's image and reputation countering various examples of aestheticism in the Gilded Age, especially those embodied in the by-then notorious Oscar

Wilde, and speaks of "a return to a realism based on the historic Teddy Roosevelt as the masculine icon and the return of virility and war as part of the American ethos."[32] The war itself is inextricably linked to the rising concerns about masculinity. James Castonguay, Charles Musser, and Kristen Whissel explain the way the early films about the Spanish-American War reveal an imperialist ethic of power espoused by Roosevelt.[33] Whissel observes that "Edison's actualities participated in a broader mass-mediated process that transformed troops such as Roosevelt's Rough Riders into 'walking advertisements' for what [Gail] Bederman calls 'a collective imperial manhood for the white American race.' "[34] And Sarah Watts argues that "for many Americans at the turn of the century, Roosevelt's rousing masculinity merged pleasingly and appropriately into the discourse on national identity. As never before in their history, Americans had identified the nation with the body of its president and believed in his struggles to preserve civilization against degeneracy and danger."[35]

It is clear that Roosevelt embodied the quintessential attributes of manhood and masculinity as understood by his contemporaries: bravery, physical power, and rigorous virility (he was a father of six). Obviously, Roosevelt was not party to whatever crisis of masculinity had been detected in American men. By a process involving metonymic association and gendered isomorphism on the one hand (soldiers in films are linked to and extensions of Roosevelt because they perform the same actions), and representational imitation on the other (soldiers are like the "real" soldiers shown in actualities and the representative soldiers shown in re-enactments), these first war films delineate men who are totally untouched by the crisis in masculinity. There is no softness or effeminacy or shirking of manly responsibilities.

In this regard, the hero of the first narrative war film, *Love and War* (James H. White, 1899; Thomas A. Edison, 1899), is a fitting archetypal figure in the genre: brave, sufficiently strong enough to withstand and recover from his wounds, and a triumphant survivor returning to claim his bride, thus confirming the heterosexual economy of the narrative. The first totally narrativized soldier in American war films, he takes his place with the soldiers seen in the actualities and in the re-enactments.[36]

Lasting a little over three minutes, *Love and War* has six scenes. It begins as the hero enters the parlor, where he finds his father sitting passively. The mise-en-scène of the parlor from which he departs includes a rifle leaning against the back wall and two crossed swords hanging over the door. Before he departs, the hero allows his little brother to hold his rifle, a weapon that is taller than the child. In the next scene the hero's mother, seated near the little brother, reads newspapers for accounts of her son. His father comes in with a dismal report; evidently the youth has been killed or wounded, and the family is distraught. The father appears to be crying as he embraces his wife and then another man who is with him in the room. The little brother clings to his mother for comfort. We then see the hero leading his men against enemy soldiers, who flee before his advance and the troop's gunfire. But the hero is shot by the retreating troops. A comrade trying to rescue him lifts him up on his shoulders; he, too, is shot and falls lifeless on the hero. The hero survives this battle and is taken to a small tent that serves as a field hospital, where he is received by nurses and doctors. One nurse in particular reacts with anguish when she sees him borne in on a stretcher, kisses him before he is taken into the tent, and raises her hands in a prayer for his recovery.[37] In the last scene he returns home. While one of the swords seen in the first two scenes has fallen slightly from its initial position, in which both were neatly crossed on the wall, the rifle is in the same position, leaning against the wall. The hero is welcomed warmly by his family and embraces his girlfriend.[38]

Love and War. The triumphant return of the hero. Courtesy: Library of Congress.

Whissel suggests that the film "begins with the dispersal of the patriarchal family" and "in the final tableau, family unity acts as a metaphor for national victory as all celebrate together."[39] Even more, the scene foregrounds the hero in relation to the other males in his family, since their status and behavior provide a context for understanding the implications of the hero's masculinity and implied sexual power: the young, untried brother, who literally clings to his mother's apron's strings, and the older father who can no longer fight. When the latter brings the bad news to his wife, he is very upset and hugs her and also another man who is with him. Like his wife, he weeps as he openly displays anguish.

The film negotiates any displays of apparent male weakness. The father's emotional display of distress can be explained in terms of the circumstance: news that the son may be dead. In fact, display of emotion under such circumstances is clearly not to be read as in any way "unmanly." Being wounded is not a sign of softness but of courage. Displays of familial and warm affection in connection with the hero's return are rationalized by the patriarchal link.

The comrade who dies saving the hero deserves comment. The film shows him picking up the wounded hero, only to be shot himself. His head falls against the hero's hip in a tableau of death that joins the living and the dead. No information is provided on the men's relationship, such as whether they were friends or rivals for the girl at home. All we have is the display of heroism and masculine power when he lifts the hero (no small man) before falling himself.[40]

These early war films, which constitute the origins of the genre, present strong, manly figures, actual or fictionalized, who embody the political and cultural values of Theodore Roosevelt and support the expansionist thrust of the United States. In so doing, they offer a positive vision of males that denies the existence of any crisis in masculinity. The heterosexual hero of *Love and War* literally embodies positive masculine power.

PERSPECTIVES

Obviously the world of the nameless hero in *Love and War* and viewers in 1899 is enormously different from that of Captain John Miller (Tom Hanks) in Steven Spielberg's *Saving Private Ryan* and contemporary audiences in 1998, separated as they are by a century of wars, the ascendancy of the United States as a world power, advances in methods of film production and distribution, and changes in spectatorship and conditions of reception. Nonetheless, looked at from one perspective, even though we know more about Miller, the distance between him and the earlier soldier might seem not all that extreme: both are heroic masculine figures and unqualifiedly heterosexual. Even though Miller doesn't make it home to his wife, that is the goal he announces to his men as his motivation for fighting. The hero of *Love and War* succeeds in returning to his love.

But from another set of perspectives, the ones that will be used in this book, the distance between Miller and the earlier hero is, in fact, immense. For one, Miller exists in a cultural context inescapably inflected by our increased awareness of the complexity of masculinity and sexuality. For example, the love in the older film is strictly romantic and familial, a situation enforced by the reunion at the film's ending. We know nothing about the comrade who died rescuing the soldier. Later films sometimes address the problematic aspects of love between comrades. The wounding of the hero in the early film has no ramifications for our sense of his masculinity—a situation quite different in today's treatment of battlefield injuries, which include both physical and mental trauma that can have profoundly debilitating effects. The gender roles in the first film are clearly aligned: women are nurses or mothers, period. But later films can and do show men performing maternal roles or, in the case of drag, literally performing gender. The weapons that proliferate in the older film are distinct from the men who wield them, as opposed to later films in which the weapons are conceived of as extensions of the male body. Finally, the logic and ideological rationales for what is shown are different. *Love and War* is an extension of a national agenda based on uncomplicated assumptions about manhood. Today we know so much more about why and how we make such assumptions, particularly as these affect representations of men. *Saving Private Ryan* was released in a country that operates uneasily with a "Don't ask, don't tell" policy about homosexuals in the military.

ORGANIZATION

In "Paradigms of the Silent Era," the first chapter, I concentrate on *The Big Parade* (King Vidor, 1925), in which male bonding and friendship exist independently of any romantic rivalry, and *What Price Glory* and *Wings* (William Wellman, 1927), in which romantic tensions complicate the men's relationship. The next chapter, "Beyond Triangles," looks at representative films of both paradigms. In the first, as in *From Here to Eternity* (Fred Zinnemann, 1953), the narrative differentiates heterosexual romance from male bonding and love by foregrounding the latter's lack of an erotic dimension. I examine films in the second category, such as *The Deer Hunter* (Michael Cimino, 1978) and *Ride with the Devil* (Ang Lee, 1999), in order to suggest that the bonds of love between men in a romantic rivalry do not mask a repressed homoerotic desire. A third paradigm includes films like *Three Kings* (David O. Russell, 1999) and *Tigerland* (Joel Schumacher, 2000), which focus on love between men with even less emphasis on heterosexual relationships.

"Disavowing Threats," the third chapter, explores aspects of war films and popular culture that counter challenges to masculinity and male sexuality. These disavowals can take a comic form, as in *The Sands of Iwo Jima* (Allan Dwan, 1949), or be serious, as in *Birdy* (Alan Parker, 1984), in which a character specifically denies the possibility of homosexuality. The threats posed to masculinity and sexuality by psychological and physiological damage are the subject matter of the fourth chapter, "Wounds." Sometimes women play an important part in bringing men with disabilities back to health, as happens in *The Best Years of Our Lives* (William Wyler, 1946) and *The Men* (Fred Zinnemann, 1950). "Drag," the next chapter, examines the implications of cross-dressing for masculinity and sexuality in two kinds of narrative situations: those in which men engage in performances, as in *This Is the Army* (Michael Curtiz, 1943), and those in which they are trying to disguise their manhood, as in *I Was a Male War Bride* (Howard

Hawks, 1949). Such narrative situations provide especially complex sites for thinking about the performative nature of gender itself.

" 'Don't Ask, Don't Tell,' " chapter 6, considers the limited filmic treatment of homosexuality in the military. Virtually incapable of being presented when the Production Code Administration was functioning, the subject entered narratives directly in *Reflections in a Golden Eye* (John Huston, 1967) once the new ratings code of the Motion Picture Association of America became operative. With hardly any exceptions, gays are presented negatively, particularly in *Basic* (John McTiernan, 2003), the first film to acknowledge the 1994 policy conceived by President Bill Clinton as a way of allowing gays in the military.

"Bodies, Weapons," chapter 7, explores the connection of male bodies to weapons in light of the famous chant given currency in *Full Metal Jacket* (Stanley Kubrick, 1987): "This is my rifle, this is my gun; this is for fighting, this is for fun." Ranging from films about Vietnam, such as *Platoon* (Oliver Stone, 1986), to the Gulf War, such as *Jarhead* (Sam Mendes, 2005), the chapter considers the narrative foregrounding of sexualized bodies and weapons.

In chapter 8, "Fathers and Sons," I focus on a number of recent films, such as *Saving Private Ryan* and *Black Hawk Down* (Ridley Scott, 2001). These films' emphasis on fatherhood suggests that the filmmakers are responding to challenges of masculinity and normative male sexuality from various directions, not the least of which could be greater visibility of gay men, particularly those who want to be in the military. In a brief concluding section, "Buddies, Then and Now," I revisit the different conceptions of "buddies" seen in criticism of the war films.

CHAPTER ONE

PARADIGMS IN THE
SILENT ERA

The short film *Love and War* (James H. White, 1899) described in the introduction establishes a number of narrative elements that will figure prominently in later war films: the hero's departure and triumphant return; the impact of the war on his family at the home front; battlefield courage and death; field hospitals and ministering nurses. These qualify as the kinds of "semantic units" Rick Altman identifies in his explanation of the foundations of genre. All of these enter into various syntactical patterns as the war film develops over time.[1]

Love, a major semantic unit of interest in this book, receives little narrative attention in the early film: a kiss before the hero departs for war and an embrace when he returns. But the word itself has primacy in the title, and the lovers in the foreground are the last image we see in the film. The scene thus anticipates the endings that will dominate classic Hollywood films of various genres that conclude with the union of heterosexual lovers in marriage (or the promise of it).[2]

The three war films to be examined in this chapter—*The Big Parade* (King Vidor, 1925), *What Price Glory* (Raoul Walsh, 1926), and *Wings* (William Wellman, 1927)—offer significant contrasts to the early work's simplicity and lack of complexity in the treatment of love. A central focus of all of them, love is inflected by war, rather than a separate thread, and is realized in two basic narrative paradigms. The first kind appears in *The Big Parade*, in which the romantic love between Jim Apperson (John Gilbert) and Melisande (Renée Adorée) is distinct from the equally moving depiction of camaraderie among Jim and his buddies Slim (Karl Dane) and Bull (Tim O'Brien). In contrast, *What Price Glory* interweaves the two threads, making the bond that exists between Sergeant Quirt (Edmund Lowe) and Captain Flagg (Victor McLaglen) a complication in their mutual love for Charmaine (Dolores Del Rio). *Flesh and the Devil* (Clarence Brown, 1927) appeared shortly after *What Price Glory*. Although it is not a war film, its principal male heroes are in the German military and are presented in a similar narrative situation: Leo (John Gilbert) and Ulrich (Lars Hanson) are friends since boyhood who both love Felicitas (Greta Garbo). *Wings*, the first film to win the Oscar for Best Picture, works with the same combination of narrative concerns as it presents the love of Jack (Buddy Rogers) and David (Richard Arlen), American pilots who are friends and also rivals for the affection of Sylvia (Jobyna Ralston).[3]

Examination of the love stories in these films takes us directly into consideration of masculinity and sexuality. I'm particularly interested in contemporary viewers' responses to these silent war films as well as later critical analyses of their treatment of masculinity and sexuality. Not only are the films significant in terms of film history; they also are the first films to produce critical commentary that deals specifically with male sexuality. One problem posed both by films and criticism comes as we try to reconstruct the epistemological field of the films' contemporary viewers. Specifically, what discourses were in place at the time of the films' release that can help us understand what contemporary viewers may have understood about sexuality and masculinity? Since the films are not widely known today, I hope more extended descriptions of their plots will be helpful.

THE BIG PARADE

King Vidor's epic film *The Big Parade* is regarded as one of the greatest war films of any era.[4] Its impressive technical accomplishments complement the powerful narrative, which includes a number of motifs and conventions in the war film, such as the varied mix of soldiers of different social stations brought together in foxhole unity and their bonding, the sharing of a cigarette with one's enemy, a mixture of high jinks in camp and deadly seriousness on the battlefield, and the difficulties of wartime romance.

The first part of *The Big Parade* introduces us to Jim, Slim, and Bull, men from very different social classes who will meet each other and become friends in the service, and shows Jim's departure from home and his girlfriend, Justyn (Claire Adams).[5] Even though Jim is wealthy and the other men are from the working class (Slim is a construction worker, Bull a bartender), they become buddies. Humorous scenes dominate the first half of the film, especially those involving basic training and the men's arrival in France. Jim first sees Melisande, a young French woman, when he and the others are digging in the road in front of her house. Their first significant contact occurs in a meet-cute scene. Jim has figured out how to rig up a makeshift shower so that the men can bathe. Because he loses the contest to decide who will find a barrel, he has to go to town for one. He finds an empty barrel and carries it by putting it over his head, thus obstructing his vision except for one viewing hole. As he walks, he sees Melisande, in what appears as an iris-shot, given his point of view looking through the hole, and they have their first verbal contact.

Once the shower has been rigged up outdoors, Melisande happens by and sees Slim and Bull nude from behind as they frolic and bathe one another. As far as I know this is the first nude bathing scene in an American war film. Vidor plays it for comedy, with Melisande laughing at the spectacle and Jim shouting at her to go away. It initiates countless shower scenes that will follow in later war films, many also involving horseplay. That this one includes a woman's look is significant, since for the first time in a war film a female character's view of a potentially erotic spectacle serves as a visual relay point for female viewers of the film, an obvious feminine counterpart of Laura Mulvey's model for male spectatorship of women.[6] One could also argue that one effect of the scene is to neutralize the clothed Jim's gaze on the nude men below him on whom he pours the water. That is, Melisande's presence and comic reaction to the men de-eroticize the narrative situation for both Jim and her.

In a short scene after this, also played for laughs, she fends off Slim's and Bull's clumsy and oafish attempts to win her attention; her real romantic interest is in Jim. The film shows their developing love in a comic scene in which Jim teaches her how to chew gum. A shift in tone in the narrative occurs when the heartbroken Melisande realizes he has a girl back in America, a discovery that occurs just as the men are called to the front. The departure of the troops, her search for Jim among the throng, and her anguish as he leaves are extraordinary moments in the film.

The second half focuses on the war itself, beginning with the justly famous long shot of the caravan of troop trucks and vehicles seen in "the big parade." The climax of this section of the film involves an intensely realized sequence on the battlefield. This begins with orders to leave the safety of their foxhole to kill Germans who are machine gunning Americans. In a counterpart to their earlier competition as to who would go for the barrel, the men have a spitting contest to determine who will first leave the foxhole for the mission. Slim goes first, and his compatriots realize he has been wounded. Jim goes in search of him, followed by Bull, only to discover his dead friend. Jim laments: "Slim, can't you just try to say goodbye?" Then he puts his face on that of the dead man. His helmet partially obscures our full view of their contact, but we see enough to realize their faces are touching. This near embrace in death is extremely moving, as the reviewer in *Variety* noted: "There is a scene there as realistic and touching as any death scene imaginable. It was heart-reaching, and had the majority of the audience in tears."[7] Jim stands up in fury and shouts: "They got him! They got him! GOD DAMN THEIR SOULS!" Then, he cries: "You got my Buddy, you b——s. Now . . . COME ON!"[8]

After the memorable death scene of Jim's buddy in *The Big Parade*, the battle continues: first Bull is killed, and then Jim is wounded. Although Jim shoots one of the Germans who killed Slim, he and his victim end up in the same foxhole. As he prepares to slit the young soldier's throat, though, the youth's imploring glance stops his fury, and he gives the doomed man a cigarette and then finishes it when the youth dies. Jim is taken to a hospital, but he steals away in search of Melisande. His search is fruitless, and he returns home, having lost one leg (like Laurence Stallings, his creator). He discovers that his girlfriend, Justyn, no longer loves him; she has fallen in love with his brother, Harry (Robert Ober). Jim returns to France to search for Melisande, and in one of the most powerful reunion scenes in a war film (or any film, for that matter), encounters her working in the fields, where they reconfirm their love.

The Big Parade. Jim's reunion with Melisande. Courtesy: Jerry Ohlinger's. © M-G-M, 1925.

There are, then, two narrative foci in the film. One displays an intense romantic love, while the other shows us the close bond of comrades. Both have various comic moments, in some cases separate from and in others connected with the two strands of narrative. The male friendships, presented most intensely as Jim embraces his dead comrade Slim, whom he designates a "buddy," have nothing to do with male sexuality, which throughout the film is presented unambiguously strictly in heterosexual terms.

WHAT PRICE GLORY

The next major war film audiences saw in the 1920s was the immensely popular *What Price Glory*.[9] Like *The Big Parade*, it includes a mixture of comic and profoundly serious scenes but, in contrast, mixes these in sometimes unsettling and jarring ways. Even more to the point, its romantic plot is inextricably bound up and resolved by the relationship of its two heroes.

Unlike the play, which introduces Captain Quirt, Sergeant Flagg, and Charmaine relatively early in the first act (with stage directions that identify her as a "drab"), Walsh's film withholds the heroine's introduction until the contentious rivalry between the heroes is well established.[10] We first see the men involved in a romantic triangle in China with Shanghai Mabel (Phyllis Haver), a flirt whose affections have shifted from the army to the marines, represented by Quirt and Flagg. Their discovery that she is involved with both of them causes the first of the numerous fights in which they'll engage. This preview of coming battles is followed by some more sparring in the Philippines, before the film's main action settles in on their experiences in France, where they meet Charmaine, who is, an intertitle announces, "thrilled by the war in her front yard, fascinated by the men who stop at her smile on their way to die." Flagg is the first man she encounters. As he did with Shanghai Mabel, he initiates their relationship by giving a garter to Charmaine, who is fascinated by his tattoos, shown when he removes his shirt.

The first prolonged battle sequence follows. An intertitle states: "Cannon fodder, young and green replacements. Boys from every walk of life." Flagg shows his sympathetic side by giving a discharge to a young soldier who "needs his mother more than the war needs him." Afterward, Quirt meets Charmaine, who shows him the same affection she displayed toward Flagg. Walsh stages this in a remarkable scene in which Charmaine cradles the sleeping Quirt in her arms, in a kind of pietà. Meanwhile Flagg has taken up temporarily with yet another woman, clearly a prostitute. He is angry when he returns to Charmaine and sees that the garter he had given her is now in Quirt's possession. He arranges a marriage of Quirt and Charmaine, but she refuses to go through with the ceremony.

The men then return to the front for the most sustained battle sequence, a spectacular cinematic tour de force that includes an impressive tracking shot through the trenches, one that anticipates by some thirty years the memorable shot in Stanley Kubrick's *Paths of Glory* (1957). When a young soldier comes in wounded to a dressing station and collapses, Flagg picks him up and carries him like a child. In a very moving scene that forces one to reassess Flagg, after the young soldier dies Flagg kisses his forehead tenderly and continues to look at him. Nothing thus far has prepared us for such a moment in which Flagg could display such tenderness, captured intensely by Walsh, who trains the camera on them in a long take as Flagg cries and puts a blanket over the corpse.

More will be said about the kiss of comrades later in the discussion of *Wings*, but for the moment it's appropriate to comment on Santanu Das's analysis of "the dying kiss" in World War I literature and records. Das describes the contents of a letter from a soldier to the mother of his dead comrade: "I held him in my arms to the end, and when his soul had departed I kissed him twice where I knew you would have kissed him—on the brow—once for his mother and once for myself." Das believes "the recurring, almost ritualistic phrase 'mother's kiss' suggests a powerful reconceptualization of both masculinity and male-male bonds through an assumed maternal impulse of charity and tenderness. . . . The phrase 'I held him in my arms,' with the subsequent connection to maternity, is almost an unconscious reworking of the *Pietà*."[11] Both the letter and this scene take us back to *What Price Glory* and R. W. Connell's conception of masculinity as "a place in gender relations" that can accommodate both male and female "practices."[12]

Here Flagg assumes the maternal role; earlier, while still retaining his masculine role, Quirt has been infantilized when Charmaine cradles him in the pietà. When Quirt discovers the kid is dead, he is distraught. Unlike the play in which the title line is given to a soldier, it is Quirt who asks (in capitalized intertitle letters): "WHAT PRICE GLORY NOW?" Flagg repeats the line, again in a capitalized intertitle. In a tense scene, he resists Quirt's desire to protect the men by keeping them out of battle.

The wounded Quirt returns to Charmaine, followed shortly by Flagg, and they resume the rivalry for her affection and fighting. Quirt boasts about having reached her sooner: "Certainly I beat you back. I can beat you fighting, and thinking, and talking and—loving." At this point, when Flagg brags he's the best pistol shot, Charmaine utters the line with which I began the introduction: "Don't fight. Don't fight. You love each other, yes?" This doesn't deter them from even more fighting and the decision to settle the matter with a draw of cards. Flagg wins, and Charmaine says, "Ah, Monsieur, you have my heart." But she realizes she can't really say that and mean it since it is Quirt, "the sergeant, he have my heart."

Flagg accepts her decision, and they salute each other as he leaves to rejoin his men at the front since he has been ordered back. Even though the wounded Quirt is not obliged to return to battle, nonetheless he decides to join Flagg, with the promise of returning to her. He cries out to his friend: "HEY, FLAGG!" The marching Flagg then "hears": "WAIT FOR BABY!" A forlorn Charmaine looks after them and predicts: "They come back once—they come back twice—They

What Price Glory. The horror of war. Courtesy: Photofest. © 20th Century Fox, 1926.

will not come back three times," and then laments: "They are so strong and beautiful, they are too young to—die—." The film ends with Quirt, with his arm around Flagg for support, marching back to the front.

Even though the boisterous fighting between Quirt and Flagg and the rampant objectification of women in general and Charmaine in particular are sometimes wearying, the film merits consideration for its complex rendering of the men and their relationship. It is clearly possible, the text says, for brawling and sexually promiscuous men to feel deeply about other men. The scene of Flagg's kiss of the dead young man is a key element here, since it suggests he is capable of a level of tenderness of a completely nonerotic nature toward another man. The pietà in which Quirt is temporarily infantilized has the effect of stripping away his bravado and implying a potential level of vulnerability in him as well. One contemporary reviewer noticed this complexity. Mordaunt Hall comments on how "the blazing jealousy of Captain Flagg and Sergeant Quirt [in *What Price Glory*] is vividly pictured . . . and these same soldiers are depicted as brothers in arms. . . . Both are shown to be men who under fire are touched by the very weakness of others."[13]

Joan Mellen's discussion of the film captures this duality, focusing on the importance of the depiction of masculinity: "[T]hough Flagg will weep at the loss of one of his boys, he orders the rest not to let up until they stop a bullet.

A real man proves his toughness by never weakening before an order. . . . [T]he men who are survive are the most masculine of all."[14] In her view,

> their rivalry . . . allows the relationship between the two of them to flourish. They enjoy each other vicariously in apparent quest of the same woman. Real men must prove their masculinity by an obligatory pursuit of any pretty woman on the scene, but neither Flagg nor Quirt is emotionally committed to Charmaine. If the film is unconscious of the emotional ramifications of this rivalry, it remains apparent that the eros coloring their feelings for each other is stoked by their rivalry over the incidental object, who happens to be female.[15]

She sees the conclusion, with Flagg supporting the wounded Quirt, as a way to legitimate their feelings:

> His war wound serves to permit this touching between the two men, to render it credible and untinged by homosexual feeling, despite the emotion trembling between them throughout the film. . . . No consummation can be more transcendent, suggests this film, than that experienced side by side with a male friend. . . . Paradoxically, it is the very dread of being unmasculine which causes the suppressed affection of men for each other to be so powerfully homosexual in character. By rejecting women and settling for sublimated emotional relations exclusively with other men, while all the time having to deny that emotional bond, the hero in the American film often is, in fact, choosing asexuality.[16]

I confess to being skeptical about her comment that "a film is unconscious" of something, or that a film doesn't know something about the characters, because it anthropomorphizes the text without acknowledging it as an artifact created by a number of different individuals, produced and marketed by a studio, and received by a heterogeneous audience. It makes a work into a person who's repressing something. From this, Mellen generalizes about "the hero in American film" who is "often . . . choosing asexuality."

Essentially, then, she attributes a textual repression to the heroes as men battling for a woman they really don't want as a way to connect with each other, something they can't do unless there is a physical lack to explain the concern and affection they feel for one another. But an alternative reading is certainly possible. In place of Mellen's "asexuality," which the men somehow are "choosing," I think Donald Spoto's suggestion cited in the introduction about the battling heroes of *Red River* (Howard Hawks, 1948) offers another possibility. He refers to the scene in which Tess (Joanne Dru) chastises Tom Dunson (John Wayne) and Matt Garth (Montgomery Clift) to stop fighting because they love one another. Spoto offers a more positive conception of what may in fact be represented:

> [M]ale bonding is a metasexual affinity. It points at the radical personal incompleteness his characters feel within themselves, an emptiness that may

be filled in some respects by a woman, but in other respects only by another man. It is, finally, one of the highest forms of spiritual love, and is quite another thing than a homosexual relationship, as it's quite another thing than a heterosexual relationship. It's the kind of affinity, in the final analysis, toward which all other beautiful and true commitments tend.[17]

Admittedly this liminal conception of sexuality—neither homosexual nor heterosexual—will clearly not be viable for critics like Mellen, who seems intent on reading in terms of strict dichotomies. Nonetheless, it has the advantage of acknowledging that human beings function in multiple registers and, to apply the suggestion of Joseph Bristow cited in the introduction, occupy complex overdetermined spaces "where sexed bodies . . . and sexual desires . . . intersect only to separate."[18]

FLESH AND THE DEVIL

Within six weeks after the premiere of *What Price Glory* in New York, *Flesh and the Devil*, another film about two men in love with the same woman, opened to critical acclaim and excellent box office on 9 January 1927. Like Quirt and Flagg at the end of the earlier film, Leo and Ulrich, the heroes and rivals of *Flesh and the Devil*, are together in the final shot. We first encounter Leo and Ulrich at a military school/installation in a vaguely movie-set Germany. Ulrich's first action is to hide information about Leo's tomcatting from his superior by covering for his friend, who has been out all night. In a flashback, we learn that their friendship began when they were little boys, and see their trip with Ulrich's sister, Hertha, to the "Isle of Friendship." As she averts her eyes, the boys cut their wrists and combine their blood using language that evokes that of a wedding ceremony: "By this rite of blood we are united . . . in riches and in poverty . . . in love and sorrow . . . in life and death."

The romantic complication in their friendship comes when the adult Leo meets Felicitas, falls in love with her at a ball, and commences an affair. When her husband discovers them, he challenges Leo to a duel but is shot. In disgrace, Leo is sent to an outpost in Africa for several years, having told Ulrich the duel was over cards and asked him to look after the widow. Not knowing of the affair between Felicitas and Leo, Ulrich falls in love with Felicitas and marries her. When Leo returns, he resumes his affair with Felicitas until Ulrich finally learns the truth. But the affair continues, to the point where Leo and Felicitas plan to flee. She has a change of heart, though, when Ulrich gives her a diamond bracelet. But when Ulrich learns of their plan, even though Felicitas says she no longer wants to go, he challenges Leo to a duel on the Isle of Friendship. The last scene in the film shows their aborted duel: neither can shoot to kill the other. Meanwhile, having being implored by Hertha to go to the men, Felicitas leaves her home and walks through the snow to find them. But she falls through the ice and drowns. Unaware of her death, the men embrace, and the film ends.

The refined intensity of their emotional attachment to one another is strikingly different from that presented in *What Price Glory*. A film full of pained glances rather than brawls, nonetheless the film invites comparison with its predecessor. Without mentioning Walsh's film, Parker Tyler cites this one as presenting an early example of a "platonic male friendship, ambiguously homosexual."[19] He ascribes a level of understanding (or lack of one) to the contemporary audience: "Only sublime innocence could be expected of Hollywood when, in 1927, two leading men (rather than Garbo and a leading man) were found in what justly used to be called the final clinch."[20]

His statement raises a major question about spectatorship in the period that I want to pursue here and in connection with *Wings*. In some ways it's the counterpart to Mellen's assumption that a film "is not conscious" of something. Here Tyler ascribes some kind of interpretive myopia (or disingenuousness) to "Hollywood." Checking the available data on the perception of the film at the time of its release complicates any attempt to understand what was or could have been known and/or supposed.

I know of three comments attributed to director Clarence Brown about his film. In an invaluable interview with Kevin Brownlow, he referred directly to his dislike of the happy ending that was shot for the film. In this added scene, some time has passed since the death of Felicitas, and Leo is preparing to leave. But as he goes, Ulrich's sister, Hertha, who has loved Leo from afar throughout the film, implores him not to depart. He realizes he can be happy with her and remains. According to Brown, he had no control over this: "They put a happy ending on *Flesh and the Devil*—I had to shoot it and it killed me. When we ran it in Paris, I told them to cut it off."[21]

Other comments attributed to Brown complicate our attempts to read the contemporary view of the work. In a commentary on the DVD of the film, Barry Paris talks about Brown's experiences with the ending. It isn't clear to me from listening which parts of the quotation are direct or indirect discourse: "The hardest thing about the film was the ending. How do you have the woman die and the two men embrace? Her drowning was enough to satisfy the censors but the exhibitors were complaining about downbeat films in general. MGM had to have a happy ending over a moral ending." The last part of Paris's vocal commentary confirms Brownlow's statement: "I had to shoot it, said Brown, and it killed me."[22]

The third quote is the most problematic. If Brown clearly disdains the happy ending, which safely heterosexualizes Leo by having him unite with Hertha, why should he complain, as he seems to be doing, in a quote attributed to him by Vito Russo and Scott Eyman, that the original ending homosexualizes both the men: "You can see my problem. How to have two leading men end up in each other's arms and not make them look like a couple of fairies?"[23]

The contemporary response from the *New York Times* reviewer Mordaunt Hall stresses the intensity of the men's friendship and acknowledges the film as "a story of passionate love and the friendship of two men who, as boys, like the knights of old, had mixed their blood; their friendship is the conquering power over their blazing affection for a conscienceless creature."[24] Clearly the reviewer sees "passionate love" in one narrative thread and "friendship" in another as being compatible and not problematic.

A reviewer who saw a preview of the film in December before its opening in January complicates matters even more:

> When previewed at a local theater, the audience roared with laughter at several of the dramatic and emotional high spots in the picture. There were several good psychological reasons for this that are easy to explain—but I will let M-G-M production geniuses figure it out for themselves. This laughter, however, takes some of the edge off the drama of the picture and results in much tittering throughout the remainder of the serious moments of the production. The ending, too, is neither convincing nor satisfying.[25]

Since it appears from these comments that it wasn't the embrace of the men at the end of the original film producing laughter, one wonders whether it was the blood oath of the little boys. That the reviewer even uses the term "psychological" in a film review is of note. Hugo Munsterberg's *The Film: A Psychological Study* had appeared ten years earlier in 1916, but the introduction of the term or concepts is atypical in reviews of this period. One is left wondering whether the reviewer has some concept of sexuality in mind and whether the potentially homoerotic interpretation had occurred to the audience at the preview.

"My Buddy"

While the word "psychological" is rarely used, a term that does appear commonly in reviews of war films of the period is "buddy." The reviewer of *The Big Parade* for the *New York Times* speaks of the "expressions of the three buddies."[26] Jim Apperson, the hero, curses the Germans for killing his "buddy." The *Variety* review of the service comedy *Behind the Front* (Edward Sutherland, 1926) speaks of the two heroes: "Shorty and Swanson mate up and become 'buddies' in camp."[27] And Mordaunt Hall's review of *Wings* describes a key plot element: "Powell plunges through the air seeking vengeance on the enemy for having, as he thinks then, slain Bruce [*sic*] Armstrong, his buddy."[28] The buddy relationship in *Wings*, the third war film involving a romantic triangle, is the most complex of them all and has provoked clear disagreements on how to interpret the sexuality of the heroes.

By the time the film appeared, the song "My Buddy" had been known to American audiences for approximately five years. While our ability to connect the language of psychology with contemporary audiences is uncertain, it is possible to look at one discourse that was indeed accessible: music. We do know that one of the most popular songs of the 1920s certainly looked back at friendship in the war, exclusive of any implications of homosexuality, "My Buddy," by Gus Kahn and Walter Donaldson:

Nights are long since you went away,
I think about you all through the day,
My Buddy, My Buddy, No Buddy quite so true.
Miss your voice, the touch of your hand,
Just long to know that you understand,
My Buddy, My Buddy, Your Buddy misses you.[29]

Glenn Watkins explains that although the song was "dedicated to Donaldson's [recently] deceased fiancée . . . the gender of *buddy*, which is defined in informal usage in the United States as a 'comrade or chum,' would not have been in doubt for the returning veterans. . . . Indeed, the notion of 'buddies,' an American expression had been extremely popular from the beginning of the war."[30]

In 1925 Donaldson wrote a song called "I Wonder Where My Baby Is Tonight," the title of which is picked up the next year as "I Wonder Where My Buddies Are Tonight," by Billy Rose and Raymond E. Egan. The speaker/singer of the lyrics specifically mentions his dead comrades, not only the living:

The world forgets, perhaps
But when day has sounded "Taps,"
I wonder where my buddies are tonight.[31]

Carl Scheele observes that "My Buddy," "which did not directly refer to the war . . . had such evocative power that most people thought of it as a war song." It would, of course, be popular later in World War II. Scheele refers to an even more striking song from 1926 not mentioned by Watkins that specifically connects buddies, mourning, and motion pictures, "My Dream of the Big Parade," by Jimmy McHugh and Al Dubin. Scheele suggests "it echoes the mood of the silent motion picture." Its lyrics are remarkable:

Last night I was dreaming of days that are gone,
Of days that you might recall,
And just like a photoplay upon my wall,
Once more I saw it all;
It was just a dream you see,
But how real it seemed to be.

The speaker/singer imagines seeing "buddies true" and also, like the hero of the film, "one-legged pals coming home to their gals,/In my dream of the Big Parade."[32]

WINGS

In the film *Wings*, Mary (Clara Bow, who received top billing) loves Jack, who is oblivious to her ardor. The relationship of Jack and David begins with tension and enmity because each knows the other loves Sylvia. The men enlist together for the war and are sent to the same camp for basic training. The scene of the preinduction physical contains a brief shot of nude men seen through the doorway in an inner room, but no specific character's point of view is attributed to the shot; it's presented as simply part of the induction process and is seen more out of the corner of the camera's eye rather than "by" any character.

Before leaving for Europe, Jack mistakenly assumes a little photograph he sees of Sylvia at her home is one she meant for him to take to the war. After Jack beats David in a rough boxing match during basic training, the men draw together in friendship, having come to recognize and respect each other's toughness. Jack wipes some of the blood off David's face as they leave the match arm and arm. At war, they develop a ritual greeting to one another before taking off on a mission. David says, "All right?" and waves his hand, and Jack responds, "OK."

A long sequence involves Mary's appearance in France with the ambulance corps, her encounter with the drunken Jack at a nightclub, and military police discovering her in Jack's hotel room. Her presence there is innocent, but she is sent home in disgrace.

Although the friendship of Jack and David is solid, they eventually quarrel when David tries to touch the photograph of Sylvia. Angered, Jack doesn't respond to their ritual greeting before leaving for their last mission together. David is shot down behind enemy lines but manages to commandeer a German plane and tries to return to his men. In the film's climax, not realizing that David is piloting a German aircraft, Jack shoots down the plane, and David is mortally injured. As David is dying, Jack tells him how important his friendship has been, insisting: "You—you know—there's nothing in the world that means so much to me as your friendship." David responds: "I knew it all the time." Jack kisses David warmly and then reprises their ritual greeting, "All right?" But David has died. Jack then puts his lifeless body on a cart. After the war, Jack returns home and gives David's grieving family the little good-luck bear David had failed to carry on his doomed flight. Eventually, Jack realizes that Mary loves him, and the film's conclusion signals their reunion.

With something of a bemused manner, Kenneth Anger recounts a conversation he had with his grandmother about her experience seeing the film when it first appeared and her description of how members of the original audience were crying when David dies. He describes the scene in this way: "The two main male characters end up in an embrace. One kisses the other on the mouth. This is OK because they're buddies. Buddy love."[33] His tone suggests that Anger, a gay filmmaker, may see more than something that's OK from the perspective of the

Wings. Jack kisses David good-bye. Courtesy: Photofest. © Paramount Famous Lasky Corp., 1927.

film's contemporary audience. If so, he is not alone in reading of the relationship as something more than "buddy love."

The film and this scene in particular have invited readings that explore a homosexual subtext. For example, Mellen calls this "one of the most resonant love scenes between two men to appear in the American cinema."[34] This and other such scenes illustrate a tendency in American films about "male bonding . . . [that] resembles the preadolescent bonding of young males who temporarily fear women and prefer each other's company, yet indulge in excessive displays of machismo to convince everyone that despite their exclusively male grouping they are really heterosexual . . . sexually chaste. . . . These are not depictions of homosexuality as a conscious choice . . . but rather of unavowed homosexual emotion."[35]

The tone of Anger's commentary certainly implies he would agree with Vito Russo, a gay critic and author of the work on which the DVD is based. In the text, Russo says: "Richard Arlen and Charles 'Buddy' Rogers have a more meaningful relationship with each other than either of them has with Jobyna Ralston or Clara Bow, both token love interests whom male adolescents all over America correctly identified as the 'boring parts' of the movie. In fact Arlen and Rogers have the only real love scene in *Wings*, and Rogers learns the true meaning of love only through his relationship with his buddy."[36]

Anthony Slide, also a gay critic, disagrees with Russo and faults *The Celluloid Closet* for being "notably weak in its examination of gay and lesbian aspects of American silent film, emphasizing as an example of homosexuality a sequence from . . . *Wings* [in which Jack kisses David]. . . . Just as this sequence has much to do with male bonding and little to do with overt homosexual love, so has an 1895 Edison short of two men dancing no kinship to lesbian and gay cinema."[37]

The contrasting positions involving both gay and straight readings define clearly opposing views of the meaning of the scene and its implications: the kiss as proof of erotic attachment versus evidence of nonerotic love and bonding between comrades. A similar kind of dichotomy figures in Sarah Cole's thoughtful assessment of the relationship between modernism and the literature of World War I. She argues that "the figure of the bereaved male friend—whose very being is constituted by the loss of war mates—becomes the war's representative *par excellence*." For her, "the crushing problem of male intimacy functioned to coalesce and crystallize a number of discourses surrounding masculinity and the male body in the First World War period, but . . . it could not ultimately resolve the contradictions inherent in the different visions of male unity that the war generated."[38] She presents a complex analysis in which she refuses to see male intimacy as necessarily a repudiation of or an indicator of homosexuality: "This conception of male intimacy neither banishes nor reduces to homosexuality."[39]

An issue in this regard is our difficulty in knowing how much the contemporary audience seeing *Wings* would have been able to understand at any level the comments of Anger, Mellen, Russo, and Slide. Although we know audiences had experienced close male friendships between soldiers in films, we can only speculate on the extent of their knowledge of the homosexual implications of close relationships in the military. The one event of which I am aware that publicly connected the military and homosexuality had occurred several years earlier in the period 1919–1921. George Chauncey Jr. and John Loughery explore in detail the famous Newport, Rhode Island, scandal of 1919 and the ensuing investigation.[40] Briefly, in order to break up homosexual activities that had involved sailors from the naval base in Newport, the navy initiated what was essentially a sting operation using sailors to trap and expose gays. The situation was complicated by the arrest of the local and highly respected Episcopalian minister, who was acquitted in both trials that followed.

Chauncey's analysis of the events leads him to describe the limited (but complicated) contemporary understanding of homosexuality:

The Newport evidence suggests how we might begin to refine and correct our analysis of the relationship between medical discourse, homosexual behavior, and identity. First, and most clearly, the Newport evidence indicates that medical discourse still played little or no role in the shaping of working-class identities and categories by [the time of] World War I. . . . More remarkably,

medical discourse appears to have had as little influence on the military hier-
archy as on the people of Newport.[41]

Essentially, whatever awareness there was regarding the status of homosexuality
as an "identity" as opposed to a "behavior" seems to have been quite indetermi-
nate. People knew that there were "fairies," understood stereotypically as limp-
wristed and effeminate, and also that there were men who weren't "fairies" who
had sex with other men. Chauncey argues that because "fairies" were assumed to
be effeminate, the noneffeminate sailors who had sex with them as part of the
sting were *not* considered homosexuals: "The stigmatized image of the queer also
helped to legitimate the behavior of men in Newport [who were used to trap those
perceived as queer]. Most observers did not label as queer either the ministers
who were intimate with their Christian brothers or the sailors who had sex with
effeminate men, because neither group conformed to the dominant image of
what a queer should be like."[42]

Acknowledging Michel Foucault's well-known conclusions regarding perceptions of the homosexual in terms of behavior and "species," Kevin White (who
does not address the Newport scandal) offers a different view. He thinks that
there was a sense of the homosexual as a being as such in the 1920s: "[T]he
homosexual was specifically presented as the antithesis of the heterosexual, the
male ideal. Indeed, in many ways, by the 1920s, men's fear of effeminacy, which
had characterized the 'masculinity crisis' of the Progressive Era, was diffused into
a whole new category, the homosexual. . . . [A]ny homosexual desire a young
man might feel now caused him to fear that he was a homosexual person rather
than someone tempted merely to commit a sin, albeit a rather venal one."[43]

Whatever memories the viewing public may have had in 1926 and 1927 about
the scandal, it's unlikely that they would have associated homosexual behavior
with deep friendships in military men. The Newport scandal involved a ring of
men who engaged in sex with other men, not friends whose demonstrable affection and love could bring an audience to tears. Thus Clarence Brown's worried
concerns about the possible audience perceptions of his heroes in *Flesh and the
Devil* seem excessive. Add to that the absolute absence of any suggestion in *any*
male character in *The Big Parade*, *What Price Glory*, and *Wings* of the stereotypical physical mannerisms associated in the public's mind with "fairies."

To what extent members of the audience might have known or guessed or
wondered about homosexuality is difficult to resolve. In addition, we do not
have an accurate sense of the actual language available to a large part of the
American public at the time to "speak" about homosexuality and to distinguish
it from displays of male affection that were perfectly consonant with rugged
masculinity, as evidenced in *What Price Glory*. Havelock Ellis's *Sexual Inversion*,
part of his *Studies in the Psychology of Sex* series, was available in the United
States. In it he talks about homosexuals as a class in much the same way they

were understood during the Newport scandal.[44] Sigmund Freud's *Three Essays on Sexuality* (1905) had also been published. Interest in psychiatry had been bolstered by treatment of psychologically traumatized soldiers in World War I, but how much specific concepts of Freud had reached the majority of Americans is not at all clear.[45]

What can be known is that by the late 1920s, two basic narrative paradigms appear in place in the war film. In one, heterosexual love is threatened by war; the principal male characters are comrades and not rivals for the same woman. In the other, the resolution of the love story depends on the outcomes of two conflicts: that of the war itself and of the tension between the rivals. *What Price Glory* is remarkable for its failure to conclude with an ending that confirms the stability of the heterosexual couple. Quirt and Flagg are with each other at the end; neither is with Charmaine. While *Wings* concludes with Jack and Mary together, his love for most of the film has been directed at Sylvia rather than her. And the most overt declaration of affection in the film is uttered by Jack to the dying David. The point is that as early as the 1920s, war films are already displaying problematic narratives that accommodate the presentation of heterosexual love stories in combination with nonsexual affection and love between men, and in the case of *What Price Glory* positioning its male heroes in the narrative space that would be expected for the traditional couple.

CHAPTER TWO

BEYOND TRIANGLES

The paradigms described in chapter 1 continue to appear in war films of the sound era. The pattern in *The Big Parade* (King Vidor, 1925), in which love of comrades can occur in conjunction with a separate romantic relationship that doesn't create conflict between men, appears most notably in *From Here to Eternity* (Fred Zinnemann, 1953). In such a case, the presence of the two kinds of relationships helps to differentiate one from the other. The paradigm observed in *What Price Glory* (Raoul Walsh, 1926) and *Wings* (William Wellman, 1927), in which the rivalry between friends is a complication in the heterosexual love relationship, figures in war films such as *The Deer Hunter* (Michael Cimino, 1978). In this chapter, I identify a third paradigm in which the bonds and love between men exist without any significant heterosexual romance, as occurs in *Three Kings* (David O. Russell, 1999) and *Tigerland* (Joel Schumacher, 2000). In such films there may be indications about characters' heterosexuality, but the relative absence of any prominent narrative attention to these has the effect of foregrounding the intensity of the men's love even more by removing a heterosexual foil to set it off. Accounts of wartime experiences by soldier/correspondents such as Philip Caputo and William J. Broyles Jr. confirm the existence of such nonerotic love.

Consideration of love between men in sound-era war films necessarily has to take into account the kinds of attention they have received from critics and scholars whose aim has been to problematize the relationships. This occurs most prominently in analyses that are incompatible with the interpretation of these as liminal, based on Donald Spoto's call for recognizing that love between men needn't be compartmentalized as heterosexual or homosexual.

Examples of such resistant approaches, mentioned in chapter 1, have their counterpart in similar kinds of arguments that have been advanced by those who in some cases draw directly on the theoretical work of Eve Kosofsky Sedgwick.[1]

All view the romantic triangle as a particularly complex structure that involves not only the rivalry of the men for the woman they both love but the men's homosexual love for each other. This chapter's title, "Beyond Triangles," points to my concern that criticism move beyond this figure and acknowledge the problems that attend schematizing human relationships. A second approach exemplified by the work of Mark Simpson doesn't specifically invoke the model of triangulation, although it also reads male love in homosexual terms. Here, too, I suggest some rethinking of his position.

From Here to Eternity

Like *The Big Parade*, *From Here to Eternity* concerns both heterosexual relationships and love between comrades. Its outstanding performances and production were rewarded with immense popularity at the box office, high critical esteem, and eight Oscars, including Best Picture, Best Director, Best Screenplay, and Best Supporting Actor and Actress. Looked at from a vantage point of some fifty years, it still is remarkable, in part because of its groundbreaking treatment of the famous love scene on the beach with Milt Warden (Burt Lancaster) and Karen Holmes (Deborah Kerr).

There are two romances in the film. The doomed relationship between Warden and Holmes is linked inextricably with the similarly hopeless one between Robert E. Lee Prewitt (Montgomery Clift) and Lorene/Alma Burke (Donna Reed). The main reason Warden doesn't want to become an officer, an act that would remove him from this base and free him to marry Karen after she divorces her husband, is his contempt of officers in general. But another motivation in particular, as he explains to Karen in their final conversation, is "this kid" (Prewitt), who has gone AWOL. At this point Warden sees a soldier whose manner and appearance suggest that of Prewitt, and he gets up to see him, only to realize his error. Meanwhile Prewitt is in Lorene's house, having been stabbed in a fight with Fatso (Ernest Borgnine), whom he battled and killed in revenge for the death of Maggio (Frank Sinatra); the latter has died as the result of an accident as he tried to escape the brutal stockade sergeant. Maggio, who was Prewitt's buddy on another base, is the first to befriend him at Scofield Barracks, sticks up for him against the oppression he faces because of his refusal to box, shares his punishment, and introduces him to the New Congress Club (and hence is instrumental in his meeting of Lorene).

Warden, Prewitt, and Maggio are together twice in the film. The first time is in a bar. After Fatso makes an insulting remark about Maggio's sister, a fight breaks out, and Warden staves off Fatso with a broken beer bottle. The second time occurs in a remarkable scene with striking displays of physical affection. Warden walks out of a bar on the base with a bottle, slightly drunk, and finds Prewitt, also drunk. The men sit down in the middle of the road and share the

From Here to Eternity. Warden drinks with Prewitt. Courtesy: Photofest. © Columbia Pictures Corporation, 1953.

bottle as they have their only sustained conversation in the film. Warden congratulates Prewitt for having beaten one of the bullies who has been trying to get him to box in the company tournament. In addition to asking Prewitt his opinion of officers, which prompts the famous line about "a man should be what he can do," Warden sympathizes with him about their mutual problems with women in general and Prewitt's specific problems with Captain Holmes (Philip Ober). During this supportive conversation, Warden puts his hand on Prewitt's back and then his head and begins to rub his hair for almost fifty seconds as he offers his support. Their conversation is interrupted by the arrival of a truck that almost runs them down. And then the battered Maggio appears. He has fallen from a truck during his escape and dies in Prewitt's arms.

I don't know of another scene in a war film in which one man shows such affection for another man by rubbing his head in this way. The point is that Warden's tender gesture for the living, which is followed by Prewitt's cradling of the dead Maggio, foregrounds the issue of intimacy. Precisely because Warden and Prewitt are unquestionably masculine and strong, their sexuality is unquestioned. Of course, the film says, Warden can show his support and affection for Prewitt in this way. The kind of bond they have is different in kind from that either one shares (unhappily) with his lover.

THE DEER HUNTER

The paradigmatic counterpart to *From Here to Eternity* is *The Deer Hunter*, which, like *Wings*, involves a romantic triangle. Mike (Robert DeNiro) and Nick (Christopher Walken), who are best friends, both love Linda (Meryl Streep). Analysis of the film in conjunction with Robin Wood's argument points to some of the problems in the kind of approach that doesn't acknowledge the full range of complexity in male sexuality.

Wood argues that Mike and Nick use Linda as their means of connecting sexually: "The male love story takes clear precedence over the heterosexual romance. . . . The triangular relationship of *The Deer Hunter* goes beyond the use/misuse of women in the buddy movies of the 1970s; the woman is present not merely to prove that the men are not gay. The film comes as close as any to articulating her function as mediator; the men make love to her because they are barred from making love to each other; she, at the same time, is ready and able to love them both."[2] He sees the presence of the typical "homophobic disclaimer" being supplied by Stanley (John Conzale), who is "characterized . . . as sexually insecure" and "*threatened* by homosexuality."[3]

Wood finds "unreadable" the one scene in which we have any direct visible erotic contact between Mike and Nick.[4] This occurs after the wedding, when Mike strips as he runs through the streets, followed by Nick. When he finds Mike lying near a lamppost, Nick throws a garment over Mike's genitals. And then the two, braced back to back (Nick clothed, Mike naked), speak about Clairton, their hometown, and the future. Nick says he loves the place and gets Mike's promise to not leave him over in Vietnam.

The glances from Mike and Nick at the men's photographs on the wall during the wedding sequence and at Linda signal how both are attracted to her. The sequence anticipates scenes later in the film when each of the men takes her photograph from his wallet and looks at it (Nick does this twice). But Cimino's point here is not to suggest a homosexual attraction between the men. For as Nick and Mike look at Linda, another scenario is being played out with Stanley, one that suggests something about his sexuality in a way that defines the relationship between Mike and Nick. While Nick and Mike look guardedly at Linda, Stanley becomes increasingly enraged with his date. He socks her when the bandleader makes a pass at her. His jealousy seems excessive, almost compensatory for what I suspect are deep feelings of sexual inadequacy and repressed homosexuality. He is constantly going for guns to prove his manhood: he threatens to get his gun when he sees the bandleader fondling his date; in the first hunting sequence he pulls a gun on Axel (Chuck Aspegren), who offers "a boot up the ass" to the improvident Stanley, who forgot his boots. On the second hunt, in response to a more insulting remark from Axel about his girlfriend and a forest ranger, Stanley draws his newest gun, thus precipitating the tense scene that ensues when Mike enters and

The Deer Hunter. The hunting trip before Vietnam. Courtesy: Jerry Ohlinger's. © EMI Films Ltd./Universal Pictures, 1978.

replays the Vietnamese roulette game. This time after spinning the chamber, he points the gun at Stanley and fires, and then throws the gun away.

Although nearly murdering Stanley is reprehensible, the event puts Mike's relationship with Nick into perspective, for it implies that Mike may be aware of Stanley's interest in him. Before Vietnam, Stanley charges that Mike is a "faggot." He claims to have fixed him up with dates a thousand times, with no results. But looking at the women Stanley himself goes out with, Mike's inactivity is understandable. The charge that Mike is a homosexual lacks any objective correlative. Why accuse him of that? If anything, Stanley seem to be emulating Mike's physical appearance, as evidenced by the mustache he grows that is similar to the one on his friend. When the group goes bowling after Mike's return, Stanley boasts that he "is getting more ass than a toilet seat," but his date that night seems comatose. On the first hunting trip, he wants to borrow Mike's boots, and we gather he has borrowed various pieces of equipment from him on earlier trips. In the sexual economy of the film, then, Stanley's presence and implied attraction for Mike provide a perspective for defining the nonsexual relationship between Mike and Nick. The terrifying replaying of the roulette game as an act of aggression foregrounds the sexual tensions between Mike and Stanley and demonstrates their difference from the love between Mike and Nick.

The Homosocial-Homosexual Continuum

We can use Wood's analysis as a point of entry to explore later arguments about the buddy film in particular and male sexuality in general. The first sees men in buddy films (a specific genre) or in buddy relationships in other kinds of films (gangsters, westerns, war) as by definition in a homosocial relationship. The second implicitly or explicitly treats the distance between homosocial (public interaction) and homosexual (private and sexual) relations as tenuous and permeable. Women used communally by the same men (either two rivals or a group of males) offer a means to connect sexually in a way that masks the actual repressed erotic desires.

For example, Henry Benshoff suggests that one way of understanding *Independence Day* (Roland Emmerich, 1996) is to see it as "a sci-fi version of the World War II war film" that displays the same conventions of that genre, including "a tightly knit group of men who must band together to fight a common enemy." This, "like many other buddy, action, and/or war films . . . celebrates masculinity and male homosocial bonds while negating their shadowy other, male homosexual bonds. Practically though, homosociality and homosexuality are inescapably intertwined, for one cannot delineate male homosocial bonds without at the same time vocally disavowing the homosexual possibility, lest the audience (or the members of the group itself) get the wrong idea." The film uses various comic moments as "inoculation, wherein counter-hegemonic ideas are addressed in order to be contained. . . . [T]raditional masculinity and male homosocial groups are on some level obsessed with forthright homosexuality—if only in their obsessive need to deny it."[5]

Such a view is consonant with the perspective offered by Eve Kosofsky Sedgwick's theory of male sexuality. Sedgwick (who, to my knowledge, has never commented on war films) draws significantly on the work of René Girard and on psychoanalytic theory, particularly Jacques Lacan's modification of Sigmund Freud. She speaks of two triangular models. The first is that of the Oedipus complex, in which the rivalry between the son and father for the mother is overcome by the son's entrance into the symbolic order identified by Lacan as the Name of the Father. The second is a variant of Girard's triangular framework involving the relationships of men who are rivals for the affection of the same woman. She describes Girard's idea of the

> calculus of power that was structured by the relation of a rivalry between the two active members of an erotic triangle. . . . [I]n any erotic rivalry, the bond that links the two rivals is as intense and potent as the bond that links either of the rivals to the betrothed. . . . Girard finds many examples in which the choice of the beloved is determined in the first place, not by the qualities of the beloved, but by the beloved's already being the choice of the person who has been chosen as a rival. . . . [H]e seems to see the bond between rivals in an erotic triangle as being even stronger, more heavily determinant of actions and

choice than anything in the bond between either of the lovers and the beloved.[6]

In her modification, whether symmetrical or asymmetrical, the triangular structure involves a homosocial-homosexual continuum supportive of patriarchy, wherein the relationship between men maintains their hegemonic power over women.

Todd R. Ramlow's analysis of *Ride with the Devil* (Ang Lee, 1999) has affinities to this model. Jake Roedel/Duchy (Tobey Maguire) and Jack Bull Chiles (Skeet Ulrich) are boyhood friends who fight for the bushwhackers, a renegade group of Southern soldiers supporting the Confederacy during the Civil War. Ramlow speaks of the men's relationship as

> the film's second story: the one of male desire and domestication[.] Various scenes demonstrate the intimacy of the central male friendships. . . . What the film shows us, but can never allude to or acknowledge that it knows, are the erotics of these homosocial associations, developed in environments devoid of women. The intimacy in the film in these friendships in the film goes far beyond good ol' boy male bonding. And yet, to ward off (presumed audience) anxieties concerning these intimacies, the film introduces a single woman [Sue Lee (Jewel)]. . . . Through Sue Lee's body, the men's desire for each other can, in a roundabout way, be expressed.[7]

In addition to the problematic assertion that the film "knows" anything, another limitation of this particular application of the homosocial-homosexual continuum lies in its omission of a crucial detail. Jack Bull has been wounded and brought to the lair the renegades have dug out for themselves. Jack Bull lies between Duchy and Sue Lee (Jewel), who is pregnant with Jack Bull's child. Duchy begins chewing an apple, and then takes out a piece of it from his mouth and puts it in the mouth of his wounded friend. Jack Bull reaches out with his hand and touches his friend's face as Sue Lee watches them both tenderly. Shortly afterward, though, Daniel Holt (Jeffrey Wright) comes in and, having observed the condition of Jack Bull's arm, decides that there will have to be an amputation. Jack Bull does not survive, and we see him lying dead, as both Duchy and Sue Lee, still on each side, weep. If anything, the repetition of the tableaux demonstrates the *opposite* of what Ramlow argues. Rather than demonstrating how two men are able to connect erotically through the body of the woman they both love, it shows us in the wounded Jack Bull someone who can simultaneously be in two different kinds of love relationships: the nonerotic bond with his childhood friend and the tie with his girlfriend. The men don't need Sue Lee to express their affection. In fact, the logic of Ramlow's argument could be turned against his conclusion. If sexual contact is made through the body of a third party, then Sue Lee and Duchy, who eventually marry, could be said to be communing through the body of Jack Bull.

Ride with the Devil. The marriage of Duchy and Sue Lee. Courtesy: Jerry Ohlinger's.
© Good Machine, 1999.

A Midnight Clear (Keith Gordon, 1992) has also been interpreted in relation
to the homosocial-homosexual model. Describing a scene in the film in which
four virginal soldiers have sex with a young woman whose fiancé has been killed,
John Belton argues:

> In enjoying sexual relations with the same woman [in war films], the men
> enjoy what psychoanalysts describe as a displaced homoerotic or homosocial
> relationship with each other in which their rivalry becomes a form not of sex-
> ual competition but of exchange. . . . *A Midnight Clear* . . . conceives of male
> camaraderie in . . . homoerotic terms. The buddies not only all sleep with the
> same young girl on their last leave together, but when one of their comrades
> dies, they also take off their clothes and ritualistically bathe him, conducting a
> sexualized communion of sort.[8]

But the four virginal soldiers who share the young woman are not now and
have never been "rivals"; they have actually been mutually supportive of one
another. The soldiers who find the young woman bring her back to share with
their friends so that all will be "men."

Arguing from a different perspective about the homosexual relationship of the
men, Mark Simpson sees the young woman "bestowing a kind of maternal bene-
diction on them through sex."[9] He finds their dead comrade, "Father" (Frank

Whaley), who had studied to be a priest, the "queerest" member of the squad, and describes the scene in which his buddies clean his wounds as

> an astonishingly moving scene that takes the homoerotic masochistic "ecstasy" of war to its limit and beyond. . . . As they wash clean the large hole in his back made by the bullet that killed him, their fingers seem to linger caressingly around it, echoing strongly the earlier sex scene with the girl. Father's love has brought the boys together in a physical expression of their love for him and for each other. His Christ-like significance takes the ultimately self-conscious form when they tie him to a wooden cross in order to fit him into the jeep when effecting their escape.[10]

But a more complex relationship connects the bathing of their dead comrade and their sexual initiation. That is, early in the film each man loses his virginity through the agency of one woman who is reliving her experience with her dead fiancé. The men are not bound together with each other sexually by having sex with her; rather, they are mutual participants in a secular ritual in which a woman brings them all to a new level of sexual maturity. The comrade/chaplain whom they bathe died a virgin, having not been part of the sexual initiation. In contrast to the initiation scene, this is a specifically nonsexualized communion, a religious counterpart to the secularized ritual they engaged in earlier when they were initiated sexually. In fact, the decision to pump out his blood and use it to make a red cross enables them to escape German attack since it appears they are part of hospital. While the woman makes them men by offering them sex, the chaplain's blood literally saves their lives.

Simpson uses this moment in *A Midnight Clear* to generalize about all "buddy war films" in which "death . . . is a sacrament: it makes love between men eternal by removing it from the male body; by canceling forever the threat of its consummation it ensures that boyish love is immortal, and that queer love, transformed into a cadaver, is buried on the battlefield."[11]

Writing of the battlefield rather than films, Santanu Das presents a diametrically opposite conclusion. Instead of burying love in death, he argues:

> [H]omoeroticism has to be understood within new conceptual parameters and a different economy of emotions. In the military, bodily contact is often one of the primary means of fostering loyalty, trust, and unity within an army unit. In the trenches of the western front, where life expectancy could be as short as a couple of weeks, same sex ardor, bodily contact, and (in some cases) eroticism should not be understood solely in contrast to heterosexuality, nor viewed only through the lenses of gender and sexuality. Such intimacy must also be understood to exist as *a triumph over death*; it must be seen as a celebration of life, of young men huddled against long winter nights, rotting corpses, and falling shells. Physical contact was the wonderful assurance of being alive, and more sex-specific eroticism, though concomitant, was subsidiary.[12]

The voice-over commentary by Ethan Hawke and Keith Gordon on the DVD makes clear that they were aware of the homoerotic potential of the bathing scene. Originally, before the bathing of Father, the soldiers were to have been nude and washing their clothes in the tub. That idea was replaced by having them act somewhat "giddy" and splash each other, but that was also rejected because of the actors' concern that the scene would be read as having too much of an erotic implication.[13] The actors' instincts were absolutely correct. While the scene could have been erotic, the somber tone and religious dimension neutralize any homosexual dimensions. In fact, the bathing scene itself is handled with almost 1940s-like reserve; no one is seen nude.

Another observation by Das is relevant in regard to this scene: "to discuss same-sex relations during war, we must introduce a different and less distinctly sexualized array of emotional intensities and bodily sensations, a continuum of nongenital tactile tenderness that goes beyond gender division, sexual binaries, or identity politics."[14] He specifically cautions against relying solely on theoretical writings such as are provided by writers like Sedgwick: "The bonds I examine are not based on triangulated desire, are far more physical than in Sedgwick, and need not be consciously erotic, nor associated with power."[15]

In a way, Anthony Easthope and Mark Simpson replace the woman in the triangle with the figure of death, arguing that the presence of death and suffering in war films in which we know something substantial about the soldiers' relationships provides a way for the narratives to negotiate the characters' homosexuality. Speaking of *The Deer Hunter*, Easthope says: "In the dominant versions of men at war, men are permitted to behave towards each other in ways that would not be allowed elsewhere, caressing and holding each other, comforting and weeping together, admitting their love. The pain of war is the price paid for the way it expresses the male bond. War's suffering is a kind of punishment for the release of homosexual desire and male femininity that only the war allows. In this special form the male bond is fully legitimated."[16] Expanding on Easthope's argument in his discussion of *Memphis Belle* (Michael Caton-Jones, 1990) and *A Midnight Clear*, Simpson suggests that

> the war film not only offers a text on masculinity and how to take one's place in patriarchy, it also offers a vision of a world in which the privileges of heterosexual manhood can be combined with boyish homoeroticism—a purely masculine world awash with femininity. ... The lesson that the buddy film has to teach boys (and remind men) is that "war" is a place where queer love can not only be expressed but *endorsed*—but only when married to death. Death justifies and romanticizes the signs but not the practice of queer love.[17]

Both Easthope and Simpson draw on psychoanalysis for their arguments. Easthope sees "four crucial elements" in representations of war: "defeat, combat, victory, and comradeship. . . . [A]ssociated with all the others, there is the moment of comradeship, the picture of the soldier weeping for his wounded buddy. For psychoanalysis these moments are to be explained in terms of the fear of castration, the triumph of the masculine ego, fathers and sons, and the sublimated intimacies of the male bond."[18] Having considered both Freudian and post-Freudian views of castration, Simpson suggests that the buddy war film presents "something of an *escape* from the Oedipus complex, given its focus on friendship rather than on conflict with the father."[19]

But it is possible to see expressions of concern and loving tenderness for wounded or dying comrades in nonerotic terms, as occurs in *Air Force* (Howard Hawks, 1943) and *The Story of G.I. Joe* (William Wellman, 1945). In *Air Force*, Irish Quincannon (John Ridgley) commands the *Mary Ann*, a B-17 caught up in the events of Pearl Harbor and thereafter. The aerial gunner Joe Winocki (John Garfield) dislikes Quincannon, who had been responsible for kicking him out of flight school earlier as a result of a fatal accident. The enmity between them abates as the crew becomes increasingly closer in response to one crisis after another. Virtually every place they land (or try to land) has been or is under siege. The most dramatic moment in the film occurs when the *Mary Ann* is hit by fighter planes, forcing the crew to abandon ship. But Winocki, who has by this time made his peace with his commander, feigns his bail out and returns to the cabin

Air Force. Winocki supports his commander. Courtesy: Jerry Ohlinger's. © Warner Bros. Pictures, 1943.

so that he can attend to the needs of Quincannon, who has been wounded and has ordered all his men to bail out. Winocki steadies him and takes over the controls, landing the plane on Manila. As it skids in, he reaches out to prevent the now-unconscious Quincannon from falling into the controls. This protective physical gesture is notable and would have been unimaginable at the beginning of the film, given their initial antipathy for one another. Winocki's heroism in keeping the plane aloft is prompted by his desire to try and rescue his former enemy. When Quincannon lies dying in the hospital, Winocki stands at the head of the bed, close to him. While there is no overt display of affection between them, it's clear that Winocki risked his life to save his commander, whom he has come to respect. While this hardly qualifies as an example of love, it does, though, belong here as a demonstration of the kind of affection that has nothing to do with any kind of erotic motivation.

The reviewer for *Variety* spoke about the bonding: "The affection of the crew of the 'Mary Ann' is genuine, manly and sentimental. It points to a type of team-work which may well be construed as a pattern for all Americans in the manner in which our team-work, on the home front and at the battle fronts, will achieve the ultimate victory."[20] The important aspect of this review comes in the suggestion that "affection" can in fact be "manly." That is, the two are not mutually exclusive, and the union of these will lead to victory.

The Story of G.I. Joe depicts various military campaigns of an infantry outfit led by Captain Bill Walker (Robert Mitchum) and Walker's interactions with the famous journalist Ernie Pyle (Burgess Meredith). This particularly melancholy war film concludes with one of the most heartbreaking scenes of mourning in the genre. Walker's body has been carried into camp on a donkey. The men gather around to pay tribute to him and, one by one, offer their farewells. One man in particular sits next to the captain, looking bleakly at his body. He takes Walker's hand and begins to stroke it tenderly, a gesture he continues even when orders are given to move out. Eventually, he stands up and joins the others, who have left the clearing. The scene illustrates poignantly the power of nonerotic love. Bernard Dick notes: "Howard Hawks claimed some of his films were male love stories. William Wellman could have said the same of *The Story of G.I. Joe*."[21] Clayton R. Koppes and Gregory D. Black claim this same film's scene of mourning for a dead soldier "came as close as the movies dared to speaking of male love."[22]

BEYOND TRIANGULATION: RIVAL BROTHERS IN WAR FILMS

Many films whose narratives certainly do not illustrate the operation of the homosocial-homosexual triangular model concern brothers who are in love with the same woman. *Hell's Angels* (Howard Hughes, 1930), one of the well-known examples, concerns Roy (James Hall) and Monte Rutledge (Ben Lyon), who are pilots in the British air force during World War I and rivals for the love of Helen

(Jean Harlow). Although the brothers are very different in character (the admirable Roy is a contrast to the playboy Monte), both fall in love with Helen. While she encourages both, neither one is really of interest to her, and she abandons them. Late in the film, the brothers have reconciled but are now prisoners of the Germans. Monte is prepared to divulge information about a surprise attack to their interrogator, Baron Von Kranz (Lucien Prival), the husband of a woman with whom Monte earlier had an affair. But Roy wants to protect the three thousand soldiers whose lives will be lost by such a disclosure. To prevent Monte from telling, he shoots him in the back. Before he dies, in an agonizing death scene, Monte realizes his error and forgives Roy. In one of many such scenes in the American war film, Roy embraces his dying brother in a pietà. Then Roy, who continues to refuse to give information, is taken out to be executed. But immediately after, the American assault on the Germans begins. Their heterosexual rivalry simply cannot be read as displaced homoerotic fraternal desire.

A related example of this appears in Lloyd Bacon's *Wings of the Navy* (1939), which concerns Cass (George Brent) and Jerry Herrington (John Payne), brothers who are rivals for Irene (Olivia de Haviland). Unlike the other films mentioned, this does not take place during a war but, rather, concentrates on the training and activities of naval pilots at the time of the film's release. The younger Jerry, who originally serves on a submarine, becomes a flier and competes with Cass both for Irene and for recognition in his new role. Ultimately, Cass, having been injured in a crash, realizes Irene loves Jerry, and acknowledges Jerry's success in the film's happy ending. Again, there is not the slightest suggestion of any hidden homosexual bond between the brothers.

Yet another film involving brothers in love with the same woman is *Love Me Tender* (Robert Webb, 1956). This film concerns Clint (Elvis Presley) and Vance Reno (Richard Egan), who both love Cathy (Debra Paget). The film opens at the end of the Civil War as Vance and his men, who are fighting for the Confederacy, take money from a train and kill Union soldiers, unaware that they committed this action after the war has ended. Pursued by the Union forces, they return to Vance's home, only to discover that Clint and Cathy have married. Even though they heard (mistakenly) that Vance was dead, Clint was unaware Vance and Cathy were in love in the first place. That is, from his perspective, there had been no rivalry before his brother left for the war. Upon his return, Vance denies he was ever in love with Cathy: "We were just good friends. I'm just happy for both of you." But tensions arise, leading the frustrated Vance to tell Cathy: "I can hear you at night" and know "you are lying together side by side." The climax of the film occurs when Clint, who beats up Cathy once he learns of her previous relation with Vance and mistakenly thinks she's about to run off, shoots his brother in the shoulder, having been goaded on by one of Vance's men. He instantly recognizes his error, but is shot by one of Vance's men. The brothers reconcile just before Clint dies. No matter how unusual the film is at times (punctuated by four songs by Elvis, making his screen debut), it is not in any way readable as a narrative that supports the homosocial-homosexual continuum.

OTHER CHALLENGES TO THE MODEL

Thunder Birds (William Wellman, 1942), a film about the training of pilots for the U.S. Air Corps, presents the story of Steve Britt (Preston Foster), an older pilot who is in love with the considerably younger Kay Saunders (Gene Tierney). We first see her when he swoops over the outdoor tub in which she is bathing as he flies into Arizona to teach in a flight school for aspiring pilots. One of the new recruits is Peter Stackhouse (John Sutton), an Englishman whose brother, another pilot, has been killed in Europe, and whose father Steve knew in World War I. Peter is not only inexperienced but also physically unfit to fly. Steve treats him supportively, even after the pilot meets and falls in love with Kay. The tensions over her between the men increase after Steve becomes Peter's champion. Her decision to accept Peter's offer of marriage occurs after he has proved himself as a pilot, primarily because of the instruction of Steve and, most immediately, his rescue of his mentor. The point is the men are already bound to one another in a kind of father-son connection before the rivalry develops, and the film doesn't admit of a narrow reading using the homosocial-homosexual triangulation model.

Another war film with a romantic triangle that resists such a reading is *Crash Dive* (Archie Mayo, 1943). Ward Stewart (Tyrone Power) and Dewey Connors (Dana Andrews) are friends and fellow officers on a submarine. Unlike *Thunder Birds*, in which one love relationship is changed by the presence of a rival, in this film the two main leads discover that each of them has already met Jean Hewlitt (Anne Baxter) and fallen in love with her. That is, neither knows until later that the woman he loves is also the object of the other's affection. Neither of them knows the other as a rival, only as a friend, until the awkward situation is revealed.

ALTERNATIVES

The examples discussed above simply don't support the validity of arguments that see the shared love of one woman as a means to disguise homosexual longing, the basic premise of those accepting the triangulation model. In contrast, I suggest that one look at heterosexual love as a way of distinguishing it from the nonsexual love between men. The two kinds of love actually complement one another. The narrative complexities generated by a situation of triangulation are all the richer precisely because each kind of love is made problematic by the presence of the other. Heterosexual love defines what the other kind of love is *not*: something predicated on sexual interaction with the other partner.

Support for this model of thinking about love between men comes from various directions. First, Richard Dyer, who has enriched our understanding of gay-themed films so rewardingly, offers an exemplary model of how to look at close male relationships in the buddy film without automatically assuming a homosexual dimension. Four years before Sedgwick's study, writing on *Papillon* (Franklin J. Schaffner, 1973), Dyer argues that a nonsexualized love between men is possible. *Papillon*, which is a prison rather than a war film (although it certainly evokes prisoner-of-war films), concerns the friendship of two men sentenced to Devil's Island. Dyer shows how the bond between Papillon (Steve McQueen) and Dega (Dustin Hoffman) displays the nature of their loving relationship in traditional ways that include common narrative strategies of the buddy film: "partly through the use of cinematic conventions for the representation of love"; "a direct recognition of the buddy movie's conventional disavowal . . . that these men cannot actually say what they feel"; and "the explicit denial of homosexuality." The narrative presents each man in a heterosexual relationship and uses a gay character, Maturette (Robert Deman), "to signal the difference between the central buddy relationship and a homosexual one." In fact, "Maturette and his . . . admirer in the hospital, in part function as a model for what Papillon and Dega's relationship is *not*."[23]

What is important to see here is that while Dyer knows and enumerates all the standard conventions of the buddy film, he warns about the dangers of seeing the conventions as a mere "smokescreen" because to do so is "to conflate love and sexuality too readily: it does not allow for the possibility of non-sexual love."[24] That is, the mere presence of some conventions of the buddy movie that have been used in the past to disavow a homosexual text doesn't necessarily mean that a particular text is *always* employing them that way. "The love between Papillon and Dega is physical and tender, but not sexual—and this is not a rejection on the film's part of homosexuality but rather an openness to the possibility of real love between men who are none the less heterosexual."[25] Dyer sees "real love between men" being expressible on its own terms: "this is important—the beauty of a non-sexual love between persons of the same sex needs representing. . . . [I]t is remarkable for a Hollywood film to represent non-sexual love between males *as love* without a concomitant rejection of homosexuality."[26] His commentary is important: someone knowing all the conventions of the buddy film, particularly the ways elements in the narrative disavow homosexuality, points out that not every buddy film is necessarily about this.[27]

ANOTHER PARADIGM: WAR FILMS WITHOUT ROMANTIC TRIANGLES

A second source of evidence demonstrating the possibility of nonsexual love is provided by the war films that do not involve romantic triangles or significant love relationships. Although the men's interest in women is established by incidental aspects of the plot (acknowledgment of girlfriends and wives, encounters with prostitutes), the primary focus remains on the bonds between the men, exclusive of any relevant narrative attention to romance.

For example, in *All Quiet on the Western Front* (Lewis Milestone, 1930), many of the young soldiers are already friends, having come from the same school. The most important bond that develops is that between Paul (Lew Ayres) and Kat (Louis Wolheim), the older soldier who forages for food, bolsters the men's confidence, and sustains them in their terror. Later Paul returns to the front after a leave at home and searches for his friend. As they walk happily along the road, Kat is wounded, and Paul picks him up. Then a plane strafes them, wounding Kat mortally, a fact Paul doesn't realize until he returns to camp and tries to give water to his friend. A medic breaks the bad news to the shattered soldier. The love at the center of this relationship is absolutely not erotic.[28]

In *Wake Island* (John Farrow, 1942), as Smacksie (William Bendix) and Joe (Robert Preston) prepare for a final and deadly assault by their Japanese attackers, Smacksie puts his hand briefly and tenderly on Joe's thigh. In the same scene, the doomed Smacksie and Joe joke about what they're going to miss because of their imminent deaths: "How many blonds are there that we didn't get to?"

David O. Russell's *Three Kings* (1999) offers a striking example of unproblematic and nonsexual love between soldiers. The film concerns the activities of Sergeant Troy Barlow (Mark Wahlberg), Private Conrad Vig (Spike Jonze), Captain Archie Gates (George Clooney), and Staff Sergeant Chief Elgin (Ice Cube), who team up to steal gold bullion from Saddam Hussein's coffers after the end of the Gulf

Three Kings. Troy and Conrad. Courtesy: Photofest. © Warner Bros. Pictures, 1999.

War.[29] Each of the main characters is introduced with a line typed in front of them on the screen. Troy's is "new father." Conrad's is "wants to be Troy Barlow." After the heist of the gold, the men and some Iraqis they are helping are gassed and get lost in the desert. Troy is kidnapped by supporters of Hussein and Conrad wounded. Conrad pushes for rescuing Troy, a feat achieved by fooling the captors into thinking Hussein himself is visiting their fortress. Once released, Troy calls out for Conrad, who, seeing his friend, gets up from the ground where he has been lying and runs toward him. But he is shot, and when Troy runs to him, he, too, is shot.

The men lie next to one another, and Troy holds Conrad's hand. Russell shoots this contact in a way that prominently displays Troy's wedding ring. Conrad dies, and Troy cries uncontrollably, totally disconsolate at his friend's death. The shot of them holding hands underscores not only that Troy is married and a new father (indeed, his last appearance in the film is with his wife and two children), but that he has loved and been loved by Conrad in a different kind of relationship. Again, the heterosexual relationship is present not as a smokescreen to hide homosexual desire but to define the nonsexual nature of the love between Troy and Conrad.

TIGERLAND

Tigerland offers a relevant complement to *Three Kings*. Set at Fort Polk in Louisiana, the film follows the lives of marine soldiers being trained for Vietnam. The climax of their training occurs when they enter a simulated replica of Vietnam called "Tigerland." Roland Bozz (Colin Farrell) is a rebellious sergeant whose behavior results in his demotion to private. He befriends Jim Paxton (Matthew Davis), an articulate person who has enlisted out of a sense of duty. The film traces the development of their bond, beginning with a trip to town where they pick up two prostitutes. Both couples appear to be in the same room in this fairly graphic sex scene.[30]

The women leave when they realize the men are not going to take them out to eat. As they do, the still-naked Bozz and Paxton are talking about their lives. This is an extraordinarily important moment in the war film in terms of the way it differentiates heterosexuality, homosociality, and homosexuality. The ease and comfort with which each man can talk with his friend without feeling the need to cover up suggests the total absence of an erotic charge at this point. Collectively naked with the women, they have enjoyed sex. Now the nature of their relationship moves to a different register. A second trip to town occasions another visit with prostitutes, although this time the sex scene is recounted, rather than shown. Bozz says he farted before having an orgasm, and Paxton says he could hear this from the next room.

Bozz has been planning to escape to Mexico from the base and wants Paxton to accompany him, but the latter can't because to do so would mean putting the

Tigerland. Bozz and Paxton. Courtesy: Photofest. © Haft Entertainment, 2000.

person who takes his place in danger. Once the men get to Tigerland, Bozz makes good on his plan to escape to Mexico, but returns out of a sense of duty to help Paxton. Both men have been the targets of the violent Private Wilson (Shea Whigham). He has tried to kill Bozz by substituting live ammunition during a training exercise, and he almost choked Paxton to death. In the film's climax, to divert the crazed Wilson, who again has substituted live ammunition, and, concurrently, to ensure that Paxton doesn't have to go to Vietnam, Bozz fires his rifle in a way that will injure but not completely damage Paxton's eye. He succeeds, with the result that Paxton gets a disability discharge. As the men part, Paxton, who is crying, acknowledges his awareness of what Bozz did and asks him to write from Vietnam. Bozz responds by saying: "No more of this phony army buddy crap." Bozz embraces him, and his face touches Paxton's cheek. In a final voice-over, Paxton says he never heard from Bozz again, but is aware of various reports about him (dead in Nam, deserted in Nam, seen in Mexico with a beautiful woman).

Like *Three Kings*, this film clearly demonstrates the love between the soldiers. While the two encounters with the prostitutes could be read as what Dyer dismisses as a "smokescreen," the point of these scenes is to contrast the totally body-driven sexual encounters with the nonsexualized bonds between the men. The line "no more phony army buddy crap" specifically acknowledges that their relationship is *not* readable as a cliché. But it can also be read another way: this affection is, in fact, real rather than phony. That is, there has been something more than conventional bonding—the love that clearly exists between them.[31]

Memoirs of War

A third source of support for the argument that nonsexual love is possible comes from commentators who speak on the basis of their experience as soldiers. Some contributions written about the Vietnam War are particularly relevant because they emerge in a context in which more is known about homosexuality and the complex aspects of love of and between men. Various autobiographical reports of wartime experiences demonstrate that bonding between and among comrades in a time of war can create intense levels of affection. Use of the word "love" to describe the relationships is common.

For example, writing about World War II, J. Glenn Gray comments on "preservative love, or concern, . . . clearly observed in combat in a soldier's care for life other than his own."[32] This is one of three kinds of love that he sees occurring during war. The other two are "erotic love between the sexes . . . and the love called friendship."[33] He distinguishes between comradeship and friendship, since he believes the former actually involves a loss of individual identity: "The essential difference between comradeship and friendship consists . . . in a heightened awareness of the self in friendship and in the suppression of self-awareness in comradeship. Friends do not seek to lose their identity, as comrades and erotic lovers do."[34] Even though he says that denial of self is a trait common to comrades and to heterosexual lovers, Gray does not conflate them. Rather, he acknowledges the complexity of love as "a genus with many species, and there is little danger of exhausting the inner relations of the species."[35]

Gerald Linderman devotes an invaluable chapter to comradeship in *The World within War*, citing a number of comments from former soldiers such as Richard Leacock, William Manchester, and Leon Uris illustrating aspects of male affection for comrades. In particular, he refers to "Watson," a soldier interviewed by Arthur Miller when Miller was researching army life in preparation for writing an early script of *The Story of G.I. Joe*. According to Watson, "Friendship is the greatest thing out there [in the field]. I mean real friendship, not because a guy can give you something you want. I tell you the truth: I would die for any one of thirty or forty men out there just as easy as I'd flick out this match. I swear that's the truth. I don't expect you to understand it, but I swear it. It never seems a terrible thing or a sacrifice after a while. I would die for them. I love them with everything in my heart."[36] Linderman comments on the awkwardness soldiers feel about their sense of affection: "Under the pressures of the battlefield, feelings of friendship intensify—and sometimes move to love. True, that word was so powerfully and indissolubly bound to heterosexual relationships that its application to comrades was almost hidden behind a curtain of reticence."[37]

Philip Caputo's *A Rumor of War*, his memoir of Vietnam, speaks of love between soldiers: "I have . . . attempted to describe the intimacy of life in infantry battalions, where the communion between men is as profound as any between

his hand is being stroked by Tom, he pushes him away. The comic gag is replayed in a different register as the two men go on stage to participate in the magician's act. They and a beautiful woman, La Belle Circe, are shut in a cabinet. Then the structure is opened, the girl has disappeared, and each man, thinking he is holding her hand, discovers himself holding the other man's hand—again for laughs.[1]

In *Gung Ho!* (Ray Enright, 1943), one of the soldiers on a troop ship asks Transport (Sam Levene): "Got any pictures of pin-ups?" After Transport comments that he doesn't have any, he says, "I got a picture of me in a bathing suit. Want me to autograph it?" A voice (unidentified) asks: "Where is it?" and produces a comic double take from Transport.

In *Wing and a Prayer* (Henry Hathaway, 1944), one husky character lying on his bunk is swatted on the behind by another walking through the cabin and says: "Do it again! I love it." That the line is strictly for laughs is confirmed when all the men are seen shortly afterward watching *Tin Pan Alley* (Walter Lang, 1940), starring Betty Grable and Alice Faye. They hoot appreciatively at the display of the stars' and dancers' bodies, and become irate when the film breaks.[2]

In *See Here, Private Hargrove* (Wesley Ruggles, 1944), an extended nightclub scene shows the singer Bob Crosby, in uniform and playing himself, singing "In My Arms" to an audience of servicemen and their dates. The sequence begins with the song serving as the diegetic dance music. The camera then closes in on a table at which a number of soldiers sit with Bob Crosby as he sings the song. The lyrics concern the imminent departure of a soldier, who laments: "You can keep your shaving cream and lotion./If I'm going to cross the ocean,/Give me a girl in my arms." At this point, Crosby makes a move to embrace the soldier on his left, who pushes him away with a grin. As the song ends, Crosby again extends his arm to show affection for another man, this one on his right. Again, for laughs, this soldier pushes Crosby away with sufficient force that he is almost knocked off his chair.

In *Objective, Burma!* (Raoul Walsh, 1945), we see Gabby (George Tobias) washing out his socks in a pond. Ordered to get moving, he responds in a purposely inflected feminine tone: "I'm washing out my last pair of nylons." Another character asks for a hand with his gear: "Give me a hand with my bustle," and is told: "Very fine, sweetheart. If it doesn't work, you can bring it back." These moments did not deter Bosley Crowther of the *New York Times* from speaking of the "hard bitten story of a group of tough, tight-lipped paratroopers."[3]

Commenting not on these films but on various defensive strategies used by servicemen in general to deal with their sexual drives and potential homosexual impulses, Allan Bérubé and John D'Emilio both draw on the work of psychiatrist William C. Menninger. In *Psychiatry in a Troubled World*, Menninger suggests that among the ways servicemen found to accommodate the absence of women, "[t]he physical substitutes were varied. . . . There were numerous psychological substitutes used: possession of 'pin-up girl' photographs; an increased interest in 'dirty' stories, in profanity, and in homosexual buffoonery."[4] Bérubé describes one of the examples:

> In some barracks joking became ritualized as "homosexual buffoonery," a spontaneous game in which recruits took turns pretending to be the company queer. An Army psychologist described how the men "kiddingly" played this striptease game with each other while they were getting undressed. "One soldier," he observed, "returning from the shower in the nude, will be greeted with cat-calls, salacious whistling, and comments like, 'hey Joe, you shouldn't go around like that—you don't know what that does to me.' Joe will respond by wriggling his hips in feminine fashion after coyly draping a towel around himself."[5]

Such overt displays publicly in films and within the barracks occur at a time when concerns had been raised by various authorities about the dangers of hav-ing homosexual soldiers.[6] Allan Bérubé and Steven Cohan both provide helpful commentary on *Psychology for the Fighting Man* (1943). This work, published in the *Infantry Journal* and circulated among soldiers, openly acknowledges the possibility of encountering homosexual behavior. The collective authors, a committee of the National Research Council, including such notable figures as G. W. Allport of Harvard and S. A. Stouffer of the Special Services Division of the War Department, note that the preinduction screening may fail, discuss the pos-sibility of what would later be called situational homosexuality, and advance a position that seems to anticipate the current argument of "don't ask, don't tell."[7] But homosexuality is clearly raised as a negative dimension of sexuality.[8]

The review in *Newsweek* described the work as a "Baedeker for the soldier's mind" and commented on its "forthright discussion of a soldier's gnawing, inces-sant hunger and what he hungers for."[9] The review quoted the following specific passages from the report on homosexuality:

> ABOUT SEX. This is the second great desire of the flesh. . . . In the course of man's life, this need is modified, changed, and disguised. . . . Although medical offices try to keep them out of the Army, a sexually abnormal man who finds satisfaction only with other men may get in. Some have no feeling of shame for their homosexuality. If they are content with quietly seeking the satisfac-tion of their sexual needs with others of their own kind, their perversion may go unnoticed. It is possible that they may even turn out to be excellent soldiers. The man whose homosexuality develops for the first time in a situation where he cannot have normal satisfaction may be only mildly disturbed, but it is more likely that he will suffer strong feelings of guilt. So long as he is thus seriously worried and dissatisfied, the chances are that he may be all right again when he returns to normal conditions of life. But he should put up a strong fight and at the same time find some other outlet for his sex drive as soon as he can.[10]

Thus after mid 1943 at least part of the viewing audience of war films would have had access to some of the information in *Psychology for the Fighting Man*, in which a complex dimension of male sexuality was acknowledged. Obviously, the strictures of the Production Code Administration (PCA) precluded any suggestion of actual homosexuality in films. The fact that such scenes just described appeared in films at all suggests that by inserting them, the creators were themselves engaged in an analogous kind of buffoonery, purposely using the display of such behavior to disavow the actual possibility of homosexuality in these characters and, by extension, all soldiers.

MASCULINITY, FEMININITY, AND THE MATERNAL

Such buffoonery can be understood in the larger context of representations of masculinity and sexuality within American culture during World War II. When films and other forms of popular culture show tough men acting in a way that acknowledges their capacity for displaying and enacting positive feminine qualities, often there will be an element that qualifies the representation by reinforcing evidence of masculinity. Significant examples of this appear in combat films and in other manifestations of culture.

Several advertisements from the period of World War II play on a denial of femininity and affirmation of masculinity in ways that suit the spirit of events shown in films and described in other venues. Three advertisements with a comic aspect to them involve a play on masculinity apparently being undermined by femininity. First, one for Monsanto Chemicals in *Newsweek* shows the drawing of a shirtless soldier holding a slip in one hand and a woman's undergarment in another, with the caption: "Hey! What goes on here? *Yes, we know—this couldn't actually happen!* You'll never encounter any lady whatcha-ma-callits in Army laundry." The ad copy goes on to argue that the detergent will work for the troops, no matter the quality of the water they have to use; hence it will be fine for "Mrs. Housewife" as well.[11]

An advertisement for the Bead Chain Manufacturing Company in *Newsweek* shows a drawing of a tough-looking soldier with the caption: "Yeah, I wear a necklace—but brother, I ain't no sissy. Every mother's son of us . . . and daughter, too . . . in the Army, Navy, Marine Corps and Coast Guard wears identification tags around his neck."[12]

B. F. Goodrich touts its newest contribution to protecting sailors on ship decks, a helmet with special rubber lining, by displaying a sailor in uniform standing before a mirror. He adjusts his helmet in a pose that suggests a woman before a mirror. The caption reads, "Latest fashion for ocean cruises," and the copy explains: "Because of dive bombers, it's healthier for exposed gunners on ship decks to wear steel helmets. But for real protection a helmet has to fit"— hence the advantages of their new process.[13]

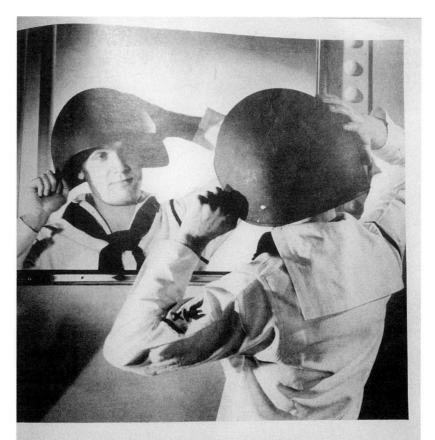

Latest fashion for ocean cruises

typical example of B. F. Goodrich development in rubber

CAUSE of dive bombers, it's healthier for exposed gunners on decks to wear steel helmets. But real protection a helmet has to fit a standard helmet would ride up on a large head and expose the man's ...; on a small head it would interfere with vision. Also it's heavy (it must be big enough to cover ear ...nes) and in the excitement of ...on many men throw away anything uncomfortable.

...avy engineers believed a helmet ...d be made to fit any head size if ... form of self-adjusting lining ...developed. A light, foamy sponge-rubber lining could be self-adjusting but open cells would absorb ocean spray, and so increase the weight and be uncomfortable.

B. F. Goodrich engineers had developed a method of coating anything with a soft film of rubber by a single dip in liquid rubber. (It is called the "Anode" process.) They made thick helmet linings of foam and covered them by this method. The rubber coating or cover keeps water out of the foam rubber beneath, and still leaves it pliable to adjust itself automatically to any head size. It protects the sponge rubber from hair and face oils—and is a special compound not irritating to the skin.

Here is only one of many examples of how B. F. Goodrich peace-time research had products and processes ready to solve scores of the problems of war-time production. That research continues, working on war now, but also to have new improvements in industrial products ready by the time war is over. *The B. F. Goodrich Co., Industrial Products Division, Akron, O.*

B.F. Goodrich

FIRST IN RUBBER

B. F. Goodrich advertisement. *Time,* 27 July 1942.

In different ways, all three ads confirm that the servicemen's toughness and masculinity are in no way compromised by being linked to the feminine. Displays of overtly and stereotypical feminine behavior or images of apparent confusion about gender identity are instantly qualified in the ads by the valorization of masculinity (the tough soldier, the guy who's not a sissy, the sailor on his way to battle), hence reassuring readers about the males' heterosexuality.

Such advertisements call to mind Judith Butler's observations about the relationship between sex and gender:

> If gender is the cultural meanings that a sexed body assumes, then a gender cannot be said to follow from a sex in any one way. Taken to its logical limit, the sex/gender distinction suggests a radical discontinuity between sexed bodies and culturally constructed genders. Assuming . . . the stability of binary sex, it does not follow that the construction of "men" will accrue exclusively to the bodies of males or that "women" will interpret only male bodies. . . . When the constructed status of gender is theorized as radically independent of sex, gender itself becomes a free-floating artifice, with the consequence that *man* and *masculine* might just as easily signify a female body as a male one, and *woman* and *feminine* a male body as easily as a female one.[14]

Clearly there is an ideological operation at work here whereby this gendered complexity is rationalized and contained as a result of the war. Thus the external situation defines and limits the temporary feminine condition of the newly rendered males. Nonetheless, these advertisements confirm the capacity for the male to adapt to the feminine while retaining his masculinity and hence, by implication, his sexuality. A counterpart to the aspects of behavior associated with femininity appears in the very few World War II films in which women are shown taking on behavior traditionally linked to masculinity. The most important example from this period is *So Proudly We Hail!* (Mark Sandrich, 1943), in which nurse Olivia D'Arcy (Veronica Lake) uses a hand grenade to kill a group of Japanese soldiers.[15]

Examples of men shown positively or sympathetically acting in maternal ways occur in *Bataan* (Tay Garnett, 1943) and *Destination Tokyo* (Delmer Daves, 1943). In the first film, as the malaria-delirious Ramirez (Desi Arnaz) succumbs, his medic stands watch over him, offering him water. Ramirez calls out for his mother. In addition, when Purckett (Robert Walker) is unable to bind his own wounds, he is assisted by Todd (Lloyd Nolan). As Todd applies a tourniquet, Purckett looks at him like a child lovingly admiring his mother, and Todd responds negatively by tightening the cloth roughly. The second scene in particular plays it both ways: showing a male acting in a maternal function and then rejecting the appreciative response this evokes in the soldier he helps.[16]

An advertisement sponsored by Nash Kelvinator reminiscent of the scene in *Bataan* appeared in *Time*. It shows a wounded and apparently dying soldier being ministered to by a medic. The top caption "MOM . . ." is followed by the supposed commentary of the medic: "It was damned hard to just lie there . . . and grind our teeth together and tighten our guts because each time he cried 'Mom' . . . it tore out our insides. . . . I put a syrette into his arm and then another, and he relaxed and his head fell back and his eyes were still wide but I could tell he thought his mother was there by his side."[17] Here the medic who is perceived as a mother accedes to the role assigned him by the wounded man in a manner that reinforces his masculinity, underscored by the language ("damned hard," "grind our teeth," "tighten our guts").

In *Destination Tokyo*, Cary Grant as Captain Cassidy is tough and assured. When one of the sailors (Robert Hutton) on the submarine needs an emergency appendectomy, Cassidy participates in the operation by administering ether to the boy who, as he would at home, says his prayers before going to "sleep" under the anesthetic. Framed with his hands clasped around a towel over the face of the boy, Cassidy displays maternal tenderness. As the kid comes out of the anesthetic after the successful surgery, Cassidy's head is practically resting on the boy's in order to hear what he is saying: the continuation of his prayers. Earlier, though, before news of the emergency reaches him, Cassidy has been seen tenderly recounting a story about taking his young son to the barbershop. The highlight of his year, he claims, was hearing his son declare that Cassidy was his dad. Thus Cassidy's maternal capacities are complemented by a monologue about his paternal role.

Significant examples of the kinds of maternal imagery and behavior appearing in combat films are visible in other manifestations of culture. One example of

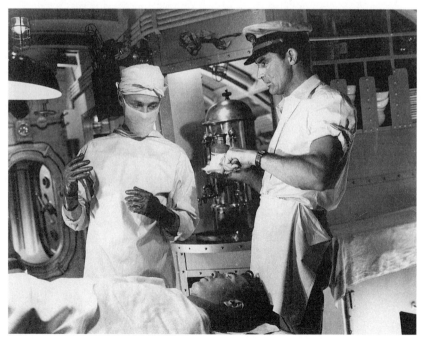

Destination Tokyo. Captain Cassidy directs surgery. Courtesy: Larry Edmunds Bookshop. © Warner Bros. Pictures, 1943.

invoking the maternal appeared in Captain Eddie Rickenbacker's account of how he and his men survived a life-threatening ordeal. His picture appears on the cover of *Life* magazine, 25 January 1943, the first of three issues containing installments of his "Pacific Mission" in which he tells a remarkable story of heroism and survival. Rickenbacker was at that time the most decorated and successful pilot in American history. When his plane ran out of fuel in October 1942, he and the seven other men of the crew ditched in the Pacific Ocean and, in two rafts, drifted for twenty-one days until being rescued. After exhausting their meager food supply—four oranges, which they divided among themselves in the first few days—they lived on raw fish, a gull, and rain water collected during squalls. One of the men, Sergeant Alexander Kacmarczyk, already weakened before the flight, became ill and did not survive the ordeal. Here is Rickenbacker describing how he tried to help:

> I asked . . . to change rafts with Sergeant Alex, thinking that Alex might rest better. It took the combined strength of Bartek, DeAngelis and myself to move him. I stretched him on the lee side of the bottom of the boat and put my arm around him, as a mother cuddles a child, hoping in that way to transfer the heat of my body to him during the night. In an hour or so his shivering stopped and sleep came—a shallow sleep in which Alex mumbled intermittently in Polish—phrases about his mother and his girl "Snooks." I kept Alex there all night, the next day and night, and the twelfth day. . . . I knew he couldn't last many hours longer. . . . We had to lift him like a baby.[18]

The essay includes a drawing of Rickenbacker cuddling the doomed sergeant.

There is a discernible pattern in these varied manifestations. Displays of the maternal are qualified by assertions of masculinity: in the language of the medic who has been called mother, in the tough response of Todd to Purkett's gaze, in the way that Cassidy's maternal caring is combined with a display of his paternal role, and here, in the way Rickenbacker describes acting in a manner as a mother cuddles a child and then identifies the sergeant as a heterosexual male with a girlfriend. Foregrounding the maternal has the effect of negotiating the problematic aspects of close physical contact by defining it as a nonsexual act of nurturing. Moreover, this confirms the logic of R. W. Connell's argument that masculinity is "a configuration of gender practice" that "exists impersonally in culture as a subject position in the process of representation, in the structures of language and other symbol systems. Individual practice may accept and produce this positioning, but may also confront and contest it."[19]

DIRECT EXAMPLES OF DISAVOWAL IN FILMS

As far as I know, no one has commented on a relevant example of nonsexual love in *Sands of Iwo Jima* (Allan Dwan, 1949), one even more remarkable for the way the issue is jokingly introduced in the film.[20] Given that it was made in 1949, a period in which the strictures of the PCA were solidly in place, an overt disavowal of love between men within the film is notable. Even more to the point, films about World War II released after 1948 must necessarily be viewed with a different set of assumptions about the audience's awareness of male sexuality because of the publication of Alfred Kinsey's *Sexual Behavior in the Human Male*. Even for those who hadn't read it, the statistics about male sexual behavior and the prevalence of homosexual behavior were available everywhere, specifically such findings as: "37 per cent of the total male population has at least some overt homosexual experience to the point of orgasm between adolescence and old age"; "30 per cent of all males have at least incidental homosexual experience"; "25 per cent of the male population has more than incidental homosexual experience"; and "10 per cent of the males are more or less exclusively homosexual."[21]

In such a context, displays of affectionate behavior take on a new significance. As Sergeant John Stryker (John Wayne) prepares to leave the base where he is stationed to hit the bars in Wellington, New Zealand, Private First Class Charlie Bass (James Brown), his only friend, tries to cheer him up. Bass is concerned because another mail delivery has left Stryker without a letter from his son and divorced wife. Bass tries to offer reasons and excuses why they might not have written, and then says: "You know, Stryker, you're a very unusual character." Stryker responds slyly: "Can this be love?" Bass says, "Ah, you know what I mean" and cautions him about drinking too much; Stryker accuses him of having "the old maid's failing: you worry," and directs him not to follow him. Against Stryker's orders, he does, and discovers him with other soldiers; one remarks that Bass "follows Stryker around like a little dog." Bass rescues the drunken sergeant once the other soldiers leave him and takes him home.

Later, on another leave, Stryker picks up Mary (Julie Bishop), a prostitute, but when he sees her dismal living conditions and realizes she's the mother of an infant, he gives her money to help support herself and her baby; he leaves without having sex. As he steps out on the porch, he finds Bass waiting for him and remarks, "Boy, you got a lot of bloodhound in you, don't you." He then asks Bass to be sure to stop him from feeling sorry for himself. When Stryker discovers that Bass was wounded and another soldier killed because of the lax incompetence of Private Al Thomas (Preston Foster), he beats the latter, who confesses to his sense of guilt for the events.[22]

If one wanted to queer the film, one could possibly argue that Bass's oversolicitous concern for Stryker (following him twice, once to check on his drinking and once to the home of a prostitute) raises questions about a possible homosexual attraction. With this logic, Stryker's fierce attack on Thomas is motivated not so much by his outrage at the death of the other soldier as much as it is anger over the near-death of his comrade Bass. By asking "Can this be love?" Stryker indicates his awareness of Bass's attraction and uses humor to deflect it, a kind of inoculation. Stryker's reference to the "old maid's failing" acknowledges his awareness and desire to disavow the significance of Bass's attraction.

The encounter with the prostitute functions like Stryker's depression over losing his wife and son as a way of demonstrating his heterosexuality.

But I think such an interpretation would be inaccurate because it fails to address the text or its reception. First, for its contemporary critics, there is a tacit assumption in play: to say someone is a "he-man" (the descriptor of masculinity used in *Time*'s review of the film) is in fact to describe his sexuality since they are seen as isomorphic.[23] Stryker's question "Can this be love?" does indeed serve an inoculating function. But it's not designed to shroud a covert recognition of Bass's homosexuality. Rather, it introduces the issue of love between men in the military and displays Stryker's embarrassment at the realization of how much Bass does in fact care about his well-being. By using language that even hints at a homosexual possibility, Stryker is saying, in effect, "Of course you *aren't* a homosexual," in order to deny love of *any* kind, whether sexualized or not. In a curious way, to admit the possibility of nonsexual love is to risk its conflation with homosexual attraction. Hence, in a complicated finesse, the line denies what it affirms in order to make another kind of love "safe." To ask "Can this be love?" is to ask and at the same time not ask "Are you a homosexual?" while saying, "Of course I know you are *not* a homosexual." The question can only be asked when an unproblematic answer is already known.[24]

It had been sixteen months since *Red River* (Howard Hawks, 1948) had appeared in theaters. There, as noted, Tess tells Tom and Matt that they love each other. Wayne's comment to Bass thus invokes intertextually yet another nonsexual love relationship. Wayne's disavowal/avowal is reconfirmed all the more in light of the totally nonsexual bond that develops in this film with Private Peter Conway (John Agar), with whom he has been in conflict.[25]

Birdy (Alan Parker, 1984), which won the Grand Prix award at Cannes, is the first American war film I know of to present a scene in which a straight character denies the presence of homosexuality seriously rather than comically. The film concerns boyhood friends who serve in Vietnam, although they are not part of the same unit. Having been wounded, Al (Nicolas Cage) returns to the United States and goes to a veterans hospital to see Birdy (Matthew Modine), who has cracked up, become catatonic, and now behaves like a bird. Before the war, Birdy had been fascinated by birds, raised them, and had tried to fly, using makeshift inventions. Al finds him in his room, hunched up like a bird.

The narrative consists of a series of interviews between Al and the psychiatrist, fruitless visits by Al to Birdy in which he tries to snap his friend out of his state, flashbacks presenting their friendship growing up before they went to war, and Birdy's dreams. In response to the psychiatrist's questions about how close they were as friends, Al responds: "We weren't queer for each other or anything." This is a shorter version of the statement made in William Wharton's novel on which the film is based. In that work, which is set during World War II, Al's first-person narrator describes how the psychiatrist "asks how long Birdy and I have been close friends. I tell him we've been friends since we were thirteen. He asks this in

Birdy. Al tries to comfort Birdy. Courtesy: Photofest. © A & M Films/TriStar Pictures, 1984.

a way so you know he really wants to know if we were queer together; or if we jacked each other off, or gave each other blow jobs."[26]

Al's overt declaration that he and Birdy "weren't queer for each other," borne out by the flashbacks and numerous scenes in which the uniformed soldier interacts with his friend, can be seen as an articulation of what could never have been said in American war films before the instituting of the new censorship ratings plan accepted by the Motion Picture Association of America in 1966. John Wayne's Stryker can jokingly ask his friend Bass "Can this be love?" and be told, "Ah, you know what I mean." But Bass can't say directly "I am not queer for you" in a 1949 film. *Birdy's* explicit statement in this regard is historically significant. It marks an important rejection of relying on the disavowal strategy described above. Al and Birdy are not "queer for each other" in the film or novel.

In addition to scenes showing them growing up, various others demonstrate that Al is actively and unambiguously heterosexual, while Birdy's erotic experiences are limited to fantasies about his favorite birds. For example, Birdy has a date with an aggressive classmate, Doris Robinson (Maud Winchester), for the prom. After it, she drives them in her car to an isolated spot, removes her bra, exposing her breasts, and volunteers to have sex with him, to no avail, since he is not interested. When Al stops by the next morning to hear what transpired, he finds Birdy naked and assumes he had sex. Instead of recounting a sexual triumph, though, Birdy describes another dream he has had in which he is actually flying. The only realized sexual experience we see involving Birdy occurs when he has a nocturnal emission while dreaming about his bird.

The extended scenes of Al talking to Birdy, particularly one in which he cradles him in his arms, demonstrate Al's love for his troubled friend. Al's heterosexuality is not in question, but neither is Birdy's. Thus *Birdy* shows the kind of possibility described by Dyer in which love between men is presented without using the typical strategies to disavow homosexuality indirectly. Only one man is actively heterosexual; the other's sexual focus is neither male nor female. Al's declaration that "we weren't queer for each other or anything" not only acknowledges the existence of such a possibility but also confronts it directly.

OTHER EXAMPLES

The process of defending masculinity and male sexuality through disavowal takes other forms as well. In *Thirty Seconds Over Tokyo* (Mervyn LeRoy, 1944), after Ted Lawson (Van Johnson) and his crew participate in the surprise raid by Lieutenant Colonel Jimmie Doolittle bombing the Japanese capital, they try but fail to return to their base. Nearly out of fuel, Lawson attempts to land the plane but crashes into the water. The survivors drag themselves to the shore. Hugging and supporting each other, the men cry out in pain and anguish as they are pelted by rain. The dazed Lawson is at the center of a triangular formation including Thatcher (Robert Walker); McClure (Don DeFore), who rests his head on Lawson's shoulder; and Davenport (Tim Murdock), whose head is cradled on Lawson's thigh. The camera dollies in to Lawson's face, and the image dissolves to his memory of a scene we saw earlier as his pregnant wife, Ellen (Phyllis Thaxter), reassured him: "Ted, look at me. The baby and I won't ever need anything. The baby is why I know you're coming home." Lawson rises, apparently coming out of his daze, and stumbles away from the men as one of them calls out his name.

One year before the appearance of *Thirty Seconds Over Tokyo*, Edward Steichen, the famous photographer who had headed the army photographic unit in World War I and who now had a commission in the navy (even though, at sixty-two, he was well over the age limit), became chief of Naval Photography. In November he was assigned to the USS *Lexington*, an aircraft carrier in the Pacific, where he was exposed to various dangers. One of the pictures he took within his first few weeks on board of sleeping sailors appears on the cover and frontispiece of this book. Three men are intertwined: one lies face down on the deck; a second rests his head on the former's back; a third rests his head on the second's stomach. A fourth man, awake, sits a few feet away, looking off to his left.

In *The Blue Ghost*, Steichen comments on this and other photographs of sailors at rest: "There are not many methods of taking things easy on a carrier, but we try all of them. Reading, studying, sleeping, poker, and in secluded corners maybe a nice little crap game."[27] "The men, in small groups, are sprawled around the deck; some choose the hot sun on the open deck, others park themselves in the shade of a plane's wing; they pillow up for each other in a fine earthly fellowship, reminiscent of colts resting under a tree or alongside the fence of a pasture, the head of one colt is draped over the neck of another, or again, something in the manner of a litter of puppies, are curled up over, under, and about each other."[28] Steichen's caption is: "Here we sprawl like pups in a kennel—pillow up together."[29]

The film and Steichen's commentary share the negotiating tendency I see manifested in representations of sexuality during World War II. *Thirty Seconds Over Tokyo* establishes a mise-en-scène consisting of a grouping of intertwined, weeping men and then undercuts the intimacy of the configuration by cutting to the leader's memory of his wife, whose comment on their unborn baby is followed by his breaking away from the men. Steichen's description of the men in his photograph explains the bonding figuratively in terms of the men's similarity to animals. The various kinds of qualifications illustrate a phenomenon found throughout films and other kinds of wartime discourses in which the heterosexuality of the men is reaffirmed.

Both the film and the commentary on the photograph are expressions of people in the period responding to manifestations of behavior that foreground the potentialities of male sexuality outside its traditional heterosexual framework. In fact, there seems almost to be a curious compulsion to show something in the mise-en-scène and images that *requires* its own containment and inoculation through qualification.[30]

The Male Body as Spectacle

Destination Tokyo and *Guadalcanal Diary* (Lewis Seiler, 1943) offer complex interpretive challenges in regard to the place of the male body as a potentially erotic object. In the first, the script establishes Wolf (John Garfield) as a promiscuous womanizer who constantly boasts of his conquests. Garfield's character as originally conceived had been a problem for the PCA. Letters from Joseph Breen to Warner Bros. identified a number of changes that would have to be made to get script approval. As far as I can tell from looking at the final film, very little of the targeted material ended up being eliminated.[31] At issue was the rampant sexuality Wolf displayed in his stories about his exploits with women.

In the first, he shows his comrades on the submarine a doll he has brought on board. He tells them he takes it to bars, and when a woman asks him if that's the best he can do, he makes a play for her. In the second story, a flashback accompanies his narration of picking up a woman outside a lingerie shop. Although she lets another sailor buy her some stockings, she leaves with Wolf rather than the other sailor. His narrative, which is interrupted by verbal sparring with Tin Can (Dane Clark), who wants to know all the details, is contradicted by the visualization of it in the silent flashback that accompanies it. She is much taller than he, thus belying his claim that she is short. As his story of the pick-up ends, we see her lips moving and hear him saying, in a feminine voice, "Going my way sailor?"

The imitation of a woman's voice is more extreme in the last of Wolf's stories. In this, he talks about randomly searching the phone book, finding the name of "Rosalie Ran," and going to her house. When he calls in at the door, she tells him

Destination Tokyo. Wolf displays his doll. Courtesy: Larry Edmunds Bookshop. © Warner Bros. Pictures, 1943.

she's taking a bath and can't come to the door, a sentence delivered by him imitating a woman's voice. He continues to imitate her voice as he tells more, again interrupted by the impatient Tin Can. In the last part of his story, he holds the female doll seen earlier, moving her like a puppet. What's remarkable in all this is that as he tells the story and interacts with the other sailors and the doll, he is removing his undershirt. The sexual longing on the faces of the men is understood as their vicarious anticipation and pleasure at *hearing* about Wolf's sexual conquest. But Daves shoots the scene in a way in which the *visual* object of their attention is a man who has exposed his chest as he tells a sex-related story and uses a woman's voice to enact one of the parts. There is no compelling narrative reason for Wolf to take off his undershirt, but the sexual dynamics of the scene seem to imply that gratuitous exposure of his (male) body alludes by implication to the sexual activity that (may or may not have) occurred with Rosalie. That is, there's a kind of metonymic function to the partial nudity of this man holding a female doll and talking about sex. This scene is certainly one of the most remarkable for conveying the sexual tensions felt by men deprived of women. The scene ends as Wolf is challenged and exposed by Pills (William Prince), who announces his disdain for such stories because of his respect for his own sweetheart. He notes that many of the others have sweethearts too, and Wolf admits that he lacks one. Thus the scene deconstructs its own sexual ambiguity.

The aural focus of the story is on (possible) sex with a randomly selected woman. The visual attention is on a man taking off his shirt. It ends by asserting that all the men except Wolf have girlfriends back home.

Although it does not involve the male body as an erotic spectacle, a related kind of narrative event occurs in *The Story of G.I. Joe* (William Wellman, 1945). The film was shot without prior script approval by the PCA. When Breen saw it, he was incensed by a number of features, especially a scene in which a group of soldiers stand outside an ambulance that has been rigged up as a honeymoon suite for a soldier and nurse who have just been married. A guitar player provides a musical background as the men watch the vehicle. The expressions of sexual longing are painful to observe and even more extreme than those seen on the faces of the men in *Destination Tokyo*. Breen wrote to Will Hays of this "unacceptable detail." After the couple enters the ambulance, "we cut again back to the boys with curious expressions on their faces—all of them quite clear in their intent." Since he thought the scene was played for laughs (the new husband is too tired to consummate the marriage), it violates "the sacred intimacies of married life." But the most compelling reason for his objection, I believe, is that the scene demonstrates the powerful urge of unfulfilled male sexuality. Thus Breen wants the producer, Lester Cowan, to cut "the several scenes of the group of soldiers staring hungrily at the ambulance."[32]

Guadalcanal Diary opens with a shipboard service led by Father Donnelly (Preston Foster) and then shows the men relaxing. Most are shirtless and closely linked physically. Taxi Potts (William Bendix) forms the apex of an extended triangular group of figures. He cradles the head of a shirtless Sosse (Anthony Quinn), on whose arm another marine's head rests; the head of a shirtless Chicken Anderson (Richard Jaeckel) rests on Taxi's stomach, close to the groin, and Taxi's hand is on Chicken's bare chest. In the second scene, shortly afterward, as the men hear their orders, Sosse rests his head on Chicken's chest. The physical intimacy displayed in the mise-en-scène is qualified by the conversations. In the first, Sosse contemplates which of his two girlfriends he would be dating if he were at home and opts for both; Taxi talks about baseball. In the second, the bonding between Chicken and Sosse takes place as they hear orders that will send them into dangerous circumstances. Writing fifty years after the film appeared, Robert Plunket suggests: "The beginning of *Guadalcanal Diary*, when soldiers sun themselves on the poop deck and then dance to the latest tunes, is reminiscent of nothing so much as a weekend on Fire Island. There is even physical intimacy—the way Richard Jaeckel and Anthony Quinn keep leaning against each other certainly raised my eyebrows—and an oddly sensitive atmosphere."[33]

Plunket's reaction to the earlier scene as a prototypically gay display of male bodies says a great deal about temporal and sociocultural perspectives in the 1990s as opposed to the 1940s. The PCA invariably warned studios that no characters should be shown nude or even with the suggestion of nudity. In their response to the initial script of this film, the Richard Jaeckel character (then named "Baby")

Guadalcanal Diary. The men relax in the sun. © 20th Century Fox Film Corporation, 1943.

specifically was singled out for caution in this regard. Two of Breen's letters to Colonel Jayson S. Joy at 20th Century Fox warn: "There must, of course, be nothing in this sequence that would suggest that Baby is swimming in the nude," and "As indicated before, we could not approve any action in this swimming sequence that would suggest Baby is swimming in the nude."[34] But no one at the PCA was concerned that this scene and its rendering of shirtless male bodies entwined in close physical contact would in any way suggest a degree of homoeroticism.

I suspect this lack of concern is a result of the qualifications (girlfriends, talk about baseball), and also because the solidarity and intimacy depicted so powerfully demonstrate the expansiveness of masculine bonds in fighting men. In this case, the trust and brotherhood remove the erotic dimension from the clear display of the sexually potent male body.[35]

This acceptance of a scene showing partially unclothed men holding each other contrasts strikingly with Breen's ire later about the Dean Martin and Jerry Lewis comedies *At War with the Army* (Hal Walker, 1950) and *Sailor Beware* (Hal Walker, 1952). Even though Lewis's character remains clothed, Breen finds the character offensive in the first film because of his unmanly behavior and mannerisms: "The portrayal was to be that of a 'sad sack' rather than a 'swish.' " He warns that in the second he must "not come through as a 'swish.' "[36] That is, gestures of affections in partially clothed men who are engaged in manly activities cast no doubts about their sexuality, as opposed to mincing characters such as Lewis portrays, who are immediately coded as homosexuals.[37]

This scene in *Guadalcanal Diary* was completely in keeping with other displays of the near or completely naked bodies of servicemen readily available in advertisements and in photographic records of the war in *Life* magazine. Bérubé in particular cites popular magazine advertisements and articles that can be read as having a potential homosexual appeal.[38] But contextualized within the framework of valorized masculinity in World War II, these serve as reassurances to their audiences that what is being shown is most assuredly *not* displaying homosexuality.

The American public did occasionally see photographs of naked soldiers in *Life* and drawings of them in certain advertisements.[39] Such displays of naked, bathing men are accompanied by qualifying material similar to what we have already seen. *Life* showed the naked male body in a state of sexual innocence, a theme that was constantly inflected in war films, mainly through the raw recruit, or kid.[40]

Life's extended coverage of the assault on Guadalcanal included two full-page photographs of naked and seminaked troops. The "Picture of the Week" for 8 February 1943 shows more than two dozen men bathing and relaxing in a river; frontal nudity is shadowed out. The explanatory caption reads: "The gray American transports steamed in near to the beaches of Guadalcanal. Over the sides into landing boats went thousands of American troops, hot and bearded and dirty from weeks at sea with no fresh water to wash in. As soon as their boats crunched up on the sand and their tents were pitched and their foxholes dug, the troops wandered over to a nearby river, gratefully pulled off their clothes, plunged into the cool fresh water."[41] The caption on the photograph itself repeats the notion of their gratitude for the relief afforded by the refreshing water. Three weeks later, *Life* ran a photograph of naked and partially clothed soldiers washing their clothes, again with dorsal but not frontal nudity.[42]

This display of naked males relaxing and washing themselves or their clothing in *Life* anticipated a remarkable series of six ads that would be run by the Cannon towel company on the inside covers of the same magazine from August 1943 to June 1944 in which naked or partially clothed servicemen were shown bathing in comic scenes. These "true towel tales" were credited to various sources, such as "a doctor in the medical corps" (16 August 1943) or "a sergeant in the tanks corps" (3 January 1944). Some reveal the kind of "homosexual buffoonery" referred to earlier. In one advertisement, a flier throws a bucket of water on a man emerging from a galvanized washing tub, thus sending his towel flying.[43] This is reminiscent of a scene in *The Immortal Sergeant* (John Stahl, 1943), which had opened ten months earlier. In this film there's a comic moment when a soldier rips off a man's towel. We do not see the result, only the setup. The "Buna Bathtub" ad, the last in the series (26 June 1944), shows a naked soldier posed seductively with a palm frond over his genitals. In its coverage of Buna Village, *Life* had run another photograph of naked soldiers bathing.[44] Each of the ads contains a small inserted drawing of a different woman discreetly covered by a towel with the same accompanying caption alerting readers that they may encounter less of a selection in towels because "[m]illions of Cannon towels are now going to the Armed Forces."

Cannon "true towel" advertisement. *Life*, 16 August 1943.

The presence of the woman not only evokes the typical Cannon towel ads, which prior to and after the "true towel" campaign featured cheesecake illustrations in which women were the objects of visual pleasure (for example, one in the 2 October 1944 issue). Even more to the point, it also inserts an image that negotiates the problematic of male sexuality by reminding viewers that women, not men, are the traditional objects of sexual desire for these tough men.[45]

The significance of this display of nakedness to a mass audience needs comment. According to George Roeder, "By late 1942 *Life* was claiming that tens of millions of civilians and two out of three Americans in the military read the magazine."[46] Such a public display should be understood in the larger context of how sexuality was negotiated in war films. Photographs of naked soldiers washing and at play in *Life* provide testimony that affirms these men *can* be observed; that is, the very act of representing their nakedness serves as an assurance that their de-eroticized sexuality is representable. The logic of representation is inevitable: the naked men shown engaged in homosexual buffoonery *must* be heterosexual. If they weren't, the advertisements couldn't be used.

Thus I would reverse the conclusion of John Costello, who argues: "An indication that public attitudes to the taboo of homosexuality were also shifting came with the appearance of homoerotic advertisements in American magazines, which began featuring male 'pinup[s]' such as those for Munsingwear underwear and Cannon bath towels."[47] I believe the opposite is the case. The very fact that naked men are shown cavorting demonstrates they are *not* homosexual.

One conclusion of the report excerpted in *Newsweek* from *Psychology for the Fighting Man* was that some homosexuals managed to get through, no matter how effective the screening, and that they are in the army. But the tenor of the description of such men suggests something hidden. The report acknowledges without welcoming the presence of homosexuals in the military. In contrast, the Cannon advertisements present a celebration of male sexuality. If something like these can be shown, then they can't be illustrating the aberrant and grudgingly accepted homosexuals who are known to be in the armed forces. Showing these manly soldiers at play, completely at ease in their sexuality, as the men are in *Guadalcanal Canal*, explicitly says: these men are heterosexual. If they were homosexual, they couldn't be represented as accepting their own easy display of sexuality. And we couldn't show them in the first place.

Although combat films made during World War II could not show a naked male body, they could and did show a hand resting casually on another man's bare chest, a man joking about a pin-up of himself, and horseplay that constantly evoked the potential range of male sexuality. But these were consistently qualified in a way demonstrating that what was potentially signified at one level needed to be understood at another. The very fact that any of these scenes were shown signified at some level that they *could* be presented—that males' sexuality was contained and inoculated by their masculinity.

CHAPTER FOUR

WOUNDS

This chapter focuses on men who display the effects of psychological and/or physical wounds and limitations. In some cases, the films show how war and battle cause the damage; in others, the narratives present characters who are already impaired in one way or another. In both cases, the resulting effects on the characters' masculinity and behavior have significant ramifications for those whom they love or those whom they lead. The most common dangers to masculinity and sexuality from psychological and physical damage center on forms of impotence, symbolic or actual. The inability of a man to function sexually because of a physical injury is potentially a sign of failed masculinity. Correspondingly, someone whose masculinity is in question because of his behavior runs the risk of being thought of as ineffective sexually.

Interest in traumatized soldiers' psychic as well as physical problems begins during World War I. Both Elaine Showalter and Joanna Bourke have documented the impact and influence of Sigmund Freud and psychoanalysis on the early treatment of shell-shocked veterans in this war.[1] Although representations of psychoanalytic treatments have appeared in films about psychologically and physiologically damaged veterans in film, more often than not psychoanalytic theories show up indirectly, in terms of understood concepts and principles rather than in depictions of analytic sessions between doctor and patient. For example, the concept of the fear of castration, originally introduced by Freud to explain aspects of male psychosexual development in terms of the Oedipus complex, has been appropriated within some films as something already understood rather than as something discovered through analysis of a patient.

While earlier films about World War I present some memorable examples of psychologically and physically wounded soldiers, none of them appears to be specifically connected to the issue of sexuality. For example, as we saw, Jim Apperson (John Gilbert), the hero of *The Big Parade* (King Vidor, 1925), loses his leg to amputation, but this has no inhibiting effect on his reunion with Melisande (Renée Adorée) at the film's conclusion. Paul (Lew Ayres) and his comrades temporarily experience psychological trauma as a result of battles or injuries in *All Quiet on the Western Front* (Lewis Milestone, 1930). That film's hospital scenes graphically depict the fear of death and physical suffering, particularly when Franz (Ben Alexander) realizes his leg has been amputated, but that trauma is not worked out in terms of sexuality as such. The montage following Franz's death grimly chronicles the way his boots are worn by a succession of men who are killed. But here, too, this is rendered solely in terms of battlefield trauma and not connected to sexuality.

After a discussion of films showing psychologically damaged soldiers, attention shifts to the physically wounded ones in *Thirty Seconds Over Tokyo* (Mervyn LeRoy, 1945), *Pride of the Marines* (Delmer Daves, 1945), *The Best Years of Our Lives* (William Wyler, 1946), *The Men* (Fred Zinnemann, 1950), *Coming Home* (Hal Ashby, 1978), and *Born on the Fourth of July* (Oliver Stone, 1989). *Home of the Brave* (Mark Robson, 1949) is of particular interest since it focuses on the psychoanalytic treatment of a soldier whose physical problem is psychosomatic. A subsidiary interest in this regard will be in the role of women as caregivers to the wounded, and of the maternal impulse as displayed in men. The topics and some of these films have already received rewarding commentary from Sonya Michel, Tania Modleski, Martin F. Norden, and Kaja Silverman.[2]

PSYCHOLOGICAL

Films made during and shortly after World War II are much more likely to present psychological trauma as a major element in the narratives and to connect it directly or indirectly to sexuality. Certainly one of the first claimants could be *I'll Be Seeing You* (William Dieterle, 1944), in which Zachary Morgan (Joseph Cotton) meets Mary Marshall (Ginger Rogers) after he is temporarily released from an army hospital where he has been treated for war stress. The film was released late in 1944, by which time the American public had ample opportunity to learn about the term "traumatic war neurosis." For example, a 1943 article in *Time* pointed out the expression had replaced "shell shock" and described how various treatments were being used in the field.[3] The fact that Zach has had to come home to be helped indicates the severity of his condition, which is underscored in the film in several scenes in which expressionistic sounds and camera movements suggest how troubled he still is. The narrative concludes as he embraces Mary, whose love has clearly been the motivation and causative agent for his return to equanimity. Mary's status as someone also on a "furlough," in her case from a women's prison where she is serving time for murder in self-defense, links them both as victims of circumstance whose healing and eventual restoration will take time. But the point is that Zach's cure really begins when he falls in love with Mary. That is, the promise of a relationship in which he can function as a whole human being—physically, emotionally, and sexually—starts his recovery.

The narrative concept of the woman who helps the veteran with severe psychological problems fight back to normalcy and the promise of a heterosexual union appears in a number of postwar films. In addition to *The Best Years of Our Lives* (discussed below), one could also cite *Till the End of Time* (Edward Dymtryk, 1946). Although the hero, Cliff Harper (Guy Madison), is not suffering major psychological damage, his disaffection and inability to adjust to the postwar world are manifested in crying and antisocial behavior. His psychological lack of ease is countered by the physical plights of two veterans: William Tabeshaw (Robert Mitchum) and Perry Kinchelow (Bill Williams). Pat Ruscomb (Dorothy McGuire), a war widow who is having her own problems adjusting to life, motivates Cliff to take a more positive attitude, and the film ends with their anticipated union.

High Wall (Curtis Bernhardt, 1947) combines the theme of rehabilitation with a murder mystery as psychiatrist Dr. Ann Lorison (Audrey Totter) helps Steven Kenet (Robert Taylor) regain his mental equilibrium. Steven, who has amnesia and is recovering from brain surgery necessitated by a war injury, is falsely accused of murdering his wife. Ann's loving help and support lead to clearing Steven of the charge. The real murderer turns out to be Willard Whitcombe (Herbert Marshall), his wife's boss. At the film's end, Steven joins with Ann in a new union with his son from the earlier marriage.

Another example is *Shadow in the Sky* (Fred M. Wilcox, 1952). Burt (Ralph Meeker) has been traumatized by his experiences in the war, and becomes dangerous during rainstorms because they trigger a battlefield memory in which he was involved in a fellow soldier's death. Part of his move toward mental health comes largely as the result of falling in love with Stella (Jean Hagen). Her love helps counteract the negative effects on his readjustment caused by the unintentionally ineffective support he receives from his sister, Betty (Nancy Davis), and brother-in-law, Lou (James Whitmore).[4]

A number of films made after 1945 return to depictions of World War II to explore or feature psychologically damaged or mentally troubled men: *Twelve O'Clock High* (Henry King, 1949), *Halls of Montezuma* (Lewis Milestone, 1950), *The Caine Mutiny* (Edward Dymtryk, 1954), *Attack* (Robert Aldrich, 1956), *Between Heaven and Hell* (Richard Fleischer, 1956), and *The Naked and the Dead* (Raoul Walsh, 1958). While none of these involves a romantic relationship, in all the effects of mental problems on the men's ability to command is central. The resulting erosion of their leadership abilities suggests various individual failures and crises in masculinity.

In *Twelve O'Clock High*, Brigadier General Frank Savage (Gregory Peck), a tough and authoritative figure who can't tolerate any signs of weakness or lack of resolve in his men, finds himself in the same position as the previous commander, who has had a nervous collapse brought on by the stress of battle and responsibility for men's lives. The narrative device of having a military leader experience the same problems he has encountered in someone else is certainly not new. For example, both versions of *The Dawn Patrol* (Howard Hawks, 1930; Edmund Goulding, 1938) involve commanders who find themselves replaying the traumatizing and challenging problems of their predecessors. In *Twelve O'Clock High*, though, General Savage finds himself subject to the same kind of psychological damage as the man he succeeds, Colonel Keith Davenport (Gary Merrill). Unlike him, though, Savage masters his problem and regains his leadership authority.

In *Halls of Montezuma*, the mental stress plaguing Lieutenant Carl Anderson (Richard Widmark) manifests itself in the disguised form of severe headaches, which he treats using excessive (and unauthorized) doses of medicine supplied him by his friend Doc Jones (Karl Malden). To my knowledge, Anderson is the first example of a military figure in an American film presented with a drug dependency. He, too, recovers, even though he has to endure the loss of a favorite soldier, Corporal Conroy (Richard Hylton), who had been his student in a college chemistry class back home before the war began.

In contrast, *The Caine Mutiny* and *Attack* offer quite different resolutions for men who fail as leaders. Humphrey Bogart's achievement as Captain Queeg in *The Caine Mutiny* was recognized by his nomination for Best Actor, although Marlon Brando received the Oscar. Bogart displays Queeg's unsuitability for command in a number of ways: the obsessive search for the strawberries, the yellow-stain debacle in which he cuts his own towline, and his general incapacity to assert authority in a way that draws his men's respect. The mutiny that prompts the court-martial of Lieutenant Steve Maryk (Van Johnson) and Willie Keith (Robert Francis) leads to the debasing revelation of his weakness, particularly signaled by his rolling of the steel balls. This habit invites analysis as a rather obvious sign of physical and mental immaturity. When Queeg cracks at the trial, he displays his lack of masculinity, made all the more pathetic by the embarrassed reactions of those in the courtroom.

In *Attack*, Eddie Albert's Captain Erskine Cooney is a hopelessly inept soldier whose tactical errors and cowardice lead to numerous deaths in his company. Although his next in command, Lieutenant Colonel Clyde Bartlett (Lee Marvin), a tough and manipulative officer, knows Cooney is unsuitable for leadership, he keeps Cooney is his position rather than kick him upstairs to his division, where he would have to deal with him. Cooney's mannerisms are never effeminate, but they constantly betray his lack of masculinity. He is peevish, snaps at his men, acts petulantly, and displays a lack of assurance in his rank or the job. Finally totally demoralized and angered, particularly when Cooney's actions cause the death of Lieutenant Joe Kosta (Jack Palance), Lieutenant Harry Woodruff (William Smithers) shoots Cooney in the back. Although Colonel Bartlett is willing to let the murder go unreported, Woodruff turns himself in at the end of the film.

While not the central characters, both Captain "Waco" Grimes in *Between Heaven and Hell* and General Cummings (Raymond Massey) in *The Naked and the Dead* represent potential dangers to the men under them because of their personal psychological problems. The former is a wild man whose instability is signaled by the ambiguous ways he talks about his home life, particularly his wives. He is not fit to be running the outfit, and Private Sam Gifford (Robert Wagner) and Private Willie Crawford (Buddy Ebsen) survive in spite of rather than because of his leadership. General Cummings makes his men miserable and challenges Lieutenant Robert Hearn (Cliff Robertson) at every opportunity he can. Toward the end of the film, we learn the probable cause of his sociopathic behavior: he is impotent and has no children.

Even though several films about the Korean War may not have had the same kind of success at the box office, they nonetheless present some of the toughest heroes in regard to masculinity. In fact, the very first film about that conflict, *The Steel Helmet* (Sam Fuller, 1951), was made within months after the war began and presents a tough-as-nails leader in Sergeant Zack (Gene Evans). Throughout the film he is cynical and hard-boiled. It is Zack who says the by-now famous line, "If you die, I'll kill you!" to an unarmed North Korean he has shot in revenge for the death of a small Korean boy who had attached himself to Zack's outfit. The child's death and the carnage take their toll on him. Still, even though he is temporarily dazed by the crushing onslaught of bullets and despair, at the end of the film he has regained some of his tough composure.[5]

PHYSICAL

Two of the earliest films dealing with the effects of physical wounding of soldiers are based on actual persons. The first, *Thirty Seconds Over Tokyo*, presents an account of Ted Lawson (Van Johnson), pilot of the *Ruptured Duck*, one of the planes engaged in the raid led by Lieutenant Colonel Jimmie Doolittle on Tokyo in 1942. Lawson is severely wounded as his plane crashes and has to have his leg amputated. While under anesthesia, as he dreams of talking to his wife, Ellen (Phyllis Thaxter), we see that he is also thinking about a tree being chopped down, an element that Martin F. Norden refers to as "one of several heavy-handed moments in this film."[6] Norden's comment pertains to the obvious symbolism on two levels: amputation of the leg as figured in the cutting of the tree, and castration: "If we accept the Freudian notion that a disabling accident is equivalent to castration, we cannot help but arrive at the conclusion that men such as Ted have been 'reduced' to the status of Freud's classic castrated Other: women."[7] Norden argues that Ellen's role is similar to that of other wives of wounded soldiers in war films: they "take on the conflicting dual role of motherlike nurturer and sexual partner for the disabled men," and, in so doing, the films essentially disempower women by subsuming their sexuality: "By asking these women to accommodate their men and thus accept symbolic male castration, [movies such as this] advocated the denial of female sexual desires."[8] Ellen serves as "a re-paternalizing agent for her heroized, feminized husband."[9]

Pride of the Marines, another film based on an actual person, released in August 1945, presents the story of Al Schmid (John Garfield), who was already familiar to Americans because of a 1943 article in *Life* describing his blinding in a battle on Guadalcanal. The first part of the film shows how Al meets and falls in love with Ruth Hartley (Eleanor Parker). On one of their dates he takes her hunting. The rest of the film depicts his battle experiences with Lee Diamond (Dane Clark) and his blinding and rehabilitation at a veterans hospital, where he receives special help from Virginia Pfeiffer (Rosemary DeCamp). She encourages him to return to Ruth, but Al refuses because he thinks he is incapable of being a proper husband to her. Al's reunion with Ruth is engineered by Virginia and Lee in a way that capitalizes on his blindness (unbeknownst to him, Ruth drives the cab that picks him up at the train station). He is angry when he learns about the ploy, but the event is important symbolically since it puts Ruth literally at the wheel of a vehicle taking him "home," inscribed as the desired norm in the sexual economy of the film. While, as is also the case with Ted Lawson, Al's injury could be read

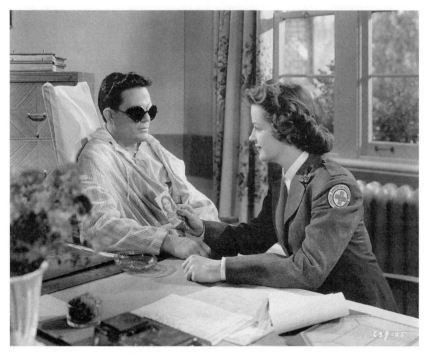

Pride of the Marines. Virginia tries to encourage Al. Courtesy: Photofest. © Warner Bros. Pictures, 1945.

from a Freudian perspective, it isn't necessary. He's afraid he can't be an adequate husband and realizes that he is capable of being one.[10]

The Best Years of Our Lives, winner of seven Oscars, including Best Picture, has received possibly the greatest amount of attention of all films about disabled veterans. The film follows the return of three men after the war. Al Stephenson (Fredric March) has not been wounded. Fred Derry (Dana Andrews) is still enduring psychological problems, signaled by his nightmares, the aftereffects of his experience as a bombardier. The primary interest is in a physically disabled veteran, Homer Parrish (Harold Russell), who has lost his hands and now wears hooks. Russell actually had been in the navy and lost his hands in an accident. Both men are helped by women to regain their equilibrium. Peggy Stephenson (Teresa Wright) comforts Fred when he awakens from a nightmare the night he stays in her parents' home. After the dissolution of Fred's marriage to Marie (Virginia Mayo), he falls in love with Peggy, and the film ends with the suggestion that they will marry.

This moment occurs during the wedding of Homer and Wilma Cameron (Cathy O'Donnell), who are at the narrative center of the film's study of adjusting to life after the war. Because of the loss of his hands, Homer does not want to marry Wilma, his fiancée, after his return. Although he tries to avoid engaging in

Best Years of Our Lives. Wilma talks to Homer in the kitchen. Courtesy: Photofest. © Samuel Goldwyn Company, 1946.

serious conversation, one day she comes to a shed where he is in engaged in target practice. Even though he has hooks, he can still fire a weapon. She observes his prowess at hitting the bull's-eye and stands admiring the paper target he removes from the wall. Then she tries to get Homer to explain why he hasn't been willing to talk to her. During this conversation, Homer holds his rifle, which is pointed upward from his legs, and cleans it using his hooks to move up and down the barrel. It's a remarkable scene, because its verbal content concerning his avoidance of a commitment of marriage is accompanied by visual content that suggests masturbation. While the scene demonstrates his prowess with the rifle (literally), more disturbingly, the masturbatory gestures with the hooks suggest, in fact, the impossibility of achieving sexual satisfaction with a woman. The scene concludes unpleasantly when Homer, aware his sister and neighborhood children have been looking at them, breaks the window of the shed with his hooks. David A. Gerber, the only critic to comment on this scene in detail, connects it to Homer's later display of anger at the drugstore and his "violent assertion of manhood."[11]

As far as I know, no one has suggested how the target practice scene relates structurally to the bedroom scene later. Wilma comes over at night to the kitchen, where Homer is having a snack, and tells him of her potential departure. He asks her to his bedroom so that she can see how he looks after removing his halter. Then she literally tucks him into bed. The scene's powerful suggestiveness fuses the maternal with the erotic. Part of its power lies in the way it answers the earlier target practice scene. There Homer is aggressive, appears dependent on his rifle as a signifier of masculinity and sexual power, and uses his hooks to break a window in anger. Here, while we can see a rifle clearly on the wall, given the deep-focus photography of Gregg Toland, who captures this detail in the mise-en-scène of Julia Herron's set decoration, Homer is separated from it as he takes off his hooks in the presence of someone he can now trust completely.[12] Thus the mise-en-scène functions to evoke the earlier scene and to contrast its violence. The obvious implication is that Homer's sexuality is henceforth linked with Wilma, whose picture next to his bed actually doubles her presence in the scene. As Wilma tucks Homer in, Wyler and Toland exclude the rifle seen earlier in the scene, thus focusing more powerfully on Wilma, who has supplanted Homer's need for the metonymic sign of sexual power.

Fred Zinnemann's *The Men* also presents a woman helping a physically damaged man to accept the limitations of his body. It also works through its mise-en-scène to address male sexuality. Ken (Marlon Brando) is a paraplegic being given extensive and exhausting rehabilitation in a veterans hospital. Much like Wilma, his fiancée, Ellie (Teresa Wright), has to contend with his indifference and anger over his injury. The film follows Ken's rehabilitation regimen, presented in extended montage sequences, and also shows us other physically disabled veterans at the hospital, including one man who dies and another, Norm (Jack Webb), who tries but fails to marry a waitress. Ken's chief physician, Dr. Brock

The Men. Ellie tries to console Ken. Courtesy: Jerry Ohlinger's. © Stanley Kramer Productions, 1950.

(Everett Sloane), plays a key role in helping Ken accept himself and, in a first for American film, explaining to wives and girlfriends of paraplegics the extent to which fatherhood is possible, given the nature of their spinal injuries. Ken and Ellie marry, but the inherent tensions in their relationship surface quickly (on their wedding day), and they separate, eventually reuniting after Ken realizes the power of her love and the wisdom of Dr. Brock's perspective on his potential.

The film's frank treatment of questions about impotency and fatherhood was notable for the time. Zinnemann and writer Carl Foreman use three scenes in particular to comment on Ken's sexuality. The first occurs when Ellie comes to Ken's bedside at night in an unauthorized visit. He has refused to see her, and this is the only way she can confront him. He tells her to go away, and then throws aside his sheet to expose the lower part of his body to her. The camera remains positioned in a way that prevents our seeing what he shows her. He says, "I'm like a baby," but Ellie is not deterred and leans over his bed and says, "I need you." Obviously the camera can't show what she sees, but her statement after his exposure suggests how strong her love is.

The second scene of note occurs after Ken's therapy has encouraged him (mistakenly) to think he is regaining the ability to feel sensation below his waist: a suggestion, therefore, that sexual feelings are returning. An extended montage of his therapy and exercising that lead him to this conclusion is followed by

Ellie's visit to the ebullient Ken, and they go outside to sit on a bench. His right leg is bouncing spasmodically as he exults in his newfound sensations. But tests determine he does not in fact have any feeling. Nonetheless, they plan on a wedding. This is preceded by another montage of physical therapy and exercise, to which is added their acquisition of and visits to a new home.

Following the wedding, at which Ken totters momentarily, they go back to their home. The awkwardness of the newlyweds is painful enough, but the tension in their relationship surfaces as Ken looks at a scrapbook Ellie had made that includes photographs of him as a high school football star. To divert his irritation about this, she offers champagne a friend has sent. She has trouble opening it; Ken takes over, and the champagne spurts out over the rug, prompting Ellie to cry out about cleaning it up with cold water. As she mops the rug, Zinnemann shoots her from an angle beside Ken's wheelchair. We see his right leg bouncing spasmodically next to the frustrated Ellie on her knees. It's a highly sexualized moment that suggests the uncertainty of sex in such a relationship. Both the spurting champagne that falls on the floor and the spasmodically bouncing leg point ironically to the opposite of sexual activity or orgasm. The scene symbolically depicts the dismal outlook for them sexually at this point in their relationship. Realizing her despair and fear, Ken forces Ellie to admit she is sorry that she married him. Although he leaves and temporarily gives up on the marriage, ultimately he returns to her, and the film ends on a hopeful note.

Given the restrictions of the Production Code Administration in place at the time this film was made, *The Men* necessarily treats the issues of sexual impotency in paraplegics and the (im)possibility of their achieving orgasm in guarded and symbolic ways. Joseph Breen used a particularly accommodating tone in his letter to producer Stanley Kramer about the script:

> [W]e note in the script a number of lines of dialogue relative to the bladder, the bowels, and the question of whether or not a paraplegic man can father children. As you know, under different circumstances much of this dialogue might prove offensive, and hence not acceptable under the requirements of the Code. However, in view of the fact that, within the framework of this story, these references seem to be used in a dignified, clinical manner, we are disposed to raise no objection to them and shall rely upon your very good taste to make certain that there will be nothing whatever objectionable in their use in the finished picture.[13]

Films about paraplegics who were wounded during the Vietnam War were made when the Motion Picture Association of America had adopted a ratings system that allowed for much more explicit treatment of such issues. Both *Coming Home* and *Born on the Fourth of July* approach the subject completely openly.

The films' narratives are quite different. *Coming Home* is a love story in which Luke Martin (Jon Voight) is able to redeem himself and his own sense of worth when he succeeds in fulfilling Sally Hyde (Jane Fonda) sexually by bringing her to orgasm.[14] The film's conclusion suggests Luke's successful sexual awakening of Sally is the counterpart to his political activism against the war. *Born on the Fourth of July*, in contrast, is a chronicle based on the life of Ron Kovic (Tom Cruise). Although there is a love interest, the story is really about how the wounded paraplegic Ron is able to fulfill himself ultimately through his political activism against the war. His lack of sexual fulfillment is addressed by his experience in a Mexican brothel in which he gives sexual pleasure to a prostitute. Curiously, his tears as he brings her to orgasm match Sally's in *Coming Home*. The film suggests that this is, in fact, Ron's first sexual experience, while Ashby's treatment of the sex scene in *Coming Home* underscores that this is Sally's first "real" experience in terms of pleasure.[15]

Born on the Fourth of July is in many ways the most explicit of all the films discussed in this section in dealing with the issue of impotency. In one particularly disturbing sequence, Ron gets drunk with his buddy Timmy (Frank Whaley) and returns home in a rage. When his mother (Caroline Kava) chastises him, he screams about his impotency and forces her to confront his anguish about the loss of his penis. She does not want to hear the term mentioned. After Ron collapses, his father carries him to bed. Earlier we have seen Mr. Kovic (Raymond Barry) helping Ron adjust his catheter, thus indicating Ron's helplessness, the exposed tubes a dismal metonymic substitute for his inoperative penis. But in a moment that underscores the issue of impotency rather than castration explicable in Freudian terms, Mr. Kovic, who has replaced Ron's mother as the source of support, carries Ron in an extraordinary pietá. Mr. Kovic joins Peggy and Wilma in *The Best Years of Our Lives* and Ellie in *The Men* as another comforting figure supporting the child being put to bed.

The nurturing figures of Peggy, Wilma, Ellie, and Mr. Kovic tending to psychologically or physically wounded soldiers at home connect visually with those in scenes in which males on and off the battlefield tend to wounded comrades or patients. At such moments, the male caregivers actually assume or can be perceived as appropriating the kinds of maternal powers suggested in the depiction of Ron's father in *Born on the Fourth of July*. The projection of the maternal function onto males is an important way of negotiating the complex relationship between men at war. As noted in the introduction and in chapter 3, the expansive conception of masculinity urged by R. W. Connell opens an interpretive space to consider situations in which "masculinity" and "femininity" are not tied to the particular biological status of being males and females. Hence the enacting of "masculine" and "feminine" behaviors can move across gender barriers.[16]

Perhaps the most complex pietà in films discussed here appears in *Home of the Brave*. Both E. Ann Kaplan and Michael Rogin explore the only narrative war film about World War II of which I'm aware that deals specifically with

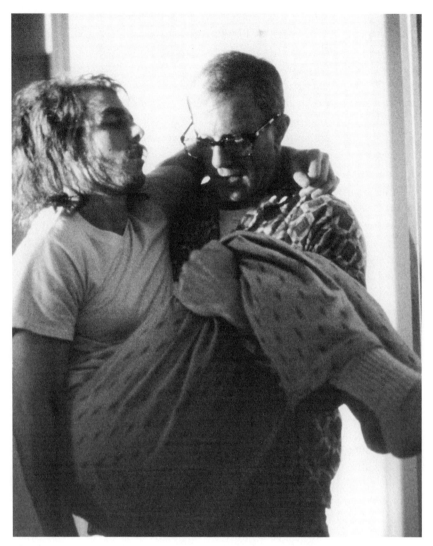

Born on the Fourth of July. Mr. Kovic carries Ron to bed. Courtesy: Jerry Ohlinger's.
© Ixtlan Corporation, 1989.

a psychologically damaged African American soldier, the troubled Peter Moss
(James Edwards). Although not physically injured, he loses his memory and ability to walk as a result of a traumatic experience in which his white friend Finch
(Lloyd Bridges) is killed. Buddies since childhood, they are part of a reconnaissance mission in which Peter has been subject to slurs from T.J. (Steve Brodie), a
racist. But when his friend begins to call him a "nigger" at a tense moment, Peter
is broken emotionally. After Finch is wounded and the men can't go into the jungle

to retrieve him, Peter suffers from a complex combination of guilt and anger that paralyzes him. When the dying Finch crawls from the jungle, Peter cradles him in his arms in a manner described by Rogin in this way: "His head on Finch's chest, Finch's head on his chest, hysterically rocking and cradling his friend's body, Moss is enacting a black and white pietà . . . Moss is thereby . . . playing mammy."[17] But in addition to this maternal image, Rogin also acknowledges the possibility, pointed out by others, of a homoerotic dimension in the relationship: "In bleeding black man into white, against the traditional model of closed-off and invulnerable manhood, *Home* provoked nervousness about homoeroticism among white reviewers" since it depicts "an African American homoerotically bonded with a white."[18]

The psychiatrist cures Peter by making him realize his paralysis is a result of survivor's guilt, a narrative strategy that Rogin sees diverting the film's initial emphasis on racism. The focus itself depended on integrating an African American into the narrative when, in fact, such a union of soldiers on a reconnaissance mission would not have been possible during World War II because of the segregation of white and African American troops.[19] The film concludes as Peter leaves with Mingo (Frank Lovejoy), whose arm has been amputated, with plans to open a restaurant together. Rogin argues that "tying Moss to the disabled veteran, the movie intends to dissolve the stigmas attaching to racial difference and amputation (and, subliminally, homosexual love), but in proclaiming that two damaged men could make a postwar life together, the movie was allying the black man with a cripple."[20]

On the one hand, one could argue that shifting the cause of Peter's trauma to survivor's guilt rather than racism is itself a way of diluting the homosexual potential even more. That is, the text is adding yet one more layer to cover what some see as a possible homosexual bond between the men. Thus the film could be said to disguise the real issue in two ways: he's mourning because he was unable to save the man he loved, and he has survivor's guilt. But on the other hand, this interpretation doesn't fully address the overall thrust of the film's narrative. While the psychiatrist's strategy of using survivor's guilt as a way to make Peter see he's like other men leads to a cure, it also explicitly demonstrates there is *not* a homosexual subtext. If Peter is like all other men in his feelings, then he is not unique or "different" in terms of the sexual economy of the film; he is not a homosexual. All men can feel guilty when they are happy they survived, even though their buddy didn't. In positing Peter's sameness, the film is not in fact disguising any potentially homosexual subtext. If so, why end by suggesting another as he goes off to form a partnership with Mingo in a restaurant? In fact, at the end Peter is in a more powerful position since he will be offering two hands to a man who now has only one.

Ann Kaplan raises another issue that complicates the possible homoerotic reading of the relationship between Moss and Finch. She reminds us that psychoanalytic

Home of the Brave. The psychiatrist helps Peter to heal. Courtesy: Jerry Ohlinger's. © Stanley Kramer Productions, 1949.

situations in films often have the effect of feminizing the analysands: "Perhaps because the successful role of analysand is inherently a 'feminized' one, most Hollywood narratives about psychoanalysis have female—that is *white* female— protagonists. When the patient is male and *black*, he too is feminized, as in a film like *Home of the Brave* (1949)."[21] From this standpoint, then, Moss can be seen to function in a female subject position both as "mammy" when he cradles Moss and as the helpless patient of the nameless psychiatrist. In either case, the gender slippage certainly can be factored in for those who would make the argument about a homosexual subtext here, one I do not find persuasive.

Significantly, the only other time African American soldiers appear in psychoanalytic situations in the 1940s is in John Huston's documentary *Let There Be Light* (1945). Suppressed at the time of its creation, the film records the treatment of shell-shocked and traumatized soldiers at a mental hospital. One of the most moving sequences shown is of an African American who has had a nervous breakdown and is crying as he describes how he has been affected by homesickness. He breaks down as he tells his white psychiatrist (all the psychiatrists are white) how her picture made him long to be back home with her.

Part of what makes this film so painful to watch comes, in fact, from seeing soldiers (not actors) in truly helpless positions trying to respond to the generally kind but still distant and aloof psychiatrists. Watching the displays of limited masculine power as the men try to keep a grip on their emotions drives home their vulnerability and, finally, their abjection caused by war.

CHAPTER FIVE

DRAG

Men in drag—the concept has a built-in potential for humor. War films and works in other genres have made extensive use of the concept for exactly that purpose, to generate laughter. In the process, though, the filmmakers who created them have provided texts that invite examination of the complex implications of drag and its challenges to masculinity and sexuality. This chapter explores and expands on some of these issues.

Drag figures in two broad narrative categories: outright performances in which men dress as women in order to entertain audiences, and disguises in which men pretend to be women to avoid being detected as men. Among the examples in the first category are *This Is the Army* (Michael Curtiz, 1943), *The Bridge on the River Kwai* (David Lean, 1958), and *South Pacific* (Joshua Logan, 1958). As far as I know, the first example of a war film in the second category is a 1927 comedy I have not seen called *Lost at the Front* (Frank Griffin, 1927), in which two American soldiers disguise themselves as Russian women. According to the review in the *New York Times*, the male leads "had hoped to escape from bullets and shells by disguising themselves as women, but to their dismay they are mixed up with the women's battalion."[1] Examples of the second kind of narrative include *Abroad with Two Yanks* (Allan Dwan, 1944), in which two servicemen have fled from jail, and *I Was a Male War Bride* (Howard Hawks, 1949), in which the character portrayed by Cary Grant pretends to be a woman so he can accompany his wife to America.

THEORETICAL CONCERNS

Drag has received extensive treatment from a number of scholars and writers: Roger Baker, Rebecca Bell-Metereau, Allan Bérubé, David A. Boxwell, Marjorie Garber, Vito Russo, Mark Simpson, Chris Straayer, and Parker Tyler.[2] Boxwell's suggestions are of particular interest. Drawing on his research into historical examples of drag in the armed services, and writing from a psychoanalytic perspective, he suggests two effects of drag performed in British stage reviews during World War I. First, drag

> satisfies the psychic demands for a defense against war's potential unmanning of the male body. This potential unmanning fosters the kind of castration anxiety that makes men extraordinarily receptive to the ritual possibility of defending themselves against the loss of "manhood" through the fetishistic opportunities afforded by drag. The transvestite permits the spectator and the performer to "play" at giving up the phallus in order to recover (the illusion of having) the phallus. Thus there is always a simultaneous acknowledgement that what the man in drag has pretended to surrender is always really there.[3]

The second effect is in offering "a 'solution' to the crises inhering in a ruptured homosocial continuum" and in permitting "the expression, through drag, of a male homosocial community less marked by anxiety about the troubling intimacy of male-male desires and identifications."[4]

Three more observations from a different perspective can be offered to complement Boxwell's suggestions and to add contradictions to those he identifies. First, one appeal of drag can be related to my argument earlier about representations of the maternal impulse. Drag may serve a need by acknowledging in comic terms the reality that men in fact do take on feminine nurturing roles. Second, drag is one way of addressing not only a "loss of manhood" or "ruptured homosocial continuum." One appeal of drag may come from the fact that it says, in effect, when men appear to be helpless like women, it is only a temporary aberration. Drag allows men to take on gender roles in which they momentarily literally behave like the gender to which, from their perspective, they have been reduced in battle when they are crying, screaming, helpless creatures on the battlefield, not the characteristically dominant males they know themselves to be.

Third, drag scenes permit the authorized looking by one male at another as spectacle, an action that simultaneously asserts and disavows the possibility of homosexual attraction: "I can take pleasure watching you, a man, perform as if you were a woman because I know you are not a woman but a man pretending to be a woman." Any potential eroticized aspect to my look is thus negated because I can't/won't watch you as an erotic object but as a performing subject. Thus I can view you in a way that disavows a homosexual dimension in my look. Steve Neale argues that one strategy for disavowing the potential anxiety caused by a male taking pleasure in watching another male is to remove the attractiveness of the image by disfiguring it through violence.[5] In contrast, I'm suggesting that one way of dealing with such anxiety is to make the male attractive as a woman in a way that necessarily disavows its own representational implications.

Boxwell is surely right to point out the inherent contradictions of drag, which denies what it shows. As Judith Butler argues, the complex process actually involves three rather than two registers: "If the anatomy of the performer is already distinct from the gender of the performer, and both of those are distinct from the gender of the performance, then the performance suggests a dissonance not only between sex and performance, but sex and gender, and gender and performance. . . . *In imitating gender, drag implicitly reveals the imitative structure of gender itself.*"[6]

The idea of imitation is important to note here, because as one looks at the various kinds of situations in which drag figures, it is clear that generally the narratives always provide reasons to explain and justify why a man is imitating that which he is not, a woman, whether in a musical show or in a comic intrigue.

There's a curious polarity and incongruity in that in performative situations, drag is there to be denied: the audience's pleasure comes from knowing the women are men. In contrast, in situations of disguise, the entertainment arises from seeing how long the act can go on without exposure. When will the men be exposed as men?[7]

"Men in Dames' Clothes"—*This Is the Army*

This Is the Army was based on the successful musical revue of 1942, originally presented on Broadway, in which servicemen performed all the numbers. The film was Warner Bros.' most successful production of the decade and the highest-grossing film made during World War II.[8] Among its significant aspects are, first, the way its depictions of drag maintain the unquestioned masculinity of the performers. Second, the manner in which African Americans are depicted is noteworthy since, for the contemporary audiences, this was the most widely viewed film during the war in which they were given visibility.[9] I'm particularly interested here in the role of African Americans in the drag numbers and the way the film makes use of them in its treatment of male sexuality. Ideologically, the film can be seen to affirm the masculinity and sexuality of white males in drag as stronger and more secure than that of African Americans.

Bérubé has discussed the film's drag numbers in *Coming Out Under Fire*. Although he comments helpfully on some aspects of race, he does not fully explore the exact relationship between race and representations of sexuality. The film's drag numbers need to be understood in relation to the government policy of segregating white and black troops. As noted earlier in connection with *Home of the Brave*, until President Harry S. Truman ordered an end to this practice, no military unit was integrated. Although two African Americans are seen briefly in the "Stage Door Canteen" number and in the finale of *This Is the Army*, in which literally hundreds of white men appear, they are kept separate in all the other musical numbers. Ironically, the segregating of the two races involved in the military and in the production numbers is foregrounded by the first drag number, which is a particularly offensive minstrel routine in which white performers are in exaggerated blackface as males while other whites impersonate black females in drag.

To get the full impact of this number's significance, it is important to understand its relation to other scenes in the show as well as to the ideological complexity of what's being naturalized for the vast viewing audience of 1943. First, the "drafting" of the performers needs comment. Although all the members of the show, whether really members of the army (like Lieutenant Ronald Reagan and Sergeant Joe Louis) or a Warner Bros. contract actor like Alan Hale, are presented narratively as already in the army, the film shows how individual members are called by commanding officers to leave their current service units and join the musical troop. While over twenty white members are displayed being picked and named, with the exception of Joe Louis, no African American is singled out for individual recognition.

The first drag number, one of four throughout the film, is in some ways the most problematic in terms of representing race and sexuality. A large chorus of white males sits on risers, while at the top of the stage, in front of a drawing of a banjo, five whites in blackface with exaggerated lip makeup sing "Mandy," after being cued by Johnny Jones (Ronald Reagan), the stage manager. As they sing, a group of white males made up as black men in drag appear (without the exaggerated lips) and descend to the stage, where they join white men in blackface and dance with them. The camera positioning generally involves long shots that keep the white chorus clearly in view along with the five whites in blackface at the top while the men in blackface and in blackface drag dance to "Mandy" and then break into "Way Down Upon the Sewanne River."

Bérubé suggests that "the all-white minstrel number . . . featured men impersonating black women who flirted and danced with men impersonating black men, so that even in blackface the taboo on interracial couples was not broken."[10] But there's more to say in terms of sexuality. This first drag number is heavily inflected by white masculinity: not only by the omnipresent chorus but also by the "females" who are twice removed from the status of "real" black women. They are impersonations (of women) created by impersonations (of black men). This first drag number sets the gendered and racial terms of impersonation that govern the film. That is, the first example of white males in drag is as blacks. With the exception of one fleeting glance of one of the white-"black"-female dancers without his wig in the dressing room, subsequent appearances of white males in drag will not be as blacks but generally as overdetermined males whose masculinity is emphasized by their gracelessness, their body hair, the timbre of their voices, the outrageousness and campiness of their routines, and camera positioning.

The first drag number initiates a strategy of disavowal that operates within the film: it's permissible for white men to be in drag because it's as incongruous and out of nature as a white man being black in the first place. This strategy approaches a level of hysteria in connection with Sergeant McGee (Alan Hale).

He's "drafted" by orders into appearing in the "Ladies of the Chorus" routine when someone doesn't appear. He's against appearing as a woman ("Men in dames' clothes! What must their mothers think," he snorts). This number, the second drag routine, occurs after a display of athletic prowess involving tumblers and human pyramids constructed by white soldiers. That is, immediately before the display of white men as white women, the film shows white men as completely in control of their bodies. Then, in a manner that emphasizes that the "ladies" are men, the group appears. Their song, "Ladies of the Chorus," is all about the fact that they are not ladies at all but men who are pretending to be ladies. Various singers identify themselves as having obviously masculine jobs: a plumber, a printer, and a farmer. The subsequent dance number with a group of men plays on the incongruity of their appearance and clumsiness. In contrast to the "black" women (played by white men playing black men in drag) who do not draw attention to their drag and disavow it, these guys are guys. In fact, the *Time* reviewer spoke of "the horsing and singing of the wool-bearing *Ladies of the Chorus*, who have taken almost excruciating care to be mistaken neither for transvestite chorusmen nor for the quite convincing young ladies they dared to be on Broadway."[11] The relevance of this comment becomes clear when one learns that the movie downplays the transvestitism as well as the potentially homosexual overtones of the theatrical revue that preceded it. Pictures in *Life* of the original stage production show that it included a sequence in which pajama-clad soldiers are served breakfast in cots by men in drag. In addition, there was one sequence in which one private did a mock, partial striptease.[12]

The disavowal of any suggestion of femininity continues immediately after the "Ladies of the Chorus" number as the now relieved Sergeant McGee can remove his wig. Following this is the only sequence that features a group of African Americans. "What the Well-Dressed Man in Harlem Will Wear" begins as a male routine sung and danced before a backdrop suggesting Harlem. Behind the backdrop are large figures of white men in blackface with the kind of exaggerated lips we saw on the white men in drag in the first sequence. Thus the real blacks are presented in relation to their prior unflattering presentation by white males. While the men sing of the olive and khaki colors they'll display in their new army clothing, Joe Louis (in uniform now), who is the only African American treated unambiguously in terms of masculinity and sexuality, incongruously works out on a punching bag to the left of the stage. The routine then moves to a jitterbug in which a single black man in drag joins the lead singer and dances energetically and effortlessly. As in the first sequence in which white males appeared as black males doing female drag number, nothing is done within the dance by way of clumsiness or silliness to disavow the transvestitism, the kind of disavowal we have just seen in "Ladies of the Chorus." Whether white or black men are in drag as black women, the dance routine doesn't disavow the femininity by overemphasizing the masculinity of its performers. This has the effect of stressing the disparity involved when *white* men do white drag as compared to when black men do black drag. That is, a white man doing a white woman in drag is instantly recognizable as a man; but a black man (whether or not he is black or being impersonated by a white man) is less easily distinguished from the woman he imitates.

In contrast to every example of white men in drag as white or black women throughout the film, the black man in drag does not have a wig or prominent headdress—a common visual source of disavowal in the film since these are generally so obvious and/or awful. Rather, he wears a strange little hat that reveals his full head plainly. His outfit is more revealing than those of the white men in drag, the sum effect being to cast the performer in a kind of competition with white men doing black drag in the earlier scene. After dancing off with his partner, in contrast to what happens to whites coming out of drag, we actually see him remove his top, thus revealing that he is, in fact, a man. While a white man in drag as a white woman cannot be confused with one visually, a black man can— hence the instant clarification by a display of the full chest in a shot. Even though one could argue that this action is motivated by the fact that he returns to the stage to conclude the number, it still draws attention to the difference in representation.

The last drag routine is the most complex because it runs the most risks of any seen so far in regard to white masculinity and sexuality. The famous "I Left My Heart at the Stage Door Canteen" is here sung by a soldier who directs his song to one of the males in drag as a hostess at the canteen. The other men in drag in this sequence are clearly just that—men in drag, especially those doing overt female impersonations of the actresses Jane Cowl and Lynn Fontanne. The film negotiates the problematic of having a love song sung by a man to a man playing a woman with camera movements and framing that obscure the face of the man in drag. We see only a partial side shot and then the figure from behind. Even more significant, as the singer turns to leave and seems about to invite the man in drag to leave with him (contrary, of course, to the canteen's taboo of fraternization outside the facility between servicemen and the women and in line with the lyrics of the song we have just heard), we see the singer positioned between two men in drag, Jane Cowl and the object of his song—the former clearly signaling that this cannot be. The soldier leaves mournfuly. As Bérubé suggests, this song and departure perform a complex ideological function by enacting another prohibition, that involving sexual contact between males.[13] No matter what affection the soldier has for the figure (a man in drag, yes—but still a man), it will not pass muster. Thus this white drag routine has the effect of reassuring its audience about the safety of white males' sexuality and masculinity, a gesture that isn't presented in the routine with the real black dancers who in fact leave the stage together arm and arm, certainly not separately as a disavowed couple.

As an added affirmation of white masculinity and power, the applause for this number is followed by one of the white men in a dress saying he can't go on with the show because "I'm having a baby." His wife is delivering right now, and he has

This Is the Army. "I'm having a baby!" Courtesy: Photofest. © Warner Bros. Pictures, 1943.

to be with her. He's allowed to leave, with the advice to take off his costume before he goes to the hospital. Tom D'Andrea adds that the child won't be able to tell who his mother is. A similar kind of reassuring textual operation is evident in the three contemporary advertisements to which I referred in chapter 3. There the masculinity of the three soldiers seen variously with a slip advertising detergent, a dog tag advertising a chain company, and a helmet before a mirror for B. F. Goodrich is confirmed since are all unquestionably male and engaged in the war effort.

"The Only Girl in the World"—*The Bridge on the River Kwai*

The drag scene in *The Bridge on the River Kwai* has special narrative interest. It is part of a combined celebration and reward for the English soldiers who, under the command of Colonel Nicholson (Alec Guinness), have built a bridge for their Japanese captors. But during its performance, while both the prisoners and their captors watch, Shears (William Holden) and Lieutenant Joyce (Geoffrey Horne) are engaged in setting the bombs on the bridge in preparation of the planned sabotage. The sequence begins with eight soldiers dressed in grass skirts dancing onto the stage. During their dance, they touch their "breasts" (stuffing of some sort in halters) and turn around to flip up their skirts from behind for the appreciative audience. The diegetic music accompanying their dance continues

Bridge on the River Kwai. Entertaining the men. Courtesy: Photofest. © Columbia Pictures Corporation/Horizon Pictures (II) 1957.

as Lean cuts to the activities of the demolition team. We return to the stage as a tall solider dressed in drag and a soldier dressed only in shorts sing "If You Were the Only Girl in the World" to each other. The song concludes as the short man jumps into the arms of the "girl," to much laughter from the audience.

"If You Were the Only Girl in the World" is an old British music hall song from World War I. The lyrics posit a romantic heterosexual idyll about a world out of time where love can thrive:

> If you were the only girl in the world
> And I were the only boy
> Nothing else would matter in the world today
> We could go on loving in the same old way
> A garden of Eden just made for two
> With nothing to mar our joy
> I would say such wonderful things to you
> There would be such wonderful things to do
> If you were the only girl in the world
> And I were the only boy.

In the narrative context of the prison camp, though, the lyrics have a special resonance. In a performative sense, the man being addressed as "the only girl in the
world" is in fact at that moment functioning as the only "girl" in the world for
the actual singer, and for the men in the audience who are enjoying the performance. Romantic heterosexual relationships in the film include those between Shears
and a nurse and between Lieutenant Joyce and one of the Burmese women assist-
ing in the sabotage. This song thus works on a number of registers. It contrasts
"real" relationships and presents a forbidden speculation: "If this man were a
woman, he/she would be the only girl for me." "He/she is not a woman; thus I can
sing to her as if she were with the built-in disavowal. I know you aren't a woman,
but at the same time, I don't want you as a man, only as the woman you are not."

"Nothing You Can Name"—*South Pacific*

Although the viewing situations are quite different, the major drag number in
South Pacific connects in an interesting way to that in *Bridge over the River Kwai*.
Nellie Forbush (Mitzie Gaynor), dressed as a sailor, sings "Honey Bun" to Luther
Billis (Ray Walston), in drag as a woman in a grass skirt. Bérubé suggests the
musical "incorporated coded gay slang in to the drag numbers. During a show
within a show, a female nurse plays a man who sings and dances with a male
sailor who plays a woman. The nurse's stage name as a man is Butch—lesbian

South Pacific. Luther and Nellie in drag. Courtesy: Photofest. © 20th Century Fox, 1958.

slang for a lesbian woman—which plays off her given name Nellie—gay male slang for an effeminate man."[14] The two drag performers are in no way mistakable for a real woman or a real man, a situation recognized by their appreciative and noisy audience. Indeed, one sailor sends a dart into the behind of Luther/Honey Bun and provokes more laughs.

As far as I know, no one has connected the drag scene with an earlier number, "There Is Nothing like a Dame." Sung by the sailors and marines, this famous song outlines the extent of deprivation faced by the men in the South Pacific, who have only the nurses and natives to look at, both of whom are off-limits. Director Joshua Logan stages the mise-en-scène in a way that lets us see the makeshift outdoor shower for the men. In front of it, the sign with the message, "Look, but don't touch," plays comically on the idea of the males as visual spectacles for anyone on the island. One phrase that follows the song title is worth consideration: "Nothing you can name." On the one hand, the denotation is simple enough: "nothing at all is like a woman." On the other hand, though, a more provocative denotation is certainly possible. That is, just as you cannot touch what you see in the shower, so too can you not name that which is not like a woman but which is capable of meeting a sexual need. That is, you can't name a man because to do so would be a sign of homosexuality.

Luther's drag act is a comic enactment of the second line in the song. He is, of course, nothing like a dame. The coconuts that serve as mock breasts, the hair on his chest, and the masculine build all "prove" that no man, or at least this man, is anything like a dame. On the other hand, he has a false name, Honey Bun. He is, in a way, the unnameable, the abject other, whose bisexuality is comically punished with a dart by the masculine sailor who is reasserting heterosexuality as the norm.[15]

SPONTANEOUS DRAG

In contrast to these drag productions that are given prominent places in the narratives are two that are spontaneous rather than planned performances. The first occurs in *Guadalcanal Diary* (Lewis Seiler, 1943). In a scene set on a ship carrying men to the site of the forthcoming battle, marines and sailors watch the comic performance of Taxi Potts (William Bendix). Dressed in semidrag as a Hawaiian "woman," Taxi dances a hula while one of the sailors plays a harmonica. The ship's chaplain, Father Donnelly (Preston Foster), enters and watches Taxi, who is embarrassed when he sees the priest and takes off some of his makeshift costume. The music changes from the Hawaiian melody to an Irish tune, and Taxi and Father Donnelly dance a jig, concluding with an arm-in-arm spin. The dancing and drag in this impromptu entertainment are presented in a context in which heterosexuality is confirmed through the inoculating element of humor (Bendix's incongruous appearance) and authority (the Irish priest who joins in a jig).[16]

Guadalcanal Diary. Taxi's dance. Courtesy: Jerry Ohlinger's. © 20th Century Fox Film Corporation, 1943.

Another spontaneous drag sequence, this one accompanied by indications of explicit sexual longing, appears in the Christmas party scene in *Stalag 17* (Billy Wilder, 1953). The sequence begins as we see a number of soldiers dancing as couples in the prison camp. A windup phonograph is playing "I Love You," which is being sung by one of the soldiers as Price (Peter Graves) provides a rhythm accompaniment on a washboard. Harry (Harvey Lembeck) has been dancing with a soldier, and when someone cuts in to take away his partner, he can't succeed in finding a new one. Frustrated, he goes over to Animal (Robert Strauss), who is in a drunken stupor gazing at his collection of Betty Grable photographs. When Animal doesn't respond, Harry makes a wig out of straw, covers it with a cap, and, primping his hair in an effeminate manner, asks another soldier to dance. He refuses him, and Harry sits on a bench with his legs partly arched. When Animal sees him in this pose, which emulates one of Grable's more well known poses, he thinks Harry *is* Grable, rises from his bunk, and starts dancing with him. He praises Harry's/Betty's legs and little nose, asks him to pinch his cheek so he knows he's not dreaming, and sings along to the words of the song. Wilder shoots the dance in such a way that we see a varied range in Harry's facial responses to Animal's comments, and, eventually, his amusing conflicted reactions, a mixture of embarrassment and chagrin, particularly when Animal starts praising his legs and little nose. Harry shouts at Animal to wake up, and the disappointed dancer breaks into tears when he realizes the truth.[17] It is not impossible to imagine that the scene, shot in a two-shot from above the waist, is meant to imply that Animal has an erection. After reading the script, Joseph Breen cautioned Luigi Luraschi at Paramount to remove any "inference of sex perversion" and the "expression [that] comes over Harry's face." Since there is no follow-up in regard to the film as produced, Breen must have been content.[18]

Unlike all the drag scenes mentioned here, Harry's assumption of the wig is done specifically to attract a male dancing partner. That is, he puts on partial female attire to gain contact with a male when he is unable to engage in the dancing, an activity authorized by his comrades. But his ruse is too successful, for Animal cannot tell the difference between the appearance and reality because of his sexual longing. His tears are not because he's embarrassed for having desired a man who turns out to be a woman, but because he cannot have the woman who is being impersonated by the man.

Wilder provides the most overt acknowledgment of the complexity of male sexuality in this scene. "Straight" dancing is authorized by the context. Cutting in, as would occur in a heterosexual situation, is permitted. Seeking a dance partner by invitation is also possible. Harry's interaction with Animal provides a comic acknowledgment of what underlines the manifest content of the scene: the basic sexual longing that in fact transcends the prohibitions.

In contrast to the two comic spontaneous drag scenes, the one that occurs in *The Thin Red Line* (Andrew Marton, 1964) is radically different and has a deadly outcome. In this film, the first of two adaptations of James Jones's 1962 novel, marines who have moved into a new camp discover boxes of women's clothing. Private Fife (Robert Kanter) begins to put on some of the dresses and headgear and is encouraged by his fellow marines to continue adding more clothes, including stockings, which he draws seductively on his legs (and which he uses as substitutes for long gloves). From the beginning of this activity, Private Doll (Keir Dullea), who is Fife's friend and who earlier has given him his watch, glowers disapprovingly. Marton cuts from the exuberant men to Fife, to Doll, and to the Japanese soldiers who are hidden underneath one of the buildings at this camp. Once Fife is completely "dressed," the men urge him to engage in a striptease, which he begins to do, beginning by pulling off his "glove." During the strip, he puts his scarf around the neck of one of the admiring and raucous men. At this point, the Japanese who have been lurking under the living quarters begin a surprise attack. Fife is killed along with many others in the bloodbath. Doll is clearly upset at his friend's death and thinks about taking back the watch from the hand of his dead friend.

In a discussion of the film adaptation, Stacy Peebles Powers points out that the novel has scenes of "circumstantial homosexuality." She observes that in the film, "Fife and Doll have a close relationship . . . and Fife is effeminate."[19] Although she comments on the striptease and its aftermath, she does not explore the

The Thin Red Line. Spontaneous drag show. © A.C.E. Films/Security Pictures Inc., 1964.

significance of Doll's disapproving glances. Stanley Kauffmann speaks of "hints of the constant possibility of homosexuality among young men cramped together and thoroughly desperate" but does not refer to this scene.[20] I suggest that Doll's glances can be read as an indication not only of his disgust but also, possibly, his anger that his buddy has exposed himself in this way to the other men. Fife's exaggerated seductive moves and glances as a temporary female define him ambiguously in terms of gender, hence sexuality in the terms of the film. That is, Doll's anger may be a result of having his friend act like a woman, hence a sexual object, when in fact there is no actual homosexual relationship. Doll may be troubled by the way Fife's behavior destabilizes the meaning of his friendship. The attack that follows can be seen, at least in part, in relation to Doll's conflicted anger. When Fife's body is discovered, he is still wearing his drag outfit. Many of the other men caught in this surprise attack are only in shorts, a telling visual contrast in which the "(sexually) healthy" male body is as exposed as it could be in a 1964 film, while Fife is covered with the wrong clothing, a female costume.[21]

In the other examples discussed thus far, the performances are kept separate from any battles. That is, whether planned or impromptu, none connects directly with actual scenes of combat. But in *The Thin Red Line*, the drag show leads directly into a battle and death, including that of the performer as well as other soldiers.

Disguise

In contrast to drag that foregrounds and acknowledges its performative aspects are narrative situations in which men are in drag to disguise themselves and avoid detection as men performing as women. Chris Straayer offers a comprehensive and extremely helpful discussion of a subgenre she calls "the temporary transvestite film." Some of its conventions include: "the narrative necessity for disguise; adoption by a character of the opposite sex's specifically gender-coded costume . . .; the simultaneous believability of this disguise to the film's characters and its unbelievability to the audience . . . ; and, finally, heterosexual coupling."[22] The inevitable conclusion of such films is always an "unmasking" that (literally) straightens out sexual identities: "Heterosexuality is the guardian of sexual difference."[23]

She discusses the comedies *Abroad with Two Yanks* and *I Was a Male War Bride*. The first is set in Australia during World War II, the second in Europe after its conclusion. Although neither contains any battle scenes, they reinforce the same sexual ideology visible in the other films. All confirm the primacy of heterosexuality by presenting transvestite moments as temporary aberrations of heterosexuality.

In *Abroad with Two Yanks*, Biff Koraski (William Bendix) and Jeff Reardon (Dennis O'Keefe) are two marines in love with Joyce Stuart (Helen Walker). The film begins with Jeff pretending to be Biff, a move that initiates the confusion of assumed identities that continues in the film as Jeff pretends to be schizophrenic, and then as they both join the "Marine Follies" as singers in drag. They have been allowed to participate in the show because, although they are prisoners in the brig for stealing a car, they are needed to fill out the chorus. Escaping from the rehearsal, they crash a party at Joyce's home, where their disguises are exposed. Joyce is really in love with Cyril North (John Loder), whom she promises to marry. The film ends as the dressed (but now wigless) Biff and Jeff are captured again by the military police.

The ending with the cross-dressing men in custody is certainly not meant as a cautionary, albeit comic, statement about transvestitism. After all, they were supposed to be part of a drag show. But it does convey in its way an affirmation about the heterosexual marriage that will occur between Joyce and Cyril. Although there are no military battles in the film, it is filled with sparring, slapstick, and physical assaults by Biff and Jeff on each other (including during the drag scenes). Their behavior appears decidedly adolescent next to that of the more assured and masculine Cyril. Heterosexual marriage is the goal not only of the characters but also of the ideological logic of the narrative. In drag, Biff sings a song about wanting a man. The film's conclusion sees the rewarding of those whose anatomy and gender are consonant and whose performances do not deviate from this linkage.

I Was a Male War Bride is probably the best-known service comedy involving drag, a result of the by now iconic image of Cary Grant dressed as a woman in a uniform. He plays Henri Rochard, a Frenchman married to an American officer in the Women's Army Corps (WACs), Lieutenant Catherine Gates (Ann Sheridan). Most of the film depicts a series of mishaps, quarrels, and misunderstandings between them before they realize they are in love and marry. Because Henri is French, the military bureaucracy impedes his ability to accompany Catherine back to the United States. Catherine hits on the idea of disguising him as a woman, using hair from a horse's tail to make his wig. The actual scenes of disguise consume a very small part of the film.

Even before the need for drag occurs, an ongoing element of the plot has involved their inability to consummate the marriage. Once the bureaucratic log-jam has been fixed, and Henri and Catherine are alone in their own room on board the ship headed for the United States, he throws the key out their stateroom window, and the film ends with the suggestion that at last they can have sexual intercourse. The delay in sexual relations is, on the one hand, a function of the Production Code Administration's standards at the time. Of course they could not have had sex before marriage. The narrative's presentation of impediments to sex after they are legally married connects to the goal mentioned by Straayer as one of the elements in this subgenre, "heterosexual coupling." Unlike any of the examples mentioned above, though, here the woman rather than the man originates the idea of using drag as a disguise, and she does so to bring about the fulfillment of her marriage. In a curious twist on the narrative logic of plots involving drag, Henri has to pretend to be a woman so he can ultimately function as the man he is for the woman who loves him. The heterosexual couple itself is engaged in the deception, not just a man.[24]

Focusing on the representation of masculinity in the film, Rebecca Bell-Metereau suggests that its ending "is charged with irony. Henri is finally allowed to consummate his marriage in the ship's brig . . . . The Freudian implications of the last shot of the Statue of Liberty through a porthole suggest sexual intercourse and liberation, but even this supposedly masculine triumph is subtly undercut by the very fact that the phallic statue is, after all, a woman. The home that should be man's castle has shrunk to a prison cell, the largest domain the male figure can successfully command."[25]

CHAPTER SIX

"DON'T ASK, DON'T TELL"

The last three chapters focus exclusively on war films released since 1966, for two reasons. The first pertains to cinematic history: in 1966 the methods by which the Production Code Administration (PCA) regulated the content of American film ended, to be replaced by a new system administered by the Motion Picture Association of America. While the PCA had made a number of accommodations in the 1950s and 1960s that involved relaxing some of its strictures, such as the use of swear words ("damn" and "hell" gradually appear more prominently), and more open treatment of illicit heterosexual behavior (premarital sex, revealing costumes), any explicit treatment of homosexuality, classified as a perversion, was still off limits. Even so, some key films appeared that approached the issue guardedly: *Rebel without a Cause* (Nicholas Ray, 1955), *Tea and Sympathy* (Vincente Minnelli, 1956), and *Suddenly, Last Summer* (Joseph Mankiewicz, 1959).[1] The second reason, which gives this chapter its title, is more obvious: in 1993 President Bill Clinton initiated a policy of toleration for gays in the military that would be known as "Don't ask, don't tell." This policy was emended in 2000, adding "Don't pursue, don't harass," as a result of the murder of a soldier, Barry Winchell (discussed below). With the new ratings system, gays in the military could be presented on screen. It would take almost thirty years for U.S. policy to acknowledge their presence. The films made after the changes in both policies provide an important perspective on masculinity and sexuality.

Allan Bérubé's *Coming Out Under Fire: The History of Gay Men and Women during World War Two* draws on a number of personal memoirs in an extensive account of how gay men and lesbians experienced the war and their sexuality, whether in casual or in committed relationships.[2] He suggests that the bonds formed among straight men actually provided a kind of enabling model for gay soldiers:

> Veterans of all kinds describe the love they felt for each other with a passion, romance, and sentimentality that often rivaled gay men's expressions of their

love for other men and made gay affections seem less out of place. "You're dealing with excesses of love and hate," explained Marine Corps veteran William Manchester, who was not gay, "and among men who fight together there is an intense love. You are closer to those men than to anyone except your immediate family when you were young."[3]

Individualized accounts and observations by soldiers regarding what they experienced or observed in the armed forces during World War II are also important sources of information about aspects of homosexuality in the military. Ted Allenby, one of Bérubé's sources, provides a fuller account of his experiences as a gay marine in Studs Terkle's *The Good War: An Oral History of World War Two*.[4] Fred Rochlin's *Old Man in a Baseball Cap: A Memoir of World War II* offers extended treatment of one of his commanding officer's romantic involvements with another soldier.[5] C. Tyler Carpenter and Edward H. Yeatts describe their own romantic experiences as lovers, soldiers, and entertainers in *Stars without Garters: The Memoirs of Two Gay GIs in WWII*.[6] Arthur Dong's *Coming Out Under Fire* (1994), a documentary about gay men and lesbians who served in World War II, was written by Dong and Bérubé and includes filmed accounts of his subjects' experiences.[7]

Almost immediately after the new censorship classification system was adopted by the Motion Picture Association of America, two films about homosexual soldiers were made and released with "R" ratings: *Reflections in a Golden Eye* (John Huston, 1967) and *The Sergeant* (John Flynn, 1968). But while homosexuality continued to figure in films such as *The Boys in the Band* (William Friedkin, 1970), *Dog Day Afternoon* (Sidney Lumet, 1975), *Cruising* (William Friedkin, 1980), and *Making Love* (Arthur Hiller, 1982), no war film having this as a central element appeared again until Robert Altman's *Streamers* (1983), an adaptation by David Rabe of his own play. There is an incidental plot element involving the exposure of homosexual soldiers in Mike Nichols's *Biloxi Blues* (1988), Neil Simon's adaptation of his successful Broadway comedy. That material is treated seriously, unlike the way soldiers' homosexuality is presented in *To Serve and Protect*, the interior "film" for which Cameron Drake (Matt Dillon) wins his Oscar in *In & Out* (Frank Oz, 1997). Chris Cooper plays a closeted marine in *American Beauty* (Sam Mendes, 1999). Besides these, though, to my knowledge, homosexual soldiers do not appear in another film until *Basic* (John McTiernan, 2003).[8]

REFLECTIONS IN A GOLDEN EYE

Based on a novel by Carson McCullers, the film adaptation of *Reflections in a Golden Eye* by Chapman Mortimer and Gladys Hill opens with a sentence from the novel: "There is a fort in the South where a few years ago a murder was committed." The film concerns Major Weldon Penderton (Marlon Brando), who

is married to Leonora (Elizabeth Taylor). She is having an affair with Lieutenant
Colonel Morris Langdon (Brian Keith), who is married to the mentally disturbed Alison (Julie Harris). The Langdons have a gay houseboy, Anacleto
(Zorro David). While Penderton appears to be oblivious to his wife's infidelity,
he is fixated on and sexually attracted to Private Williams (Robert Forster).

We first observe Penderton exercising furiously with weights as Leonora, on
her way to a liaison with Langdon, bids him good-bye. Then he preens before the
mirror, admiring his biceps and tough physique. Given the revelation that he is a
homosexual, here his hypermasculinity serves as his way for him to deny his
homosexuality to himself. This scene sets the pattern for his behavior for the rest
of the film as he acts in ways that serve to prove how masculine he is: by his manner of teaching cadets in the classroom, by riding horses and attending boxing
matches, and by showing contempt for unmanly personnel. But the point is that
his masculine behavior is in fact false and a masquerade.

This becomes clear in a number of ways. First, in a later scene that echoes the
early one in which he admires himself in the mirror, Penderton stands in the
bathroom before the mirror and slathers on cold cream. Second, his ongoing
criticism of Captain Waincheck (Irvin Dugan) becomes a way for Penderton to
use his masculinity as a cover for his sexuality. Waincheck appears only once in
the film but is mentioned several times as being dubiously unmasculine. He

Reflections in a Golden Eye. Penderton exercises. Courtesy: Photofest. © Warner Bros.
Pictures/Seven Arts, 1967.

plays the violin, likes classical music, and reads Proust; he invites people over for tea and conversation; he's upset because at one of his social functions someone has stolen a silver spoon. Penderton later refuses to promote him on the basis of his alleged lack of strength and leadership abilities.

But we quickly learn early on that Penderton himself stole the spoon. It is part of the cache of forbidden objects that he keeps in a box hidden in his room. He first opens it after a fight with Leonora. She tries to entice him into having sex, but he doesn't respond to her taunting behavior, which includes stripping before him and walking naked up the stairs, prompting him to threaten to kill her. After this he retreats to his room and opens the box, which also contains a photograph of a statue of a fig-leaved Perseus.

This photograph introduces the theme of Penderton's homosexuality and desire to look at naked men. Such opportunities are afforded by Private Williams. Introduced as someone from the base sent over to clear brush at the Penderton home, Williams clearly has evoked the attraction of the major, who recalls how two years earlier the private spilled a pot of coffee on his uniform. We next see him as Penderton, Leonora, and Langdon are riding horses. They spy Williams, who is out riding his horse naked. Penderton is clearly obsessed by the man and seeks to observe him again. This time he goes out by himself, riding Leonora's horse. Encountering the naked soldier lying on a rock, he is so agitated that he whips the horse violently to the point of bloodying it before he falls off. When Leonora discovers what has happened to her horse, she publicly lashes Penderton with a whip at a party in their home.

The heterosexual counterpart of Penderton, Williams is obsessed with Leonora and hides outside the Penderton home to catch a glimpse of her. After observing her striptease and taunting of Penderton, he steals into their home and into her bedroom, where he spends the first of several nights watching her sleep.

His ongoing fascination with voyeuristically seeing her is echoed by Penderton's stalking of him. The major follows him from a boxing match and picks up a candy wrapper that Williams dropped, almost as if the private is purposely leaving it because he knows he's being followed. Penderton hangs around outside Williams's barracks, hoping to get a chance to see him.

The climax of the film occurs after an evening in which Penderton, Leonora, and the recently widowed Langdon are together. Langdon says he'd like to have gotten the gay servant Anacleto into the service, reflecting the he "might've made a man out of him." Penderton clumsily knocks a figurine off the fireplace, breaking it. When Leonora criticizes him, he blames it on the clutter in their home, contrasting it with the spareness of army life. Leonora dismisses this and asks, "Why don't you start all over again as an enlisted man?" His response is illuminating:

Of course you're laughing, but there's much to be said about the life of men among men, with no luxuries, no ornamentation, utter simplicity. It's rough and it's coarse perhaps, but it's also clean as a rifle. There's no speck of dust inside or out, and it's immaculate in its hard young fitness. It's chivalry. Men are seldom out of one another's sight. They train and they drink and they shower, play jokes on one another, go to brothels together, sleep side by side. They guard their privacy. And the friendships, the friendships my lord! Friendships are formed that are stronger than the fear of death and they're never lonely, they're never lonely. And sometimes I envy them.[9]

After this, the two retire to their separate bedrooms, but Penderton spies Williams entering the home. For a moment, it appears as if he thinks Williams may in fact be sneaking in to see him, and he uses his hands to smooth down his hair, but he is quickly disabused of this fantasy. He realizes Williams is here for his wife and confronts him in the bedroom of Leonora, who is asleep. He kills him, producing shrieks from her and his own agonized moans.

Montgomery Clift was originally scheduled to star as Penderton.[10] Given his previous work with Elizabeth Taylor in *A Place in the Sun* (George Stevens, 1951), *Raintree County* (Edward Dymtryk, 1957), and *Suddenly, Last Summer*, it would have been interesting to see the effects of intertextuality on their relationship in film. As it is, Brando's performance works quite effectively to convey the repression of a closeted gay man, including his rage. From the standpoint of Taylor as a sexual icon, for contemporary viewers, a man who isn't at all interested in her must have been perceived as already having serious problems. The speech in which he valorizes the military life exposes how a gay man could welcome the intimacy of army life as a way of permitting him the displaced enjoyment of other men at a safe sexual distance.

But as the first commercial war film about a gay soldier, *Reflections in a Golden Eye* sets a tone: gay men are devious, dangerous, and killers. And ridiculous. Pauline Kael's review at the time noted that "the fat, ugly Major putting cold cream on his face, or preening himself at the mirror, or patting his hair nervously when he thinks he has a gentleman caller, is so ghastly that some members of the audience invariably cut themselves off from him by laughter."[11] As such, his performance initiates what will become the main (although not completely dominant) mode of representing gays in the military.[12]

STREAMERS

Streamers, whose cast won the collective acting award at the Venice Film Festival, depicts life in an American barracks during the Vietnam War, particularly the racial and the sexual tensions generated by the gay Richie (Mitchell Lichtenstein) and the African American Carlisle (Michael Wright). These lead to the death of Billy (Matthew Modine), who is presented as the object of Richie's desire and as possibly conflicted about his own sexuality.[13] Perhaps because the film is not set within an actual theater of war, the sexual and racial tensions are not specifically contextualized in relation to Vietnam.

Streamers. Richie and Carlisle. Courtesy: Photofest. © Streamers International, 1983.

Richie, who is clearly attracted to Billy, is played as a not-very-closeted gay male. Roger (David Alan Grier), another African American, tells his barracks mates that Richie is not gay, basing his evidence on the fact that Richie has a pin-up on his locker door. But it appears to be a photograph of the transvestite Hollie Woodlawn, hence in strong contrast to the Playboy bunny on Billy's door.[14] Billy also doesn't think Richie is gay. Carlisle functions rather obviously as the disruptive force whose presence will unsettle the hitherto unexamined sexual economy within the barracks and cause tension. The issue of Richie's sexuality prompts various speculations and, in Billy's case, his recounting of an anecdote about a supposedly straight friend of his who was in the habit of baiting gay men. Eventually, this friend came to terms with and accepted his own homosexuality. Richie speculates that Billy is actually describing himself.

Carlisle, Billy, and Roger leave to go into town and, evidently, a whorehouse. As tensions mount after their return, Richie flirts with Carlisle, who is on the bunk above him, by using his foot to play with Carlisle's dog tags. Carlisle becomes increasingly agitated and, ultimately, violent, and stabs Billy as a way of venting his rage and frustration about his status. At the end, after the bloodbath that also results in the killing of Sergeant Rooney (Guy Boyd), Richie lies in his bunk crying. When Sergeant Cokes (George Dzundza) asks why Richie is crying, Roger, who now recognizes Richie's sexuality, says: "He's crying because he's queer." Sergeant Cokes, who is drunk, asks if this is true, and when told that it is, accepts it, saying that it is not as bad as having leukemia.

In some ways the film's setting in a barracks is not so much disingenuous as irrelevant. The talky presentation of tensions could just as well have been played out in a college dormitory. Nonetheless, the issue at the center of the film is of interest: What happens when there is someone gay in the barracks? The narrative seems to suggest that Roger, who is convinced at the beginning that Richie is straight and dismayed and disillusioned to find that he isn't, is probably the only straight man in the barracks.

The film's revelation that there are gay and bisexual soldiers whose sexual and racial tensions can lead to murder remains enclosed by the narratively claustrophobic setting. Moreover, its implications for a contemporary audience are unclear since in 1983 acknowledgment of the presence of gay soldiers was still muted and limited.[15] The legal aspects of the Leonard Matlovich affair, in which a gay member of the air force sued the government for dismissing him and won a settlement, first surfaced in 1975. It probably would have been more on the minds of the audience for the play when it appeared in 1976 than in 1983 when the movie opened. Matlovich's revelation that he had AIDS did not occur until 1987. Agitation for acceptance would build in the next ten years, leading to the "Don't ask, don't tell" directive.

COMEDIES

Use of the plot device of pretending to be a homosexual to avoid getting drafted had appeared as an element in *Alice's Restaurant* (Arthur Penn, 1969), a film from the Vietnam era, and constituted the entire plot of *The Gay Deceivers* (Bruce Kessler, 1969). The narrative situation was still being used as a plot device in *The Boys in Company C* (Sidney J. Furie, 1978) and *Hair* (Milos Forman, 1979).

The comedy *Biloxi Blues* is an adaptation of the second play in Neil Simon's autobiographical trilogy that also includes *Brighton Beach Memoirs* and *Broadway Bound*. Its main focus is on the developing heterosexual love life of its narrator-hero, Eugene Jerome (Matthew Broderick, re-creating his role on the stage); his experiences in training camp with buddies and with Sergeant Toomey (Christopher Walken); and his assimilation into the army during World War II. In an incidental and minor subplot, two soldiers who are seen kissing in the bathroom are exposed and ignominiously removed from the service. There is simply not enough narrative information provided to let us determine the exact relationship of the two soldiers. In addition, they are narratively irrelevant in terms of the main focus on Jerome's development. Their only function seems to be to foreground the heterosexuality of the other characters.

A quite different treatment of the exposure of gay soldiers occurs in *To Serve and Protect*, a "film" that is watched by the characters of *In & Out*. This 1997 work appeared three years after the formal institutionalization of the "Don't ask, don't tell" policy announced by President Bill Clinton on 19 July 1993 and approved by the Department of Defense on 28 February 1994.[16] *In & Out*, written by Paul Rudnick, is the first work of any sort of which I'm aware that acknowledges, however indirectly, the implications of the policy.

The film concerns Howard Brackett (Kevin Kline), an English teacher about to be married to his longtime fiancée, Emily Montgomery (Joan Cusack). Cameron Drake, a graduate from the high school in Indiana where both Howard and Emily teach, is a nominee for a Best Actor award for his performance in the war film *To Serve and Protect*.

On the night of the Oscar ceremonies, we see various audiences in Howard's town watching clips of Cameron's film. The film within a film depicts three scenes. First, we see Billy Stevens (Drake) carrying Danny (Gus Rogerson) in what is obviously supposed to be a Vietnamese jungle as they are under attack. Danny says: "I love you, Billy." He responds: "Do you mean you love me as a friend?" to which Danny says, "No, another way." Then Billy asks, "Do you mean as a brother?" Same answer. Then, "As a cousin?" and finally, "As a pen pal?" At this point Danny screams in pain, and the film cuts to Billy's court-martial. Even though he has been awarded two Purple Hearts and the Congressional Medal of Honor, he is being tried because the following have been discovered in his locker: "a personal letter to a soldier," "a photograph of a soldier sent from San Francisco," and "a tape of *Beaches* with Bette Midler." Billy shouts, "Give that back!" and he is declared guilty. The interior film ends with Billy and Danny on the courthouse steps, now out of uniform, having been drummed out of the army for being gay. Billy asks whether it was worth it, talks to the statue of George Washington (Danny points out it's a statue and can't respond), and then declares: "Danny, I love you. Come on, let's go home." Then Billy walks away triumphantly as Danny, who is legless in a wheelchair at the top of the steps, can't accompany him and desperately calls his name.

As Cameron accepts his award, he thanks his agents and pays tribute "to all the gay soldiers, sailors, and women who do so much for this country but can't date." Then he thanks Howard for his inspiration. Much to the surprise of everyone, especially Howard and Emily, Cameron says Howard is gay. The rest of the film deals amusingly with Howard's denial and ultimate acceptance of his sexuality.

James Keller and William Glass explain how the interior film's allusions to *Forrest Gump* (Robert Zemeckis, 1994) relate the narrative situation of *In & Out* to the revelation during the 1994 Oscar ceremony by Tom Hanks that his inspiring high school teacher was gay. They also connect specific scenes in the interior film to the war sequence of *Forrest Gump*: "*In & Out* satirizes the scene in which Gump carries his platoon to safety after they are overwhelmed by Vietnamese soldiers. The conversation that Cameron Drake's character and his buddy share in *In & Out*'s interior film is reminiscent of Gump and his buddy Bubba's efforts to communicate and their subsequent incomprehension. . . . *To Serve and Protect* is a satire of Hollywood politics and efforts to intercede in national, social, and ethical debates."[17]

More can be said about the interior film. First, unlike the moments of homo-sexual buffoonery mentioned in earlier films such as *Objective, Burma!* (Raoul Walsh, 1945), in which a straight man can joke about washing out his nylons, playing for laughs from his comrades, here a supposedly serious film about out-ing a couple of gay soldiers is played entirely for laughs, but only for us, the view-ers of *In & Out*, and not the interior viewers of the film. Everyone within that film takes the interior film and its message absolutely seriously. Responding to the court-martial, Howard's brother, Walter (Gregory Jbara), remarks on the unfairness of what's happening to Billy since, after all, "he killed people." This response foreshadows the ultimate acceptance the outed Howard will receive at the film's climax, which takes place in the high school auditorium.

This disparity between the appreciation of the interior film by its immediate viewers who take it seriously in Hollywood and Indiana and the amusement it generates for the "real" audiences who take it comically underscores the incon-gruity that the first post-1994 film about being outed in the military is a comedy. Granted, the interior film takes place during the Vietnam era, where exposure of homosexuality would undoubtedly have resulted in dismissal according to the Code of Military Justice. Thus *To Protect and Serve* finesses the issue of "Don't ask, don't tell" by setting the action at a time before the policy was authorized. Nonetheless, it is notable that evidence of Billy's homosexuality was discovered in his locker, and not as the result of anyone "asking" or "telling." In 1997, sup-posedly, snooping in lockers wouldn't be authorized, but it could be during the Vietnam War.

Moreover, Cameron Drake's own persona is unambiguously heterosexual (as is Matt Dillon's, who plays him). Thus there's a kind of double layering of safety in terms of representing gays in the military that exceeds what Tom Hanks did in *Philadelphia* (Jonathan Demme, 1993). There a straight actor plays Andrew Beckett, a gay man with AIDS. Here a straight actor (Dillon) plays a straight actor (Drake) playing a gay soldier.

The point is that the only audience that can take seriously a film about gays in the military is the one in the film. I haven't read anything that suggests Rudnick, who is gay, was trying to make a statement about this incongruity. But given my interest in the ways Hollywood had dealt with homosexuality in the military up to that point, *To Serve and Protect* is particularly significant since it becomes an extended gag on the issue.

Serious Treatment of the Issue

Although it is not a war film, *American Beauty* needs consideration in relation to the concerns of this chapter. The film's perspective on contemporary sexual activi-ties is extremely broad, ranging from the sexual obsession of Lester Burnham (Kevin Spacey) for Angela Hayes (Mena Survari), to the adulterous relationship of Carolyn Burnham (Annette Bening) and Buddy Kane (Peter Gallagher), to the youthful sexual involvement of Jane Burnham (Thora Birch) with Ricky Fitts (Wes Bentley). As has been observed, the only truly happy people in the film appear to be the gay couple Jim Olmeyer (Scott Bakula) and Jim Berkely (Sam Robards), who are seen jogging or welcoming retired marine Colonel Fitts (Chris Cooper) to the neighborhood.

Fitts is a tyrant at home, treasuring his Nazi memorabilia, bullying his son, Ricky, and subjugating his wife, Barbara (Allison Janney), into a semicomatose state. He is also a closeted gay man. Colonel Fitts has more than a passing resemblance to Major Penderton. Both are uncompromising in their hyperassertions of masculinity, Fitts to the point of caricature. Similar to Penderton's spying on the naked Private Williams, Fitts, too, is a voyeur, looking down from his window at Lester exercising. Because of his spying, he mistakenly thinks Lester and Ricky are engaged in fellatio, a scene that provokes him to make a direct overture to Lester. But the suggestion of lipstick on Fitts's lips when he goes to the Burnham house is more grotesque than Penderton's simply smoothing his hair when he thinks Williams has come to see him.[18] Both men are disappointed: Williams is here to see Leonora, not Penderton; Lester is not gay and gently rebuffs Fitts's advances. Both Penderton and Fitts kill the men to whom they are attracted.

But *American Beauty*'s treatment of the closeted gay character admits of another kind of homosexual life in the neighbors. In *Reflections in a Golden Eye*, Anacleto, the openly gay character, is, for all his kindness to Alison, still rendered as stereotypically flamboyant, hence more a reinforcement of than a contrast to Penderton's sexuality. He is completely unmasculine, with no suggestion of healthy manly exercise, like that shown in the jogging gay couple that suggests an alternative to Fitts's repressed homosexuality, which finally erupts in violence. Even if audiences respond to the gay couple more as a gag element than as a genuine and positive alternative to Fitts, the men are nonetheless there as genuine alternatives to him.

The first serious treatment of gays in the military in a film about soldiers after the "Don't ask, don't tell" policy went into effect was in *Soldier's Girl* (Frank Pierson, 2003), a Showtime-produced made-for-cable dramatization written by Ron Nyswaner (who wrote *Philadelphia*).[19] The film presents the true and horrible events that occurred at Fort Campbell, Kentucky, in 1999 when Barry Winchell (Troy Garity), a soldier, fell in love with Calpurnia Addams (Lee Pace), a singer whom he met in a gay club featuring transvestites. Winchell was brutally murdered by Private Calvin Glover (Philip Eddols), who had been goaded into killing him by Winchell's homophobic roommate, Private Justin Fischer (Shawn Hatosy). This murder resulted in the addition of "Don't pursue, don't harass" in 2000 to the original policy statement approved in 1994.

Unlike the works about gays in the military made for commercial television, the freedom from censorship accorded the Showtime film allows for much more intense and graphic treatment of the story, especially of the love that develops between Winchell and Addams and, shockingly, the violence of his murder. There's the definite suggestion that the homophobic Fischer is possibly a closeted gay, but this suggestion of his homosexuality is made in a way that doesn't make that the basis of his criminality, as is clearly the intent in *Reflections in a Golden Eye*. Rather, he's a monster because of his surreptitious homophobic goading of the truly homophobic Glover to murder Winchell.

The issue of "Don't ask, don't tell" surfaces directly in the plot as Winchell's superiors, alerted to the possibility that he may be gay, acknowledge the policy. Sergeant Diaz (Andre Braugher) scrupulously observes it; but Sergeant Paxton (Barclay Hope) purposely violates it as he tries to determine if the rumors about Winchell are true.

BASIC

Basic is the first American war film both to address the policy of "Don't ask, don't tell" and to include the actual words in dialogue. They occur in a speech delivered by Tom Hardy (John Travolta) to Levi Kendall (Giovanni Ribisi), as far as I know the first soldier in an American war film to say "I am a homosexual." The scene takes place in a hospital room where Hardy and Julia Osborne (Connie Nielsen) are interrogating Kendall as to what has happened on a training exercise in the Panamanian jungle in which, apparently, a number of soldiers died or were murdered.

The film has been widely criticized for its incoherent plot, which seems to be cobbled together as the work proceeds.[20] The inciting event, the apparent murder of Sergeant Nathan West (Samuel L. Jackson), prompts an investigation by Colonel Bill Styles (Tim Daly). The film consists of increasingly unreliable interviews with the characters, whose contradictory stories evoke *Rashomon* (Akira Kurosawa, 1950), to the decided disadvantage of this film. The film's revelation is that military personnel in Panama have been heavily involved in conveying drugs from Colombia to the mainland of the United States. A secret unit to which Hardy and West belong finally exposes the complex scheme.

Kendall's first response to his interrogators turns out to be false, like those of others, but his is unique in that he adds (quite gratuitously) the information, "I am a homosexual." Because his father has a high rank in the army, he is safe from being dismissed. Upon hearing this revelation, Hardy says: "Well that certainly blows 'Don't ask, don't tell' out of the water." Kendall, as played by Ribisi, is consistently obnoxious: whiney, evasive, and infantile. During their final interrogation of him, though, he starts vomiting blood, as a result of having been poisoned by Colonel Styles, the mastermind behind the drug scheme. In contrast to most of the other deaths seen thus far in the film, which turn out to be fabrications in false flashbacks, his is decidedly real and occurs graphically.

There's a troubling dimension to the film's presentation and treatment of the gay soldier. Not only is Kendall totally unsympathetic, his character and death are rendered in a way that actually feeds into and supports the arguments against "Don't ask, don't tell" and allowing gays in the military. First, although like several straight characters he can't be trusted, his duplicity comes on top of his already compromised status. He is openly gay and still present in the force because of his connections. Technically, following the directive, he should not, in fact, be there in the first place. Now that he is, since the legally correct process is being ignored, he's protected. But this intruder has abused his safety and engaged in criminal activity. His criminality is overdetermined: he's someone in the drug trade and also a gay man who can't be booted out because of his father. Unlike the crimes of the straight characters, his are inflected additionally by his sexuality. That is, given the ideology of the film, his homosexuality is also implicitly criminal.

Second, the blood that spurts from him mouth and sprays over the bed and floor evokes the worst nightmare scenario about hospital workers exposed to blood from people with AIDS. There's no suggestion whatsoever that the character has this, but the image of a gay soldier coughing up blood suggests how potentially dangerous a gay soldier could be—as a source of disease through unwanted sexual contact, the ultimate homophobic nightmare that drives the fear of having gays in the military at all, in shower stalls, in barracks.

Thus the film's ideological content is especially pernicious. The gay character is a villain because he's a drug dealer. Worse, he shouldn't be in the army in the first place—because he's a gay man who has been sufficiently empowered by connections to be able to *say* what he is, which is itself an infraction of the rules.[21]

CHAPTER SEVEN

BODIES, WEAPONS

Before "Don't ask, don't tell" became a widely known statement in the 1990s, another expression related to the military had already attained recognition, in part because of its use in films and in fiction. This one, in the form of a chant, pertains to the obvious connections between weapons and conceptions about masculinity and male sexuality: "This is my rifle, this is my gun; this is for fighting, this is for fun." Since referring to the chant has become a critical commonplace in discussions of the war film, I hope the following commentary will lead to some new insights about the relationship. Five of the works examined here deal with the Vietnam War: *The Boys in Company C* (Sidney J. Furie, 1978), *Apocalypse Now* (Francis Ford Coppola, 1979), *Platoon* (Oliver Stone, 1986), *Full Metal Jacket* (Stanley Kubrick, 1987), and *Casualties of War* (Brian De Palma, 1989). *Saving Private Ryan* (Steven Spielberg, 1998) is about World War II, and *Jarhead* (Sam Mendes, 2005) concerns the Gulf War. The major link connecting all of these is how at certain key moments weapons are consciously foregrounded as objects of narrative attention specifically connected to the male body and sexuality. In fact, all these films revisit the clichéd connection of weapons and genitals in most striking ways.

THE BOYS IN COMPANY C

The Boys in Company C follows a group of young recruits from their induction, training, and immersion in war. R. Lee Ermey makes his first appearance in a film as Staff Sergeant Loyce. The moral focus of the film is on the incompetence of the military leadership, with the exception of Lieutenant Archer (James Whitmore Jr.), and the insanity of the Vietnam War. Not much in the film centers directly on sexual issues. Early in the film, a recruit pretends to be gay to avoid being inducted, a comic scene played for laughs in a way that had been presented earlier in *Alice's Restaurant* (Arthur Penn, 1969) and would be repeated a year later in *Hair*

(Milos Forman, 1979). Once they arrive in Vietnam, all the recruits have to undergo a test for venereal diseases. One recruit, Billy Ray Pike (Andrew Stevens), finds out his girlfriend is pregnant. Some recruits hang out in a club looking for women to pick up.

The most sexualized moment in the film comes as Tyrone Washington (Stan Shaw) and the other soldiers are bathing at a pond on a sunny hillside. The scene begins with shots of large artillery howitzers firing shells from on top of a hill, then opens up to show a number of naked men sitting around the water, celebrating the shelling from behind them and commenting on the relative success of shells as they land and burst on the hills in front of them. They also cheer on the U.S. planes overhead dropping bombs and strafing. The scene both compresses and expands the logic of the rifle/gun chant. On the one hand, the men are naked, without any weapons in their own hands. On the other, they are metonymically linked to the large howitzers. And they are, in fact, having fun as, naked, they watch the destruction. In a curious way, Furie has established the mise-en-scène like the interior of a movie theater: the action (the firing of the guns) proceeds from behind the men, who can watch the effects of the firing in front of them. They are physically between the source of death and its effects, exulting.

What binds the men at this point in the narrative is a temporary escape from direct interaction with their hopelessly incompetent commander and a chance to

The Boys in Company C. Exulting in the destruction. © Golden Harvest Company Ltd./ Good Times Films S.A., 1978.

watch destruction as pure spectacle. It's simultaneously sexual (the naked male bodies linked to large guns spewing forth destruction) and nonsexual (cheering from men whose attention is on the effects of the weapons and not on their own bodies). The men in this scene are very different from those naked soldiers pictured at play in the "true towel" advertisements discussed in chapter 3. Those men were momentarily free of the weapons of war. Here, though, the men's nakedness in the presence of the booming guns and airplanes spewing fire underscores their vulnerability.

APOCALYPSE NOW

In contrast to Furie's depiction of weapons and bodies, in *Apocalypse Now* Coppola constructs a dark world in which Colonel Kurtz (Marlon Brando) and his death squad operate in what seems like perpetual half-light or darkness. But what this film shares with Furie's work is an interest in bodies and weapons. The arrival of Captain Willard (Martin Sheen), Lance (Sam Bottoms), and Chef (Frederic Forrest) into Kurtz's compound occurs at night. The assassination team enters the dense jungle populated by hundreds of men in loincloths. As Willard talks to the spaced-out unnamed journalist (Dennis Hopper), Coppola frames the conversation so that we see a naked dead man dangling from a wire in the background; his body turns randomly as Hopper expounds on Kurtz's uniqueness.

When Willard meets Kurtz for the first time, it is as if he's encountering a human penis. Kurtz himself is the ultimate weapon in this disturbed world and functions as the phallus in terms of the sexual economy of power. Coppola frames the first sight of him in an erotic manner, letting us see Kurtz's bald head bathed eerily in yellow light in a manner that literally suggests the head of a penis. To show who, in fact, controls the phallus, Kurtz brings Chef's head to Willard, who is now a captive with his hands bound. Kurtz throws Chef's head onto Willard's lap in a way that suggests an indirect sexual violation of him—an incomplete, displaced, and grotesque form of fellatio imposed on a helpless victim. The film actually evokes aspects of science fiction and horror films in terms of the difficulties of dispatching this "monster" who has a different (nonhuman) set of attributes. That Kurtz is the inevitable and symbolic outcome of U.S. policy in Vietnam only makes him more horrible and frightening. His ultimate display of evil is as the tyrannical killer who demonstrates his superiority with the head that is both a sign of his castrating power and his pan-sexual rule.

It is hard to know how to describe accurately the sexualized world of *Apocalypse Now*. Although a few women and young girls are visible in two scenes, the majority of figures are all male (both living and dead). It seems a world in which sex and sensuousness are themselves a function of the collapse of reason associated with the mad Kurtz. It's a world of indiscriminately arrayed pieces of flesh, both dead and alive.

Apocalypse Now. The arrival. Courtesy: Photofest. © Zoetrope Studios, 1979.

Lance, whose prowess as a surfer so interested Colonel Kilgore (Robert Duvall), quickly succumbs to the sexual abandon of his empire, dons a loincloth, and paints his face and body with the same kinds of markings seen on Kurtz's men. His immediate acceptance of this world suggests how quickly sanity and male sexuality can be deranged and subverted by Kurtz. It's not that we are to take Kurtz or his acolytes as homosexuals, or that Lance is succumbing to homosexual longings. Rather, it's that as we see him, literally entranced, in his loincloth moving sensuously in tai-chi-like motions, he has abandoned normative male sexuality having heterosexual union as its goal. This turning away from women has already occurred in the behavior of both Kurtz and one of his American supporters, Lieutenant Colby (Scott Glenn). Lance looks like someone who is not interested in ever leaving such a world. Willard not only destroys the phallic rule of Kurtz; he also restores the normal parameters of male sexuality, signaled by Lance's behavior once they return to the boat. He lets the rain wash off his painting.

PLATOON

Oliver Stone draws narrative attention to male sexuality in two parts of *Platoon*. The first of these significant moments comes in a remarkable sequence that crosscuts between two areas of Charlie Company's headquarters showing how each of the two opposing factions relaxes when off duty. The men linked to Elias (Willem Dafoe) are high on pot and dancing uninhibitedly in Elias's "Underground," a grotto lit in warm (and lurid) tones of red and orange. Barnes (Tom Berenger) and his supporters like Bunny (Kevin Dillon) are drinking and playing cards in naturally lit quarters. The men in the Underground listen to Jefferson Airplane and Smokey Robinson, those in Barnes's area to country music. The sequence begins as Chris Taylor (Charlie Sheen), recently returned from the hospital after being wounded, is led by King (Keith David) into Elias's grotto.[1] Once he enters, he's given a marijuana cigarette. Unused to smoking it, he chokes. Then Elias approaches, asks if this is his "first time," and lifts a large Remington shotgun to his lips and blows smoke into the barrel after telling Chris to "put your mouth around this." John Newsinger and Margaret O'Brien, among others, have remarked on the sexual nature of the action that obviously simulates fellatio. The query about "first time" suggests not only an initiation to dope but to sex as well.[2]

Stone cuts on motion from King lighting a joint to Bunny lighting a cigarette. Bunny is ranting on to Junior (Reggie Johnson) about the potheads and talking about how much he likes pussy. This comment foregrounds his heterosexuality against the apparently homoerotic encounter we have just seen. When Stone cuts back to the Underground, the men are dancing to Smokey Robinson's "Tracks of My Tears." Elias is holding a soldier in a traditional dance position as if he were a woman.

This scene introduces Chris not only to marijuana but also to a world in which weapons are a source of pleasure as well as pain and death. It's not just that Elias appears to be engaging in a symbolic homosexual act with Chris. Rather, Stone uses this scene to suggest something about the complex aspects of sexuality associated with the weapon itself and how using the gun is, in fact, like engaging in a sexual act. Rather than a symbolic blowjob, it's an attempt to suggest something about the eroticism involved in the use of weapons.

In addition, the scene offers a complex statement about male sexuality. First, while Chris and Elias are linked in a sexual manner, they do not engage in any

Platoon. "First Time?" © Cinema 86/Hemdale Film Corporation, 1986.

sex act. This is not fellatio. Both are unambiguously heterosexual.[3] As to why the film should present a scene that depicts male intimacy in a way that suggests homosexuality, I think Stone is using the rifle (and dope) to signal what the relationship is *not* (in a way such as Richard Dyer explained the strategic use of the homosexual in *Papillon* [Franklin J. Schaffner, 1973], discussed earlier).

The very outrageousness of linking them in this way suggests an appropriation of a gesture that denies its own implications.

On the one hand, Stone provides an elaborately conceived mise-en-scène and sexual gesture as a way to show in a displaced manner the bond being established between Chris and Elias. To suggest the depth of the intimacy that is forming between them, Stone uses a sexually suggestive action as a vehicle. On the other hand, the contrast between the homosexual implication of the action and the heterosexuality of the participants suggests the practice described by Mikhail Bakhtin in his commentary on the "carnivalesque": "carnival celebrated temporary liberation from the prevailing truth and from the established order; it marked the suspension of all hierarchical rank, privileges, norms, and prohibitions."[4] In the rituals of the "Feasts of Fools," traditional decorum, status, and behaviors are abandoned, as the participants engage in a "grotesque degradation of various church rituals and symbols and their transfer to the material bodily level: gluttony and drunken orgies on the altar table, indecent gestures, disrobing."[5] Here, though, instead of jesters acting like kings, the soldiers playfully abandon their ordinary heterosexual roles and symbolically appropriate the gestures of gay men. As Gilbert Adair has noted, "In a scene of soldiers dancing together one catches a potent whiff of the louche homosexual bar which takes us way beyond the customary depiction of buddy-buddy affectivity peculiar to every all-male society. And when, with a maliciously enigmatic smile on his face, Elias persuades Chris to insert the end of his (Elias's) rifle in his mouth and then coquettishly blows marijuana smoke along its barrel, the phallic analogy could hardly be rendered more explicit."[6] The war unsettles traditional gendered expectations about sexuality. While Stone presents a temporary reversal of sexual roles, he is nonetheless careful to keep clear reminders of the heterosexual world that has been temporally displaced. He does this by showing Rhah (Francesco Quinn) cradling a naked female doll in a shot that recalls John Garfield's Wolf in *Destination Tokyo* (Delmer Daves, 1943).

The second scene in which male sexuality is displayed occurs after the My-Lai-like massacre in the village. As Chris moves out, he sees Bunny, Junior, and other soldiers engaged in raping two young Vietnamese girls. He forces them to stop. Bunny asks him contemptuously if he is a homosexual, to which Taylor responds, "You just don't get it." As the men disperse, Stone cuts to Elias, who has obviously seen the interchange between Chris and the rapists. He shouts to the men to get out.

It's interesting that Stone chooses to link Chris, Elias, and Bunny again in a way that contrasts aspects of male sexuality. The responses of Chris and Elias to the attempted rapes not only display their decency and values, but also replay the contrast Stone set up by cutting from Elias, Chris, the shotgun, and the symbolic suggestion of homosexual intimacy to Bunny's talk about getting pussy. It is Bunny who has taken perverse pleasure in using his rifle to stomp out the brains of the retarded boy during the massacre in the village. His use of the rifle as an instrument to kill with pleasure thus underscores the connection of the sex and violence in the earlier scene.

FULL METAL JACKET

Platoon premiered 19 December 1986, preempting by six months the next major Vietnam War film, *Full Metal Jacket*, which opened 17 June 1987. While the capability of a weapon to serve as a source of pleasure and pain is worked out implicitly in *Platoon*, Kubrick's film presents the issue explicitly in two well-known scenes in which Sergeant Hartman (R. Lee Ermey) gives his recruits directives about the relationship between weapons and the body. Looking at what appear to be the origins of these linkages in reports about English and American soldiers at war can help one understand how the complex and contradictory relationships posited in these equations underscore the tenuous gendering of the armed male body and its connection to sexuality. In the first important scene, Sergeant Hartman orders his recruits to treat their rifles as women; in the second, the sergeant leads the men through the famous chant, "This is my rifle, this is my gun; this is for fighting, this is for fun."

Full Metal Jacket. The chant. © Natant/Warner Bros. Pictures, 1987.

Early in the basic training process, the tyrannical Sergeant Hartman instructs his men about their weapons before they go to bed. All the new recruits hold rifles and stand at attention in their underwear next to their cots. Sergeant Hartman tells them: "Tonight you pukes will sleep with your rifle. You will give your rifle a girl's name because it is the only pussy you people are going to get. Your days of finger-banging old Mary Jane Rottencrotch through her pretty pink panties are over! You're married to this piece, this weapon of iron and wood, and you will be faithful." He orders the recruits to mount their cots. They do and hold their rifles lengthwise on top of their bodies, with the barrels close to their mouths. Hartman orders them to "Pray!" Their response is: "This is my rifle. There are many like it, but this one is mine. I must master it as I must master my life. Without me it is useless. Without it I am useless. I must fire my rifle true. I must shoot my enemy who is trying to kill me. I must shoot him before he shoots me. I will. Before God I swear this creed: my rifle and I are defenders of my country; we are the masters of our enemy; we are the saviors of our life. So be it, until there is no enemy, but peace. Amen."

This "prayer" closely follows "The Infantryman's Creed, My Rifle" by Major General William H. Rupertus, who is said to have written it after Pearl Harbor. The original "Creed" does not contain any lines suggesting that the soldier is married to the rifle or that it is in any way a substitute for a woman. Rather, it conceives of the rifle as a brother. The fourth section of the poem reads:

> My rifle is human, even as I, because it is my life.
>   Thus, I will learn it as a brother.
> I will learn its weakness, its strength, its parts, its accessories,
>   Its sights and its barrel.
> I will keep my rifle clean and ready,
>   Even as I am clean and ready.
> We will become part of each other.
>   We will . . .

This section in which the rifle is referred to as a brother is included in *The Short-Timers*, the novel by Gustav Hasford on which *Full Metal Jacket* is based.[7]

The second scene occurs shortly afterward, as Sergeant Hartman leads his men around the barracks. Again, Hartman is in uniform, the men in their underwear. All, including Hartman, carry rifles and chant: "This is my rifle, this is my gun; this is for fighting, this is for fun." As the group speaks the words "gun" and "fun," each man grabs his genitals and then shakes them.

As far as I know, the first reference to the rifle/gun relationship in any film (war or otherwise) occurs in *Take the High Ground* (Richard Brooks, 1953). Not surprisingly, given the restrictions of the Production Code Administration at that time, the version there is considerably sanitized. The scene begins as Sergeant Thorne Ryan (Richard Widmark) introduces recruits to the rifle: "This is your best friend." After Private William Hazard (William Hairston) is issued his rifle by Ryan, Hazard, who is African American, refers to the rifle as his gun, and prompts Ryan's ire. Oddly, Ryan accuses Hazard of probably liking the poetry of Elizabeth Barrett Browning. Although Ryan says he does not read her ("Never touch the stuff"), he lists a number of her poems. He then recites another kind of poem for Hazard: "This is your rifle; it's not your gun; it's made for shooting and not for fun."[8]

The concept of being married to a rifle makes its first filmic appearance here in *Full Metal Jacket*. Joanna Bourke has found examples of linkages between rifles and women as early as World War I and cites examples demonstrating that soldiers could think "that guns were like women and to be treated as such."[9] In *Band of Brothers* (1992), Stephen Ambrose describes how the members of the airborne division that would become Easy Company, a unit that participated in D-Day, received instructions that are similar to Hartman's comment about being married to the rifle: "When they were issued rifles, they were told to treat the weapon as they would a wife, gently. It was theirs to have and to hold, to sleep with in the field, to know intimately."[10]

The earliest instance of the rifle/gun chant and practice I have been able to find documented in records from the U.S. military appears in personal histories of wartime experiences by William T. Paull and Leonard E. Skinner, who were in marine boot camp in San Diego in 1942. Both offer versions of what happened to anyone who mistakenly called his rifle a gun. According to Paull,

> There were two standard punishments for this sacrilege. The first time the DI heard a recruit say the forbidden word, "gun," the hapless offender would be required to sleep with his rifle beside him in the narrow cot. If he slipped up again, he would be stationed in front of the company headquarters with rifle on shoulder, fly open, and pecker hanging out. He'd recite to all who passed by: "This is my rifle" while pointing to the rifle, and "this is my gun" while pointing to his crotch, then "this is for fighting" and "this is for fun."

Skinner discusses a similar punishment: "One evening a recruit from another platoon opened the door to our hut and stepped inside, holding his rifle in one hand and his penis in the other. First presenting one, then the other, he loudly recited the following poem: 'This is my rifle and this is my gun, This is for shooting and this is for fun.' He then went on to the next hut, as he had to repeat his performance to everyone in the entire recruit depot!"[11]

The complexity of such an identification becomes apparent in the context of a number of comments about the relation of the killing instruments (guns, bayonets) to male anatomy. Several commentators on the Vietnam War quote a passage from Mark Baker's *Nam* in which one of his sources states: "A gun is power. To some people carrying a gun constantly was like having a permanent hard on. It was a pure sexual trip every time you got to pull the trigger."[12] Both David

Grossman and Joshua Goldstein describe an inextricable connection between killing and sexual violence. Grossman observes "the phallic character of weapons has seemingly persisted as technology has evolved—from spears to guns to missiles."[13] Grossman believes that "many men who have carried and fired a gun—especially a full automatic weapon—must confess in their hearts that the power and pleasure of explosively spewing a stream of bullets is akin to the emotions felt when explosively spewing a stream of semen."[14]

Bourke sees weapons as capable of being interpreted as "both the paternal and maternal phallus."[15] Cynthia Fuchs also sees a duality. Granting that "guns and penises are old bedfellows," she comments on the implications of the rifle/gun relationship and chant in *Full Metal Jacket*.[16] She points to two kinds of anomalies. First, there is "a desperate contradiction between loyalties to self (body-gun) and other (gun-body)." The "creed … weds them heart and soul to their weapons, while denigrating the other that the rifle represents." But to the extent that the weapons are "extensions of themselves," there is "an impossible contradiction" between weapon as "girl" and weapon as "self." She explains this as a result of "the patriarchal system's dread of the woman as representative of sexuality and potential loss of (male) self/control. No more 'Mary Jane Rottencrotch' for these recruits. Their sexual energy is channeled into grossly representable military action: that is, the destruction of the other."[17]

But this "impossible contradiction" of gender in regard to the rifle itself is matched by the incongruity in seeing the gun/penis as "for fun," since it, too, is a killing machine, as much an agent for destruction and domination as the rifle. Many have pointed out the link between military and sexual aggression. Fuchs and others cite Adrienne Rich's argument that

> rape is a part of war; but it may be more accurate to say that the capacity for depersonalizing another which so corrodes male sexuality is carried over from sex to war. The chant of the basic training drill: ("This is my rifle, this is my gun [cock]; This is for killing, this is for fun") is not a piece of bizarre brainwashing invented by some infantry sergeant's fertile imagination; it is a recognition of the fact that when you strike the chord of sexuality in the patriarchal psyche, the chord of violence is likely to vibrate in response, and vice versa.[18]

In a related observation, Grossman states:

The concept of sex as a process of domination and defeat is closely related to the lust for rape and the trauma associated with the rape victim. Thrusting the sexual appendage (the penis) deep into the body of the victim can be perversely linked to thrusting the killing appendage (a bayonet or knife) deep into the body of the victim. The process can be seen in pornographic movies in which the sexual act is twisted, such that the male ejaculates—or "shoots his wad"—into a female's face. The grip of a firer on the pistol grip of his gun is much like the grip on an erect penis, and holding the penis in this fashion while ejaculating into the victim's face is at some level an act of domination and symbolic destruction.[19]

The chant thus defines two kinds of potential assertions of male power in two separate regimes: as wielder of a weapon (rifle), he can kill; he should not confuse that weapon linguistically with the other one, for the gun refers to a different exertion of his power.

Carol Burke's analysis of the chant in *Full Metal Jacket* partially addresses yet another complexity of the gun/penis connection: "In step, the barefooted, scantily clad trainees stroke their genitals in perfect beat to the command of the uniformed drill instructor, a form of collective autoeroticism."[20] More can be said. In effect, this choreographed circlejerk is yet another application of power by Hartman in which even the suggestion of sexual gratification (in this case, mutual masturbation) is under the domination of the ultimate male power in the barracks, the sergeant. Hartman's constant taunts generally about the men's sexual orientation (calling them "ladies") and his particular assault on Private Leonard Pyle (Vincent D'Onofrio) make clear his contempt for homosexuality. Yet the chanting scene, unlike those reported by individuals being punished, is a collective experience that both denies and affirms a homoerotic element: my penis is for having sex with women; I am grabbing my penis with a group of other men at the same time.

In the accounts of the punishment cited above from Paull and Skinner, the way to chastise the erring marine was to have him expose his unerect penis in the presence of other men who have not had to unbutton. Thus his ineffectiveness as a soldier (I don't know the correct language for my rifle) is centered on his (temporary) impotency as a male (a limp penis/gun held helplessly in his hand) as he is singled out for exposure and criticism, either as he stands in front of other men or moves around the barracks.

R. Wayne Eisenhart recalls in his basic training as a marine at Parris Island that "whenever I failed at task or performed poorly, I was physically assaulted. At the same time my drill instructor screamed in my face something like, 'You can't hack it, you goddamned faggot.' The means by which the military socialization process forged this link between an individual's sexuality and his military mission was proportional in intensity to the resistance encountered." He describes an event in which punishment involved forcing a man to insert his penis in the rifle: "One night three men who had been censured for ineffectiveness in their assigned tasks were called forward in front of the assembled platoon, ordered to insert their penises into the breeches of their weapons, close the bolt and run the length of the squad bay singing the Marine Corps Hymn. This violent ritual ended as the drill instructor left and the three men sank to the floor, penises still clamped to their weapons."[21]

The chant as displayed in *Full Metal Jacket* underscores the collective sexual identification of the men: all are in their underwear; all go through exactly the same aggressive and sexual motions at the same time. And given the way ineptitude is linked with sexuality in Eisenhart's anecdote, as well as the way Sergeant Hartman constantly calls the men "ladies," it is possible to see Hartman's imposing of a collective physical action as yet another way of suggesting their limitations as sexual beings. Equally relevant, James McBride's analysis of the chant leads him to argue persuasively that

> the association of the soldier's phallus with his rifle occurs in a context in which the soldier's identity as a man is stripped away. He is rhetorically castrated by the incessant badgering of drill instructors who variously call their recruits "ladies" or "girls." In this initiation into the warrior community, humiliated individuals are compelled to seek their manhood from the collective, embodied by the drill instructor. And it is he who gives the recruit back his masculinity in the form of a weapon, the infantryman's rifle.[22]

The authorization for the recruits' sexual activities, using their penises for fun, has significant implications for our consideration of manhood and sexuality in this film, *Platoon*, *Casualties of War*, and *Saving Private Ryan*. In *Full Metal Jacket*, the chanting scene should be seen as the first of three in which implied collective sexual activity occurs: the "circlejerk" is followed by a "blanket party," in which Private Pyle is assaulted; the film's climax includes the rapelike killing of the sniper.

Private Pyle immediately becomes the butt of the company. In his first interaction with Sergeant Hartman, the hapless recruit has to attempt to strangle himself to wipe the smile off his face. His constant mishaps during field exercises, physical limitations, and general ineptitude climax in the sergeant's punishment of the other men in the barracks when he discovers Pyle has secreted away a doughnut. The intensifying frustration in the company angered by having to be punished for Pyle's mistakes climaxes in the collective beating of him at night. The men, including his one ally, Joker (Matthew Modine), approach Pyle's bunk and, as he is held down and gagged to stifle his cries, beat him with their weapons—towels in which they have put bars of soap. Kubrick carefully positions his camera to catch the expressions of anguish and pain on Pyle's face during the extended beating.

On the one hand, the event is of interest as the first example I'm aware of in a film to depict what is known as a "blanket party." As far as I have been able to determine, blanket parties, "towel parties," and "soap parties" first began occurring in barracks during the Vietnam War. All were used in one way or another to punish a member of the group whose behavior was offensive to his fellow soldiers. Towel and soap parties were given as punishment to men who did not bathe and who smelled. In these parties, the offender would be dragged into the shower and forcibly cleaned by his captors. The blanket party itself seems to have

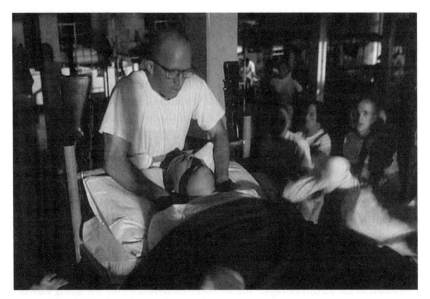

Full Metal Jacket. The attack on Pyle. © Natant/Warner Bros. Pictures, 1987.

been used for people like Private Pyle, whose behavior brings punishment on the group.[23]

On the other hand, the scene in the film merits consideration because of its potential sexual implications. I have read two reports that describe a blanket party as punishment for a man suspected to be gay by his companions.[24] Sergeant Hartman's sexually demeaning tirades notwithstanding, nothing in the film seems to suggest that Pyle isn't heterosexual. Some of his punishments infantalize him (thumb sucking, having to walk with his pants down around his ankles), but nothing said by the other men implies any anger at him for his sexuality.

What seems more viable as a line of inquiry concerns the physical appearance of Private Pyle. Unlike his companions, he is ungainly and extremely fat. D'Onofrio is reported to have gained an enormous amount of weight for the part. What is more, Pyle is the only marine ever shown without a T-shirt on in the barracks. Kubrick positions his camera almost mercilessly on the shirtless Pyle in a manner that gives embarrassing prominence to his pendulous and unmasculine breasts. He is the opposite of the hard-bodied soldier such as audiences had witnessed in the two Rambo movies with Sylvester Stallone in 1982 and 1985 or the soldiers in *Platoon*. One could argue that Kubrick here not only infantalizes him but also feminizes him, in a way reminiscent of the visual and narrative treatment of Ned Beatty in *Deliverance* (John Boorman, 1972).[25]

The attack on Pyle is connected to the killing of the female sniper at the end of the film. Susan White speaks of "the strange dialogue between the men, who stand over the woman's body as though this were a gang rape, as they had stood

Casualties of War. Meserve challenges Erikson. Courtesy: Rick's Movie Graphics. ©
Columbia Pictures Corporation, 1989.

that your problem?" Clark asks: "Are you a faggot?" When Eriksson tries to make
eye contact with Diaz, hoping the latter will not engage in the rape, Meserve and
Clark interpret his glance in a sexual manner. Asking why he looks at Diaz that
way, Meserve says: "Maybe he is a queer . . . a homosexual," and puts his own rifle
in his mouth, simulating fellatio. Eriksson adopts what Meserve calls an "attack
posture" with his rifle, infuriating him. After noting that all the men have weapons,
which is appropriate, Meserve reworks the rifle/gun chant in a significant manner. He holds his genitals in one hand, as the men had done in *Full Metal Jacket.*
But as he shakes them, he says, "*This* is a weapon," and, gesturing toward his rifle,
says, "This is a gun." Grabbing his genitals again, he says: "This is for fighting";
the rifle is "for fun." In so doing, Meserve makes explicit the kind of association
articulated by Adrienne Rich above. His penis is the organ of aggression; his rifle
provides a source of fun.

Gavin Smith connects the symbolic rape of the sniper in *Full Metal Jacket* to
Casualties of War. Referring to the latter film as "De Palma's Wargasm," he says it
is about "the indiscriminate release of sexuality and aggression engendered by
the removal of all civilized controls in war. . . . It replaces Kubrick's cinematic
rape of a girl sniper with the literal rape of a Vietnamese civilian."[31]

Ruth Seifert also explores the function of rape, citing Susan Brownmiller's
essential work on this topic. In addition to the fact that "rape is used to regulate
the power relations between the two genders," during war "the rape of women

carries a message: a man-to-man communication, as it were, telling the other side that [they] are incapable of protecting 'their' women and thus hurting their manly pride." Commenting on charges of gang rape during the Vietnamese War, she notes: "[I]nflicting additional cruelty on the victim had been seen a kind of virility contest. A few of these crimes were reported by soldiers who had been present but had not participated in the rapes or sexual tortures. Before the court martial the rapists typically questioned the masculinity of the man who had reported the incident or called him a sissy or a weakling."[32]

Of particular interest, given the way he and Clark taunt Eriksson about being homosexual since Eriksson doesn't want to rape the girl, is Meserve's threat to rape Eriksson. "After I get done humpin' her, I might come out here and hump you." He doesn't carry out his threat, but the fact he could and not be seen as gay speaks to complex aspects of male sexuality. First, Meserve has accused Eriksson not only of being a homosexual but also of being a Vietcong sympathizer and feminine: "We got two girls here." But the linguistic charge of being a woman is supplanted by the threat of homosexual rape. Joshua S. Goldstein has investigated various forms of aggression in military history. Discussing homosexual rape, he explains: "A third method of feminizing enemy soldiers in the ancient world was anal rape, with the victor in the dominant/active position and the vanquished in the subordinate/passive one." He cites historical examples of this practice, ranging from ancient Greece to the wars in Bosnia and Kosovo.[33]

Meserve's threat evokes consideration of the complex relationship between homosexual and heterosexual appearances such as we saw in *Platoon*. Jeremy M. Devine suggests that earlier in the film, "Meserve homoerotically reserves compassion solely for his troops."[34] Earl Ingersoll explores the implications of the homosexual threat by connecting it to the "very (il)logic that has allowed heterosexual males in masculinist cultures like those of the Arab Middle East to engage in same-sex encounters as long as they maintain the subject position."[35] Ingersoll discusses the homophobic and homosexual aspects of the film rewardingly, pointing in particular to the way the reluctant rapist Diaz is himself feminized by De Palma's framing. Diaz is the only nude male we see during the rape:

> Viewers—at least, male viewers—are drawn into a kind of homosexual "rape" of Eriksson through his surrogate Diaz as the object of Meserve's desiring gaze. Meserve is "too much a man" to act out his threat to "hump" Eriksson.... However, in his earlier innuendo that Eriksson desires Diaz rather than the Vietnamese woman, Meserve is demonstrating that *he*, Meserve, can "have" Diaz by forcing him into the place of heterosexual desire he has just prepared for Diaz/Eriksson as his successor to the hootch.[36]

The fact that Diaz himself is made a spectacle suggests the relevance of Susan Jeffords's analysis of the behavior of collective rapists. Commenting on

Brownmiller's description of the rape that would become the basis of *Casualties of War*, Jeffords suggests how much spectacle itself becomes an element in rape: "Soldier after soldier remarks that he was aware that others were watching him commit the rape. . . . Gang-rape is testimony to the function of display in establishing and enforcing the status of the collective. Collectivity is finally nothing more, and nothing less, than its power to create and re-create spectacle."[37]

SAVING PRIVATE RYAN

While my emphasis on *Platoon* and *Full Metal Jacket* has been on rifles and their connection to male sexuality, here the focus is on a scene in *Saving Private Ryan* in which a German soldier uses a knife to kill the Jewish soldier Melish (Adam Goldberg). The insights of Peter Ehrenhaus and Thomas Doherty provide a helpful perspective on Melish's death.

One of the most obvious conventions in Spielberg's epic is that of the "melting pot" makeup of the company engaged in finding and saving Ryan. The most pronouncedly ethnic member of the group is Melish, whose Jewish identity is foregrounded in the film in two scenes. After one battle, as he encounters German prisoners of war, he takes a knife from one and says he'll use it to cut challah. Later, he grasps the Star of David he wears around his neck and flaunts it at the German POWs, saying, "*Juden! Juden!*"

In one of the film's most disturbing scenes, Melish, who is out of ammunition because Upham (Jeremy Davies) has panicked and been unable to bring him a new bandolier, fights hand to hand with a German. He bites the German's face, drawing blood. As they struggle, the German manages to grab Melish's knife. Now on top, he slowly pushes the knife into the helpless Melish. The German's language, untranslated in the film with subtitles, is difficult to make out. Ehrenhaus translates his speech as saying: "Let's put an end to this. This will be easier for you. Much easier. It will soon be over."[38] Karen Jaehne translates part of his words as "Let's just end it all."[39]

Amy Taubin, who comments on the conventional makeup of the troop, suggests "the film veers wildly between realism and allegory. A horribly disturbing scene in which a German soldier disembowels a Jewish American soldier while an all-American boy cowers in fear is forced to carry the entire weight of the Holocaust."[40] Ehrenhaus presents a much more extended discussion of the significance of Melish's death in terms of the Holocaust: "As the unit's Jewish member, Melish is the vehicle through which viewers can engage the Holocaust and participate in construction of its memory as an American phenomenon." He points out the contrast between Melish and the WASP, Corporal Upham, whom he takes as emblematic of a national weakness: "an American Christian incapable of acting despite hearing the cries of the Jew."[41] Upham's "inability to act" explains,

for Ehrenhaus, the reason Americans have devoted so much energy to memori-
alizing the Holocaust: "guilt for not having acted, for not having acted soon, for
not having done enough."[42]

In terms of this chapter's emphasis on weapons and their relation to sexuality,
Ehrenhaus's description of the battle is notable: "In a close-up of Melish, mouth
agape, the German's face enters the frame, dripping sweat, their lips nearly close
enough to kiss. . . . The intimacy of Melish's rape-like struggle and his blood sacrifice are horrific."[43] Doherty also suggests the sexual aspects of the German's attack
on Melish, pointing out "he is penetrated by a blade in a deadly pas de deux that
plays like an act of coitus."[44]

Clearly the German's attack can be read as an allegorical rape of Jews. Ehrenhaus's comment on the "rapelike" attack and Doherty's remark about "an act of
coitus" suggest another aspect to explore. Interpretation of the scene has been
complicated by a situation of "too much information." Spielberg has (notoriously)
been quoted as saying he identifies with Upham, whose inaction leads directly to
Melish's death: "He was me in the movie. That's how I would have been in the
war," a statement that both Christopher Caldwell and I find puzzling.[45] Spielberg
told Stephen J. Dubner in the *Guardian Unlimited* that he "chose the Jewish soldier [to die in this way] because all the other squad members were accounted for,
and I'd already shot their whereabouts." The form of Melish's death as the German
soldier "hushes like a baby" was something Spielberg claims to have "made ... up
on the spot." According to Dubner, Tom Hanks disagrees with Spielberg's claim
that Upham is his "alter-ego": "I think who Steven fantasises himself being is
Mellish [*sic*]... who pulls out his Star of David, and says 'Juden, Juden' as the
German POWS are going by."[46] Thus interpretations of the scene see not only an
allegory for American weakness and impotency, but also the director projecting
himself into both victim and causative agent.

Another dimension of this riveting scene that has not been explored by Spielberg or any the film's commentators relates to two conversations that transpire
immediately before it: one involving Upham, Melish, Private Reiben (Edward
Burns), and Private Horvath (Tom Sizemore); and one between Captain Miller
(Tom Hanks) and Private Ryan (Matt Damon). These provide an ironic and
complex perspective for witnessing the rapelike death of Melish. Prior to the sustained battle that takes up the last thirty minutes of the film, we see Miller fum-
bling with a broken coffee urn and hear, faintly, the sound of music: the singing
of Edith Piaf on a record being played by Upham. Miller tells Ryan that Piaf is
singing about her lost love. Then the film cuts to Upham, who stands next to the
diegetic source of the music, an old phonograph; Melish, Reiben, and Horvath
are arranged in a triangular composition on the steps. Upham translates more of
the song: "I dream I'm with you. You say things that make my eyes close." This
prompts Melish to say: "Upham, to be honest with you, I find myself curiously

aroused by you"—a line that gets a laugh from the men. Reiben tells Upham, "You're a strange one," and then tells a story he is reminded of by the song. On his last day home before leaving for the army, he was working in his mother's clothing store when their superintendent's wife came in to try on a brassiere. A buxom woman (44EE), she insists on trying on a 42D. Her breasts are pouring out of the brassiere, and she can see that Reiben "has a hard on the size of the Statue of Liberty." She tells Reiben: "If you see anything that upsets you, close your eyes and think of these." Then Spielberg cuts to Miller, who suggests Ryan try to remember a context so he can recall his brothers' faces. This prompts Ryan's story about surprising his oldest brother in the barn as the latter tried to have sex with an unattractive girl.

Since nothing thus far in the film has been about sex, the back-to-back introduction of two specifically erotic (albeit mildly so) stories about encounters seems unusual. Reiben's story of being sexually aroused by the buxom woman follows Melish's comic claim of finding himself "strangely aroused" by Upham's explanation of the Piaf song.

I think the song, the two stories, and the two references to arousal provide a powerful context for watching the death of Melish. Piaf sings of loss; Reiben talks of large breasts and his erection; Melish jokes about being aroused; Ryan describes a sexual encounter that was interrupted. And then we watch a German soldier kill Melish in a manner that recalls the observation from Grossman, cited earlier: "Thrusting the sexual appendage (the penis) deep into the body of the victim can be perversely linked to thrusting the killing appendage (a bayonet or knife) deep into the body of the victim."[47] Thus Melish's death occurs in a narrative context that has been filled with references to heterosexual encounters and one joking comment about how hearing about heterosexual sex produces a homosexual response in the auditor. In addition to the killing's significance as a statement about Jews and about the responsibility of those who didn't stop the Holocaust, the scene can also be seen as concerning male sexuality in war and the complex forms it takes. The German's urging of Melish not to fight his attack is a troubling emblem of the effects of war on male sexuality. This symbolic rape replays actual rapes of males performed by victors. As I noted in the previous section, Goldstein explains that one way "of feminizing enemy soldiers in the ancient world was anal rape, with the victor in the dominant/active position and the vanquished in the subordinate/passive one."[48] This symbolic subjugation has continued to the present, as Goldstein notes in his comments on Bosnia and Kosovo. Whether actual, as is historically the case, or symbolic, as it is here in Melish's death, the rapes feminize the victim. But this symbolic rape occurs in a context in which the potential varieties of sexual behavior are all present, rendered in comic terms with the accompanying laughter. Part of the death scene's power comes, I think, from turning the laughter into horror.

JARHEAD

Although it received generally unenthusiastic reviews, some of them comparing it negatively to *Three Kings* (David O. Russell, 1999), *Jarhead* deserves attention in relation to the issues being explored in this chapter. Based on Anthony Swofford's autobiographical record of his experiences as a marine gunner in the Gulf War, the film, written by William Broyles Jr., a Vietnam veteran, effectively depicts a situation in which frustration caused by bodily impotency can't be corrected by displacing sexual power onto that of weapons. This film's rendering of that connection provides a totally opposite alternative to that depicted in the exultant naked soldiers in *The Boys in Company C.*

In many ways *Jarhead* is the most explicit of any war film discussed regarding the effects of sexual deprivation on the men. Swofford (Jake Gyllenhaal) talks openly about the men's conversations regarding masturbation (which is better to use, left or right hand?). In one scene we see him in a bathroom stall trying to masturbate but failing to achieve orgasm. To embarrass the brass as well as to shock journalists there to interview them, the marines stage a "field fuck" in which they grapple in and then begin removing their uniforms as they simulate intercourse and fellatio. When the marines watch a videotape of *The Deer Hunter* (Michael Cimino, 1978) sent to one of the men, they discover added footage has been interpolated that shows the recipient's wife having sex with another man. Swofford wants to keep watching, even though the cuckolded marine is distraught.

They learn a version of the rifleman's prayer, described above, as they all hold their weapons. The connection of warlike enthusiasm to sexual arousal appears in two comments by Colonel Kazinski (Chris Cooper). As he encourages the men and hypes them up for the war, he responds to their first satisfactory burst of enthusiasm by saying, "I just felt my dick move." When the men produce an even more vociferous response, he tells them, "I just got a hard on."

The most significant connection with rifles, guns, and bodies comes at a moment when Swofford becomes enraged with Fergus (Brian Geraghty). Swofford has staged a bacchanalian Christmas Eve party at which he wears only a Santa Claus hat and a G-string. While the men party, Fergus holds watch, but his carelessness results in an explosion and loss of ammunition. Swofford receives an ignominious punishment and has to wear his Christmas hat and clean toilets long after the holiday is over. As he drills Fergus in assembling his rifle, Swofford puts his rifle on Fergus's face and insists he recite that part of the "Infantryman's Creed" with the words, "This is my rifle. There are many like it, but without me, it is useless." Fergus becomes increasingly terrified by Swofford, who then turns the gun around on his own face and tells Fergus to shoot him. Now his rationale is not continued anger for Fergus's inept behavior, but his own frustration at *not* being able to kill. Both he and his fellow rifleman Troy (Peter Sarsgaard) are desperate for the opportunity to use their weapons but are prevented from doing so

openly gay soldier in a film in which that policy is mentioned by name is despicable.

The Greatest Generation

One explanation for the emphasis on the family and generations in these war films is to see it as an example of an ideological operation supporting and valorizing conservative patriarchal values in American culture. Certainly the three films about World War II (*Saving Private Ryan*, *Pearl Harbor*, and *Hart's War*) directly evoke those who fought in what Studs Terkel designates "the good war."[1] Catherine Kodat's observation is relevant:

> From the first word in the dialogue of the film ("Dad?" the aging Ryan's son exclaims as his father crumples to the ground before Captain Miller's grave) to the last ("Tell me I'm a good man," Ryan asks his wife, who firmly replies, "You are"), *Saving Private Ryan* casts itself as a reverent tribute to our fathers' generation, a gesture Spielberg sought to underline when, upon receiving the 1999 Oscar for Best Director, he thanked his own father, a World War II veteran, "for showing me that there is honor in looking back and respecting the past."[2]

Jeanine Basinger suggests one possible explanation for the "reactivated . . . combat genre" as a result of "male directors who watched combat films as boys and now want to make their own; a new conservatism that takes us backward to simpler times, the millennium that makes us want to reevaluate the century." She concludes with a provisional advisory that "until we see a full decade of the new combat films, however, we cannot really know what they will add up to."[3] Thomas Doherty sees *Saving Private Ryan* as "not just a motion picture event but a cultural milestone, an occasion for another solemn encounter with the meaning of World War II and perhaps the last chance for a face-to-face salute to the surviving warriors."[4] Albert Auster sees the film serving as a corrective to the United States' limited successes in foreign wars in the 1990s. He finds World War II "the indispensable symbol of American patriotic virtue and triumph. . . . *Saving Private Ryan* was a perfect anodyne to the somewhat equivocal glory of the low-key American victories in the Cold War and the Gulf War."[5]

Such a conception that speaks to a present lack of satisfaction in this particular case would illustrate what Linda Hutcheon says about the function of nostalgia in general. She believes nostalgia

> may depend precisely on the irrecoverable nature of the past for its emotional impact and appeal. It is the very pastness of the past, its inaccessibility, that likely accounts for a large part of nostalgia's power. . . . This is rarely the past as actually experienced . . . ; it is the past as imagined, as idealized through

memory and desire. . . . The aesthetics of nostalgia might . . . be less a matter of simple memory than of complex projection; the invocation of a partial, idealized history merges with a dissatisfaction for the present.[6]

If such dissatisfaction as Hutcheon describes theoretically includes discomfort with the "Don't ask, don't tell" policy, then the attention given in these films to supporting and fathering new generations has a special resonance.

Because Private James Ryan (Matt Damon) was saved as a result of the mission led by Captain Miller, he has lived to create a family. Its members surround the aged Ryan at Miller's grave, offering literal and figurative support. Since we know nothing of the later Ryan except that he has prospered and been fruitful, his wife's assertion that he has been a good man is readable in necessarily limited terms. The evidence of what has made him "good" in the moral and sexual economy of the film would appear to be provided by the proof that he heads a closely bound nuclear family. Miller's enjoinder to the young Ryan to "earn this" takes on an unintentionally ironic quality, since Ryan's goodness is measurable by the fact he has helped create more Ryans who honor their father/grandfather.[7] Certainly the scene is moving, but ideologically it works quite emphatically to say something about what makes the "Greatest Generation" so important. The revival of interest in World War II and its heroes is not only a valorization of patriarchy. It is also confirms the *present* generation as the children and grandchildren of men who were capable of the pure love that arises in wartime among comrades.

Saving Private Ryan. Captain Miller as father figure to Private Ryan. Courtesy: Photofest. © Amblin Entertainment/Dreamworks SKG, 1998.

One reason for the greatness of this generation is precisely the fact that it created new generations. The imminent deaths of World War II veterans underscore the inadequacies of the present generation that openly acknowledges the possibility of a military that has in it gay soldiers whose sexuality will not result in new generations.[8]

LOOKING BACK AT WORLD WAR II—*PEARL HARBOR*,
HART'S WAR, AND *THE GREAT RAID*

Pearl Harbor fades out with another family in view as a plane carries a father, Rafe McCawley (Ben Affleck), and his stepson, Danny, the child of Danny Walker (Josh Hartnett) and Evelyn Johnson (Kate Beckinsale), into the sunset. This image of dual fatherhood is particularly striking in the context of a number of war films that emphasize the fecundity of their heterosexual heroes.

Pearl Harbor's narrative trajectory builds to an excess of heterosexual affirmation about fatherhood in the final dialogue between Danny and Rafe. The two, seen first as childhood friends, are fliers. Rafe volunteers to serve in the British Royal Air Force (a patent impossibility, historically), but gives Danny the impression he had no choice. By the time Rafe leaves for England, he has fallen in love with Evelyn, a nurse. Danny, Evelyn, and their other friends are assigned to Pearl Harbor. Hearing that Rafe has been killed, Danny and Evelyn comfort each other and fall in love. But Rafe was not killed, and is angry when he returns and finds out about their love. During the attack on Pearl Harbor, Danny and Rafe successfully shoot down some Japanese planes. Because of their skill in flying, General Jimmy Doolittle (Alec Baldwin) enlists them for the raid on Tokyo. Before they leave Hawaii, Evelyn tells Rafe (but not Danny) that she is pregnant. Although the raid is successful, Rafe's plane is shot down, and Danny saves him by strafing the Japanese who are about to kill his friend. But Danny's plane crashes, he is injured, and then shot. Knowing he is going to die, Danny tells Rafe he isn't

Pearl Harbor. The new family. © Touchstone Pictures/Jerry Bruckheimer Films, 2001.

going to make it. Rafe tells him he must: "Danny . . . you're my family. You can't leave me like this. . . . You can't die. You can't. You're going to be a father." When Danny hears that, he tells Rafe: "No. You are," and then he dies, cradled in the arms of the tearful Rafe.[9]

The film ends by showing us the family formed by Rafe, Evelyn, and Danny's son (also named Danny) back in Tennessee. Rafe takes his (that is, Danny's) "son" up in an old biplane like the one he and Danny played in as children, thus framing the film with a kind of reunion of Rafe and the next generation fathered by Danny. This excess of fatherhood at the conclusion of *Pearl Harbor* illustrates the operation of an ideological discourse about generations that extends well beyond the film.

Such a discourse is apparent in the promotional articles and advertising for *Pearl Harbor*. The cover of the 18–20 May 2001 *USA Weekend* Sunday supplement shows Ben Affleck and Tom Brokaw standing next to each other on the deck of the USS *Intrepid*. The caption reads: "War & Remembrance. Patriotism. Loyalty. The Greatest Generation. That's just the beginning when Tom Brokaw and Ben Affleck sit down to talk about *Pearl Harbor*. AN EXCLUSIVE CONVERSATION."[10] The article simultaneously promotes *Pearl Harbor*, which would open the following week, and Brokaw's *An Album of Memories*, which was being published in May. At least one critic at the time could see the obvious kind of advertising synergies. For example, Owen Gleiberman finds the film "nearly painstaking in its traditionalism, a tale of love, war, and valor in which nostalgia for 'simpler times' gets mashed together, almost fetishically, with nostalgia for old movies and for the spirit of knightly self-sacrifice during World War II that *Saving Private Ryan* and Tom Brokaw helped make fashionable again."[11]

This excess of commentary on generational love and the ending of *Pearl Harbor* are reinforced ideologically by another kind of discourse that appears in popular magazines published at the time of the film's release dealing with Josh Hartnett and Michael Bay and their respective fathers. Even though their fathers were not in the military, the information relates in some way to the film's production. In the case of Hartnett, there is a happy bond between father and son. In an article in *People* titled "Ready for Takeoff," Hartnett discusses his father's influence on his decision to make the film: "We had this great discussion while we were washing the car. . . . He reminded me that I said when I got into acting, I wanted to ride it as far as I could."[12] Hartnett, presented on the cover of the June 2001 *Movieline* as "The Reluctant Hero," again talks about his decision to act in *Pearl Harbor*. In language that might be used more appropriately to describe a decision to enlist in the armed services and depart for war, he responds to the question of "what finally convinced you to take *Pearl Harbor*": "A conversation I had with my dad. I told him that the film would change my life and maybe my whole family's too, and that I didn't know if it was the right thing to do. He said, 'It's your decision. But fame is temporary. You can quit and it'll go away or you can keep going and it'll go away anyhow. But regret can be permanent.' One of the last things I said to my dad before I got on the plane to go off and shoot *Pearl Harbor* was, 'I'm going to go for the ride until it lets me off.'" The reporter observes: "Sounds like you're very close to your father," and is told: "Oh man, he's a great guy."[13]

Information about a different kind of father-son relationship surfaced during the production of the film in connection with Michael Bay and his adoptive father, who died during the filming of *Pearl Harbor*. In an interview with *Esquire*, Bay says: "I got to see him at the very end. . . . It's sad because, you know, he said, 'One thing I want to live to see is your movie.'" His father had actually contributed to one aspect of the film:

> I showed him the rough trailer, the teasers, and, you know, he's very down to earth, not into all the hoopla bullshit, and the trailer had words—*peace, hope, love*, you know—all those words floating up on the screen. And he was like, "What is that crap? *Get rid of all that crap!* It happened on a Sunday morning—that's all it should say. Because that's when the attack on Pearl Harbor happened. Get rid of all that crap!" . . . So I called the marketing guys . . . and that became the campaign.[14]

The importance of father-son relations is worked out in a symbolic register in *Hart's War*. Set in a German prison camp during World War II, the film concerns the conflicted relationships between Lieutenant Thomas Hart (Colin Farrell) and Colonel William McNamara (Bruce Willis). After being captured and interrogated by German captors, Hart has evidently succumbed to their torture and revealed information crucial to the Nazis. McNamara, who when taken prisoner earlier never revealed anything to his interrogators, appears to be aware of Hart's failure when Hart is brought to the prison camp. The complicated relationship between the men is initially signaled by the relegation of Hart to an enlisted men's cabin rather than to one with other officers. Tensions mount when two African American fliers, also officers, are brought into the camp and assigned to the same cabin as Hart. Even more tension occurs after the Germans summarily kill one of the fliers because he was cruelly set up by the racist Vic Bedford (Cole Hauser). When the racist is killed and the other flier, Lieutenant Lincoln Scott (Terrence Howard), is accused of his murder, Hart is tapped to defend him in a trial.

But the manifest scenario in which Hart thinks he is working (defending Scott) turns out to be much more complicated. In fact, McNamara is heading an escape operation and using the trial as a diversionary ploy to absorb their captors' attention. Hart discovers this and realizes that McNamara himself murdered Bedford. As the film moves to its climax, Hart announces that he and not Scott was the murderer. But once the successful escape is revealed, McNamara appears (wearing the Nazi uniform appropriated for him as part of the plan) and exonerates Hart by admitting his role in all the plotting. Colonel Visser (Marcell

Iuris), the commander of the camp, kills McNamara by shooting him in the head. The film ends with a written commentary indicating that the camp was liberated shortly afterward.

McNamara loses his life to save Lieutenant Hart from certain execution. Even though there is pronounced tension between them, he refers to Hart as "son." Looked at in the context of the other films about World War II, and the ongoing valorization of the "Greatest Generation," McNamara's sacrifice seems readable as evidence that the truly heroic figures who save younger men are gone. Moreover, even though he has redeemed himself by his actions in the prison camp, Hart earlier was not as strong as McNamara, who couldn't be broken. Nonetheless Hart's willingness to die at the end by lying about the murder signals his growth into the kind of standards represented by McNamara. Thus the latter's sacrifice for his son suggests that Hart has, in fact, met his symbolic parent's standards.

The focus of *The Great Raid* is on the successful rescue operation that freed American soldiers imprisoned at the Japanese camp Cabcaben in the Philippines rather than on paternal continuity and support. Based on Hampton Sides's 2001 book about the men who survived the Bataan death march, the film stresses the toughness and uncompromising courage of the prisoners, especially the doomed Major Gibson (Joseph Fiennes) and the leaders of the raid, Lieutenant Colonel Mucci (Benjamin Bratt) and Captain Prince (James Franco). Gibson's unconsummated love with the heroic nurse Margaret Utinski (Connie Nielsen) revives memories of similarly doomed romances in World War II films like that between Rusty Ryan (John Wayne) and Sandy Davyss (Donna Reed) in *They Were Expendable* (John Ford, 1945). Its consistently somber examination of the rescue operation and the increasingly cruel treatment of the prisoners of war by the Japanese underscores the men's masculine power. In this regard, its depiction of prisoners of war evokes an unrelievedly serious film like *The Purple Heart* (Lewis Milestone, 1944) rather than *Stalag 17* (Billy Wilder, 1953) or *The Great Escape* (John Sturges, 1963).

LATER WARS—*WE WERE SOLDIERS*, *BLACK HAWK DOWN*, *SPY GAME*, AND *BEHIND ENEMY LINES*

We Were Soldiers draws on real events and people, in this case Lieutenant Colonel Hal Moore (Mel Gibson), who leads his men to a horribly bloody and violent victory in the first major battle involving the United States in Vietnam. *We Were Soldiers* is notable for its refusal to demonize the enemy. The film begins with the arrival of Moore; his wife, Julie (Madeline Stowe); and their five children on an army base. The opening shots show the Moores in a station wagon singing. That night Moore prepares the children to say their prayers together by ordering them to "fall in." As Thomas Doherty has explained, "Colonel Moore and his troops may be fighting machines but they are also husbands and fathers, women-centered and God-fearing."[15] The image of Moore leading his children in prayer and the decorous shots of him with Julie in bed confirm him as a family man of the first order, a quality that is underscored in a conversation he has with Lieutenant Jack Geoghegan (Chris Klein) in the chapel after the birth of the Geoghegan baby.

Moore's return to the base after surviving the battle emphasizes the importance of fatherhood. Knowing that taxi drivers are being used to deliver death notices, Julie becomes alarmed when she sees one outside and sends the children upstairs, out of earshot. But it turns out the cab has brought Moore home, and she shouts up the stairs, "Children, come and say hello to your daddy."[16]

Black Hawk Down involves a rescue operation based on actual events that occurred in Somalia during a military operation that failed when Army Rangers became trapped in Mogadishu after their helicopters were downed. A key figure in the rescue operation is Michael Durant (Ron Eldard). Although he eventually is released by the Somalis, the film's story ends with him still a prisoner. His capture is presented in a graphically disturbing way, as a large group of Somalis discover him in hiding. One hits him in the head with a blunt object, and the mob seems about to attack him when the leader claims Durant in the name of the head of his army. Immediately before being discovered, Durant has been looking at a two-sided photograph that has images of his wife and children. As he's attacked, he tries to maintain the photograph in his grasp but can't, a fact registered in a close-up. A matching shot shows the hands of one of his captors on the

We Were Soldiers. Colonel Moore leads his children in prayer. Courtesy: Photofest. © Icon Entertainment International, 2002.

photograph. The blond Durant and his similarly fair-skinned family are thus seen to be collectively vulnerable to the attack of the Somalis, an aspect of the film that certainly supports the concerns raised about its racism.

The film ends with Staff Sergeant Matt Eversmann (Josh Hartnett) saying good-bye to the body of a comrade who didn't survive and then a closing shot of the hold of a troop plane. As the screen goes black and the credits begin to roll, we hear Durant's voice reading a letter to his wife: "My love, be strong and you will do well in life. I love you and my children deeply. Today, tomorrow and every day keep smiling, even when things get you down. So, in closing my love, tuck the children in bed warmly. Tell them I love them and give them a big kiss from Daddy." Toward the end of the credits, information is given about Durant's eventual release. Ending the film with Durant's letter to his wife and information about his survival confirms the ideological process I see operating in recent films. Here, though, the continuation of the ideal nuclear heterosexual *white* family is foregrounded by the particular nature of the battle in which Durant was involved.[17]

Like *Hart's War*, which suggests a symbolic father-son relationship, both *Spy Game* and *Behind Enemy Lines* concern older men who sacrifice themselves in various ways so that younger men can be saved. While only the first of these directly addresses the sexual relationships of the young man who is rescued, both the narratives occur in a hermetically sealed heterosexual world.

Spy Game is about a rescue conceived and successfully coordinated by Nathan Muir (Robert Redford), who wants to save his protégé, Tom Bishop (Brad Pitt),

Spy Game. Muir and his symbolic son. Courtesy: Photofest. © Beacon Communications LLC/Universal Studios, 2001.

from execution by the Chinese government. Flashbacks show how Muir recruited and trained Bishop as an assassin and operative for the Central Intelligence Agency (CIA). On one of his assignments Bishop meets and falls in love with Elizabeth Hadley (Catherine McCormack). When she is taken prisoner by the Chinese, Bishop breaks into the prison to rescue her, but the plan fails, and both are in imminent danger of execution. Through his connections with various contacts such as Harry Duncan (David Hemmings), Muir sets up a rescue operation funded out of his own retirement money.

The present-day action involving the rescue takes place on Muir's last day at work at the CIA, where he is questioned by his superiors. They are quite willing to have Bishop killed because his presence is an embarrassment, given delicate trade negotiations occurring between the Chinese and the United States. At various points the film makes clear what Muir's ideal retirement will include: an island retreat that costs over $200,000. Through Duncan, Muir commits his own money to negotiate a deal that will get Bishop and Hadley safely out of China. The film ends by showing Muir driving away from the Pentagon, and Bishop and Hadley, battered but alive, being flown safely out of danger.

No indication is provided of what Muir will do now, given the depletion of the nest egg he had accumulated to buy his retirement home. Throughout the film there have been teasing references to his marital status, but these ambiguous comments about his various marriages and divorces make it impossible to determine whether he is or has ever been married. Thus his rescue of Tom has an even more significant resonance. He has, in fact, sacrificed his dream of a retirement home, which is not clearly going to be shared with anyone, so that both Tom and Elizabeth can live.

A different kind of sacrifice occurs in *Behind Enemy Lines.* Chris Burnett (Owen Wilson) is a navy flier engaged in a reconnaissance mission with his partner, Stackhouse (Gabriel Macht). Having gotten off their assigned course and strayed inappropriately into a no-fly zone, they are shot down in Bosnia and crash. Stackhouse is shot in cold blood by Sasha (Vladimer Mashkov), and Burnet tries to escape. Fortunately, he has been able to maintain contact with Admiral Leslie Reigart (Gene Hackman). Initially hostile to Burnett for his flippant attitude about wanting more action in the first place, and angry about his violation of his flight plan, Reigart nonetheless actively engages in trying to rescue Burnett, whom he constantly calls "son" in their communications. But this brings Reigart in conflict with the North Atlantic Treaty Organization (NATO) commander Admiral Piquet (Joaquim de Almeida), who prohibits Reigart from sending in a rescue team.

Violating the NATO commands, Reigart sends men in to rescue Burnett. As it turns out, the documentation Burnett is able to provide about atrocities is essential to NATO in prosecuting the head of the Serbs. Even so, Reigart ends his career in a kind of polite disgrace. Threatened with reassignment to a desk job in Washington, Reigart resigns in a way that leaves him some dignity, and certainly the respect of his men, but not what could have been anticipated before this incident damaged his reputation with his superiors.

Looking Backward, Looking Forward

With the exception of *Jarhead*, all the films discussed in this chapter display a variety of untroubled men whose masculinity and sexuality are not in question: there is no need to "explain" anything such as being in drag; no one shows signs of mental instability; no one makes jokes about homosexuals. Unlike the bleak, despairing *Jarhead*, these films depict a safe world removed from the complexities of the present. A comparable positive treatment of masculinity and sexuality appears in Clint Eastwood's *Flags of Our Fathers* (2006), based on James Bradley's book about his father, John, one of the six men who raised the flag on Mount Suribachi. The screenplay by Williams Broyles Jr. and Paul Haggis focuses on the battlefield experiences of the flag raisers, and concentrates on the three survivors who were tapped by the U.S. government to lead a bond drive. One of the narrative emphases in the film is on James Bradley's search for information about his father. Near the film's conclusion, James speaks to his dying father in a hospital. John expresses regrets for not being a good father. James asserts that he was, in fact, "the best father a man could ever have." The scene in this film, coproduced by Steven Spielberg, evokes the moment at the graveside in *Saving Private Ryan* in which Ryan's goodness is confirmed by his wife. It will be interesting to see to what extent the anticipated films about the Iraq war support or reject such affirmations.[18]

BUDDIES, THEN AND NOW

In a brief analysis of war films from the silent era to the present in which he discusses their themes, conventions, generic continuities, and connections to the historical moment, Steve Neale observes: "Coinciding with a renewed interest in the topic of masculinity in Film, Media and Cultural Studies, war films of all kinds have been studied . . . not only in terms of their Oedipal dynamics and their sado-masochistic scenarios, but also in light of the fact that the war film is one of the few genres in which, as *Saving Private Ryan* ([Steven Spielberg,] 1998) has recently confirmed, male characters are permitted to weep as a means of expressing their physical and emotional stress and hence their physical and emotional vulnerability."[1]

Neale's point about the way recent war films have been studied in relation to a particular critical emphasis has even broader implications. Just as narrative elements can move from one genre to another, so, too, has the question of what male bonding between buddies is *really* about emerged over time as a topic of concern in relation to films that focus on male relationships in a variety of genres, including the war film.

For people in the 1920s, the noun "buddy" was innocuous and unambiguous: it referred to a soldier who fought in World War I. As we saw in chapter 1, reviewers regularly used it in commentaries on war films. "My Buddy," a song written for the composer's dead fiancée, was appropriated as a signifier for male soldiers. Now the term "buddy" is inescapably embedded in a complex linguistic, socio-cultural matrix that is most certainly not innocuous or unambiguous. The noun can refer to a kind of genre, "the buddy film," or a semantic feature that crosses over from one genre to another. But now it has a sexual valence.

Ironically, a term used initially to refer to a dead female lover, and subsequently to a man, has gone through an even more complex transformation. In Mark Simpson's essay "Don't Die on Me Buddy, Homoeroticism and Masochism in

War Movies," the term refers to both to a male soldier and a dying lover. Like the fiancée of the songwriter who memorialized her, buddies are seen as the objects of desire. But unlike the woman in the heterosexual relationship, who was intended as a lover, the men are unattainable lost objects over whom one can weep copious tears precisely because death protects one from the problem or suspicion of sexual inter-action. Simpson argues that death in a film like A Midnight Clear (Keith Gordon, 1992) "makes love between men eternal by removing it from the male body; by can-celing forever the threat of its consummation it ensures that boyish love is immor-tal, and that queer love, transformed into a cadaver, is buried on the battlefield."[2]

This is not the place to begin a history of criticism of gays in films, but it is possible to suggest that recent discussions such as Simpson's of the meaning of male bonding between buddies occur in a context inflected by a different epis-teme than that of the 1970s and early 1980s, which saw the appearance of the early feminist criticism of Molly Haskell and Joan Mellen and the first histories of gays in film by Parker Tyler and Vito Russo.

Emanuel Levy describes the advent of buddy films depicting "[m]ale friend-ships, with their robust macho romanticism. . . . A spate of male buddy movies was produced in the 1970s, as a backlash against the Women's Movement. According to Molly Haskell, the emotional intensity of these films exists between the men; feminism gave filmmakers the freedom to drop the token women from the narrative altogether."[3]

Obviously, Leslie Fiedler provided a major impetus for arguments about homo-erotic subtexts in "buddy" relationships in films. His earlier reading of Mark Twain's Huckleberry Finn posited a subtextual homoerotic relationship between Huck and Jim and other figures in American literature.[4] Haskell acknowledges him as she explores how buddy films and relationships confirm the authority of male hegemony:

> [T]he buddy system that Fiedler uncovers in literature with obsessive (and depressing) regularity is just as present in American film. Once the backbone of the genre film, the male friendship has become, in recent womanless melo-dramas ... the overt and exclusive "love interest" as well. . . . The theme of male camaraderie has cropped up with increasing self-consciousness and sentimen-tality in recent years. . . . Sexual desire is not the point, nor "homoeroticism" the term for these relationships or for men fighting together shoulder to shoulder at the front. . . . Rather, the point is love—love in which men under-stand and support each other, speak the same language, and risk their lives to gain each other's respect. But this is also a delusion; the difficulties of the adventure disguise the fact that this is the easiest of loves: a love that is adoles-cent, presexual, tacit, the love of one's semblable, one's mirror reflection.[5]

Some of the films she mentions in this category as evidence of Fiedler's thesis include Easy Rider (Dennis Hopper, 1969), Midnight Cowboy (John Schlesinger,

1969), *Butch Cassidy and the Sundance Kid* (George Roy Hill, 1969), *Wild Rovers* (Blake Edwards, 1971), *Bad Company* (Robert Benton, 1972), *Deliverance* (John Boorman, 1972), and *Scarecrow* (Jerry Schatzberg, 1973).[6] Another notable buddy film of the early 1970s is *The Sting* (George Roy Hill, 1973), which paired Paul Newman and Robert Redford again after a four-year interval from *Butch Cassidy*.

Following Levy's logic, if the buddy films that constitute this genre (or figure as elements in other genres) are a backlash against the women's movement, one can argue that aspects of feminist criticism, especially such as that offered by Haskell and Mellen, who identified the genre, represent a corresponding backlash against the films that exclude women. Identifying potentially homoerotic subtexts in buddy films could be seen as a challenge to the masculinity celebrated and valorized in these films.

The results of the 27 June 1969 revolt against sexual oppression by occupants of the Stonewall Inn reverberated throughout American culture in a number of ways. One of the most significant outcomes was to foreground gay men (and lesbians), their sexuality, and their needs as human beings for respect. The burgeoning of the gay rights movement in the 1970s occurs simultaneously with the increased visibility of films that include or are about gay men: *Boys in the Band* (William Friedken, 1970), *Fortune and Men's Eyes* (Harvey Hart, 1971), *Sunday, Bloody Sunday* (John Schlesinger, 1971), *Cabaret* (Bob Fosse, 1972), and *Dog Day Afternoon* (Sidney Lumet, 1975). Films in the early 1980s with gay characters and themes include *Cruising* (William Friedken, 1980), *Making Love* (Arthur Hiller, 1982), *Victor/Victoria* (Blake Edwards, 1982), *Partners* (James Burrows, 1982), and *Deathtrap* (Sidney Lumet, 1982). Obviously, some of these offer decidedly negative images of gay men, especially *Cruising*.

As I suggested earlier, the presence of openly gay characters in films owes much to the Motion Picture Association of America ratings system adopted in 1966. What is interesting to observe is that around the time of early feminist explorations of the buddy films and their homoerotic subtext, Parker Tyler and Vito Russo, in their histories of gays in film, discuss apparently straight characters in works in which they see a homoerotic subtext. These include war films such as *Wings* (William Wellman, 1927) and *The Great Escape* (John Sturges, 1967).[7] I wonder to what extent their exposure of gay subtexts shares an analogous motivation and resentment with that of the feminists in that both want to show what hasn't been adequately acknowledged: that masculinity needs to be seen as more problematic than the works suggest.

Such a motivation certainly seems readable in Tyler's complaint about *The Great Escape*. While he says he is "far from imputing to the film-makers here a homosexual conspiracy," he faults the film for not acknowledging that homosexuality must in fact be present in such a context as a prison camp:

> It is not a whole human picture that we get in *The Great Escape*, but only an elaborately executed trick plot. . . . The only logical thing to infer, humanly, is

that beneath the visible surface, hiding as it were in the unphotographed interstices, is buddy-buddy homosexuality. No one need bother to pretend that such a thing doesn't exist in armies; it is more than amply documented. . . . Humanly, sexually, emotionally, such deep personal attachments are not to be accounted for by the dedication of the prisoners to escape. . . . One can offer the obvious excuse: the human factors of sexuality and related emotions have been eliminated here. But why should they have been? Why should artistic representation *ever* eliminate those factors?[8]

If the feminist exposure of homoerotic elements in buddy films that exclude women can be seen as a backlash that suggests a level of resentment, Tyler's response bespeaks an analogous kind of resentment, in this case not for the exclusion of men but, rather, of gay men from a context in which they must have been present.

If the possibility of resentment seems an inappropriate hypothesis, one could also speculate that construing such affection in the war film as queer love is to limit conceptions of masculinity. The kinds of expansive definitions advanced by R. W. Connell and Joseph Bristow, who understand masculinity as "a place in gender relations" and "a place where sexed bodies (in all their shapes and sizes) and sexual desires (in all their multifariousness) intersect only to separate," extend its range conceptually. Simpson's view implicitly rejects the possibility of such a broad conception.

Yet another aspect about which to speculate in thinking about the way buddy relationships are interpreted concerns the representation of gay men. In the 1987 revised edition of *The Celluloid Closet*, Russo discusses some of the early films that addressed the onslaught of AIDS. By the mid 1980s, awareness of AIDS had increased markedly, displacing the early lack of understanding of the disease's severity and its dangers. Even before the publication of Randy Shilts's *And the Band Played On* (1987), which chronicled the medical response to AIDS, its dangers were underscored for the American public in terms of the entertainment industry by the shocking death of Rock Hudson in October 1985. According to Russo, *Buddies* (Arthur J. Bressan Jr., 1985), which premiered at the Chicago Gay and Lesbian Festival in July 1985, is "the first feature film about AIDS . . . [and] tells the simple story of a gay man dying of AIDS and how his assigned volunteer 'buddy' from the 'gay center' copes with his illness and death. The film, however, goes far beyond the AIDS crisis and examines the foundations of gay love and desire, which transcend politics."[9] In November of that year, NBC broadcast *An Early Frost* (John Erman), a made-for-television movie that undoubtedly reached a larger audience than that of the independently produced film by Bressan. It depicts the conflicted response of a family to the revelation that their son, Michael Pierson (Aidan Quinn), is gay and has AIDS. In February 1986, Bill Sherwood's *Parting Glances*, a commercial film treating the issue, examined the disease's impact on a group of gay men, one of whom, Nick (Steve Buscemi), is dying of AIDS.

Rob Epstein and Jeffrey Friedman, who would later make *The Celluloid Closet*, based on Russo's book, directed *Threads: Stories from the Quilt*, which concerns the memorial quilt made for people who had died from AIDS and which won the Oscar for Best Documentary for 1989. *The Ryan White Story* (John Herzfeld 1989) is about the hemophiliac White (Lucas Haas), who contracted AIDS through a blood transfusion. Norman René's *Longtime Companion* (1990) portrayed the effects of ten years of devastation on a group of gay friends, beginning with their initial uninformed response to the "gay flu," followed by the relentless deaths of one character after another. One section of Todd Hayne's *Poison* (1991) is an allegory about the spread of AIDS. *The Living End* (Gregg Araki, 1992) presented a violent and searing chronicle of two HIV-positive men who engage in violent criminal acts. But except for television shows and independently produced films, there was no regular studio film of any note until Columbia's TriStar Pictures released *Philadelphia* (Jonathan Demme, 1993), for which Tom Hanks won an Oscar for Best Actor.

Some of these films, especially *Longtime Companion* and *Philadelphia*, contain extremely moving scenes in which the living comfort the dying. David (Bruce Davison) in the former is a particularly notable character in this regard. Given the ten-year scope of the film, he is first a caregiver and supporter of his dying friends, and then one of the victims himself at the end of the work. Many of the scenes occur in a hospital, as does the penultimate scene in *Philadelphia*, in which Miguel (Antonio Banderas) tenderly watches over his dying lover, Andrew Beckett (Hanks).

These films participate in a larger cultural discourse that focused on and displayed people with AIDS. Susan Sontag's story "The Way We Live Now," which appeared in the 24 November 1986 issue of the *New Yorker*, depicts the reaction of a group of friends to their friend's HIV status. The photographs by Nicholas Nixon of "People with AIDS" were featured in an exhibition at the Museum of Modern Art in 1988 and later published in a collection. Robert Mapplethorpe's ghostly face, which appears in a self-photograph of him holding a cane with a skull on its top, became a defining image of a man dying of AIDS.

I cite all these films and works because they may have some bearing on how buddy relationships are viewed by some critics today. I wonder to what extent these films showing gay characters and men dying of AIDS surrounded by their grieving lovers have provided a kind of visual frame of reference (almost like a Kantian set of spectacles) through which viewers observe straight comrades and dying soldiers in war films. The only weeping to be found in *Saving Private Ryan*, the film Neale mentions, occurs when the aged Ryan stands at the gravesite of Colonel John Miller. In "Don't Die on Me Buddy," Simpson quotes Anthony Easthope's comment about how, "in the dominant visions of war, men are permitted to behave towards each other in ways that would not be allowed elsewhere, caressing and holding each other, comforting and weeping together, admitting their love."[10]

Neither Simpson nor Easthope provides much by way of specific examples of weeping from actual war films in support of their assertions. Nonetheless, I think that the references to weeping are significant, for they may be symptomatic of the changed viewing perspective of the present. That is, even though there have not been that many films about gays and men dying of AIDS, I wonder if a structure of imagery associated with them inflects comments about straight soldiers in a way it could not prior to the advent of AIDS. It may be that the arguments of Easthope and Simpson, made after the proliferation of images about gay men dying of AIDS, at some level appropriate a kind of meta-iconography from the AIDS films and graft images of weeping, grieving gay men onto heterosexual buddies that makes them lovers, not only men who love one another.

Looking back at *Ride with the Devil* (Ang Lee, 1999), I think it's instructive to consider Jack Bull (Skeet Ulrich), the dying hero, in this regard. His friend Duchy (Tobey Maguire) masticates food so that his helpless friend can consume it, maintains a deathbed vigil, and receives a tender touch on the cheek from him. While I doubt that Lee is consciously or purposely drawing on the iconography of AIDS films at this moment, it's difficult to watch the scene without thinking of comparable scenes involving homosexual lovers rather than heterosexual friends. But the fact that the scene has a visual similarity to others doesn't prove it has the same meaning in terms of its depiction of sexuality. Jack Bull's pregnant girlfriend, Sue Lee (Jewel), is on the other side of him. His position between his male friend and his female lover underscores the difference in the relationships. While we need to acknowledge why the scene might be read this way, we need also to understand how our temporal viewing positions affect its interpretation.

Thus, buddies then and now. An extreme explanation of the current homoerotic readings might point to the possibility of resentment about the ways gays have been excluded or unacknowledged in films; of a limited conception of the potential range of masculinity that denies its capabilities of expressing nonerotic feelings between men; and the influence of an iconography of suffering associated with dying gay men in AIDS films.

A more practical and charitable explanation—and the one with which I conclude—is that we are all struggling with the only discourses available to us as we try to explore dauntingly complex issues. Often we find that the meanings of relationships outrun the language we use to try to describe them. War films will continue to offer us challenging texts that engage our efforts to understand the complexities of masculinity and sexuality.

NOTES

1. In the comparable scene in the play on which the film is based, Charmaine simply says: "No! No! You must be friends." Shortly after that she says: "I love you both"—a line that does not appear in the film. Maxwell Anderson and Laurence Stallings, *What Price Glory?* in *Famous American Plays of the 1920s*, ed. Kenneth MacGowan (New York: Dell, 1959), 124. The film's title lacks the question mark of the play, as does John Ford's remake in 1952.

2. Jeanine Basinger, *The World War II Combat Film: Anatomy of a Genre* (Middletown, Conn.: Wesleyan University Press, 2003); Allan Bérubé, *Coming Out Under Fire: The History of Gay Men and Women in World War II* (New York: Plume, 1991); Joanna Bourke, *Dismembering the Male: Men's Bodies, Britain and the Great War* (Chicago: University of Chicago Press, 1996); Joanna Bourke, *An Intimate History of Killing: Face to Face Killing in Twentieth Century Warfare* (London: Basic Books, 1999); Steven Cohan, *Masked Men: Masculinity and Movies in the Fifties* (Bloomington: Indiana University Press, 1997); John Costello, *Virtue Under Fire: How World War II Changed Our Social and Sexual Attitudes* (Boston: Little, Brown, 1985); John D'Emilio and Estelle B. Freedman, *Intimate Matters: A History of Sexuality in America*, 2nd ed. (Chicago: University of Chicago Press, 1997); Thomas Doherty, *Projections of War: Hollywood, American Culture, and World War II*, rev. ed. (New York: Columbia University Press, 1999); Paul Fussell, *The Great War and Modern Memory* (New York: Oxford University Press, 2002); Paul Fussell, *Wartime: Understanding and Behavior in the Second World War* (New York: Oxford University Press, 1989); Joshua A. Goldstein, *War and Gender: How Gender Shapes the War System and Vice Versa* (Cambridge: Cambridge University Press, 2001); Susan Jeffords, *The Remasculinization of America: Gender and the Vietnam War* (Bloomington: Indiana University Press, 1989); Susan Jeffords, *Hard Bodies: Hollywood Masculinity in the Reagan Era* (New Brunswick, N.J.: Rutgers University Press, 1994); Michael S. Kimmel, *Manhood in America: A Cultural History*, 2nd ed. (New York: Oxford University Press, 2006); Katherine Kinney, *Friendly Fire: American Images of the Vietnam War* (New York: Oxford University Press, 2000); Dana Polan, *Power and Paranoia: History, Narrative, and the American Cinema, 1940–1950* (New York: Columbia University Press, 1986); Lawrence H. Suid, *Guts and Glory: The Making of the American Military Image in Film*, rev. ed. (Lexington: University of Kentucky Press, 2002).

3. Donald Spoto, *Camerado: Hollywood and the American Man* (New York: Plume, 1978), 210.

4. I draw my use of "liminal" from Victor Turner, *The Ritual Process: Structure and Anti-Structure* (Chicago: Aldine, 1969), 95: "The attributes of liminality or of liminal *personae* are necessarily ambiguous, since this condition and these persons elude or slip through the network of classifications that normally locate states and positions in culture space. Liminal entities are neither here nor there; they are betwixt and between the positions assigned by law, custom, convention, and ceremonial." Eve Kosofsky Sedgwick applies the term "liminality" in a different framework, focusing specifically on "transitivity between genders." *Epistemology of the Closet* (Berkeley: University of California Press, 1990), 1–2.

5. Basinger, *World War II Combat Film*, 236–237.

6. Ibid., 239.

7. Rick Altman, *Film/Genre* (London: BFI, 1999), 219.

8. Ibid., 222.

9. Steve Neale, *Genre and Hollywood* (London: Routledge, 2000), 126.

10. Basinger, *World War II Combat Film*, 239.

11. Barbara Ehrenreich, *Blood Rites: Origins and History of the Passions of War* (New York: Henry Holt, 1997), 91.

12. Ibid., 125.

13. Ibid., 127.

14. Ibid., 129.

15. R. W. Connell, *Masculinities* (Berkeley: University of California Press, 1995), 68–70.

16. Ibid., 71.

17. R. W. Connell, *The Men and the Boys* (Berkeley: University of California Press, 2000), 29. See also R. W. Connell and James W. Messerschmidt, "Hegemonic Masculinity: Rethinking the Concept," *Gender and Society* 19.6 (December 2005): 829–859.

18. Stevi Jackson and Sue Scott, "Sexual Skirmishes and Feminist Factions: Twenty-five Years of Debate on Woman and Sexuality," in *Feminism and Sexuality: A Reader*, ed. Stevi Jackson and Sue Scott (New York: Columbia University Press, 1996), 2.

19. Joseph Bristow, *Sexuality* (New York: Routledge, 1997), 1. He says the term was first used by an editor in 1836 commenting on William Cowper's "The Lives of Plants" (3). Michael S. Kimmel and Jeffrey Fracher ground their conception of "masculinity" in sexuality, which they see as "socially constructed, a learned set of both behaviors and cognitive interpretations of those behaviors. . . . *That* we are sexual is determined by a biological imperative toward reproduction, but *how* we are sexual—where, when, how often, and with whom, and why—has to do with cultural learning, with meanings transmitted in a cultural setting." "Hard Issues and Soft Spots: Counseling Men about Sexuality," in *Men's Lives*, ed. Michael S. Kimmel and Michael A. Messner, 2nd ed. (New York: Macmillan, 1992), 440–441. Kimmel bases his concept of masculinity on Sigmund Freud's theory that a male's successful identification with the father after renouncing the Oedipal fixation on the mother produces a healthy pattern of psycho-sexual development: "Masculinity, in this model, is irrevocably tied to sexuality." "Masculinity as Homophobia," in *Theorizing Masculinity*, ed. Harry Brod and Michael Kaufman (Thousand Oaks, Calif.: Sage, 1994), 126. Ethyl Spector Person thinks that "sexuality is a biological force, grounded in the anatomy, physiology, and hormonal secretions of the human body." In addition, she points out its sociocultural valence: "Nonetheless, each individual's sexual practices and attitudes are shaped and colored by cultural attitudes and directives. These are themselves powerfully affected not only by medical advances but by

the studies of sexologists and sexual theorists." *The Sexual Century* (New Haven, Conn.: Yale University Press, 1998), 14. Arguing from a politicized ideological position, both Michel Foucault and Judith Butler reject essentialist conceptions of sexuality and gender rooted in biology. According to Foucault, "sexuality is the set of effects produced in bodies, behaviors, and social relations by a certain deployment deriving from a complex political technology." *The History of Sexuality*, Vol. 1, *Introduction*, trans. Robert Hurley (New York: Vintage Books, 1980), 127. Butler follows Foucault in wanting "to expose the foundational categories of sex, gender, and desire as effects of a specific formation of power." *Gender Trouble: Feminism and the Subversion of Identity* (New York: Routledge, 1990), x.

20. Judith A. Allen, "Men Interminably in Crisis? Historians on Masculinity, Sexual Boundaries, and Manhood," *Radical History Review* 82 (2002): 199. See also Melissa Dabakis, "Douglas Tilden's Mechanics Fountain: Labor and the 'Crisis of Masculinity' in the 1890s," *American Quarterly* 47.2 (June 1995): 204–235.

21. K. A. Cuordileone, " 'Politics in an Age of Anxiety': Cold War Political Culture and the Crisis in American Masculinity, 1949–1960," *Journal of American History* 87.2 (September 2000): 525.

22. Kristen Whissel, "Uncle Tom, Goldilocks, and the Rough Riders: Early Cinema's Encounter with Empire," *Screen* 40.4 (Winter 1999): 384.

23. For commentary on Spanish-American War films, see James Castonguay, "The Spanish-American War in United States Media Culture," *Hypertext Scholarship in American Studies*, section on "Media Culture in the 1890s," http://chnm.gmu.edu.aq/war/index. html (accessed 8 November 2005); Charles Musser, *The Emergence of Cinema: The American Screen to 1907* (New York: Charles Scribner's Sons, 1990), 240–261; Whissel, "Uncle Tom," 384–404; Kristen Whissel, "The Gender of Empire: American Modernity, Masculinity, and Edison's War Actualities," in *A Feminist Reader in Early Cinema*, ed. Jennifer M. Bean and Diane Negra (Durham, N.C.: Duke University Press, 2002), 141–165; and Kristen Whissel, "Placing the Spectator on the Scene of History: the Battle Re-enactment at the Turn of the Century, from Buffalo Bill's Wild West to the Early Cinema," *Historical Journal of Film, Radio and Television* 22.3 (2002): 225–243. See also Oscar V. Campomanes, "Casualty Figures of the American Soldier and the Other: Post 1898 Allegories of Imperial Nation-Building as 'Love and War,' " and "Imperialist Fictions: The Filipino in the Imperialist Imaginary," in *Vestiges of War: The Philippine-American War and the Aftermath of an Imperial Dream 1899–1999*, ed. Angel Velasco Shaw and Luis H. Francia (New York: New York University Press, 2002), 134–162, 224–236; Amy Kaplan, *The Anarchy of Empire in the Making of U.S. Culture* (Cambridge, Mass.: Harvard University Press, 2002), 146–170; and Robert Sklar, *Movie-Made America: A Cultural History of American Movies* (New York: Vintage, 1976), 22.

24. Cohan, *Masked Men*, xii.

25. Jeffords, *Remasculinization of America*, xi. In a later study of the 1980s and early 1990s that includes commentary on the various Rambo films starring Sylvester Stallone, Jeffords demonstrates how the depiction of Vietnam veterans, including POWs, reveals a link between government and conceptions of masculinity: "These hostages come to represent a crisis in the national body, an effort to suppress a part of the national body that has been, presumably, 'forgotten' but has, in fact . . . actively been suppressed by a weakened government." *Hard Bodies*, 37. She attributes the popularity of Ronald Reagan in large part to the way he represented a "hard body" in contrast to the "soft body" associated with "the errant body containing sexually transmitted disease, immorality, illegal

chemicals, 'laziness,' and endangered fetuses"—that is, gays, immigrants, and women. *Hard Bodies*, 24. Similarly, David Savran argues that "*The Right Stuff* [Philip Kaufman, 1983] and Rambo trilogy reexamine and replay crucial battles of the Cold War in order to consolidate the delusion, so dear to Reagan's heart, that the American empire remains triumphant and invulnerable. . . . Both reconstruct masculinity in the ruins of Cold War culture, turning the 'macho' man into a spectacle in the hope that his self-inflicted pain will redeem that heroism which a cynical culture finds both embarrassing and irresistibly alluring." *Taking It Like a Man: White Masculinity, Masochism, and Contemporary Culture* (Princeton, N.J.: Princeton University Press, 1998), 204.

26. *American Film Institute Catalog of Motion Pictures Produced in the United States. Film Beginnings, 1893–1910, A Work in Progress*, comp. Elias Savada (Lanham, Md.: Scarecrow, 1995), 1:918.

27. Theodore Roosevelt, "The Manly Virtues and Practical Politics," in *The Theodore Roosevelt Treasury: A Self-Portrait from His Writings*, comp. Hermann Hagedor (New York: G. P. Putnam's Sons, 1957), 111.

28. Theodore Roosevelt, "The Strenuous Life," in *The Works of Theodore Roosevelt in Fourteen Volumes*, executive ed. (New York: P. F. Collier and Son, 1900), 14:4.

29. Ibid., 14:9.

30. Gail Bederman, *Manliness and Civilization: A Cultural History of Gender and Race in the United States, 1880–1917* (Chicago: University of Chicago Press, 1995); Kristen L. Hoganson, *Fighting for American Manhood: How Gender Politics Provoked the Spanish-American and Philippine-American Wars* (New Haven, Conn.: Yale University Press, 1998). Bederman suggests: "Ostensibly, 'The Strenuous Life' preached the virtues of military preparedness and imperialism, but contemporaries understood it as a speech about manhood. The practical import of the speech was to urge the nation to build up its army, to maintain its strong navy, and to take control of Puerto Rico, Cuba, and the Philippines. But underlying these immediate objectives lay the message that American manhood—both the manly race and the individual white men—must retain the strength of their Indian-fighter ancestors, or another race would prove itself more manly and overtake America in the Darwinian struggle to be the world's most dominant race." *Manliness and Civilization*, 193.

31. Kimmel, *Manhood in America*, 120.

32. Mary W. Blanchard, "The Soldier and the Aesthete: Homosexuality and Popular Culture in Gilded Age America," *Journal of American Studies* 30 (1996): 45. See also E. Anthony Rotundo's commentary on Roosevelt in *American Manhood: Transformations in Masculinity from the Revolution to the Modern Era* (New York: Basic Books, 1993).

33. Castonguay, "Spanish-American War"; Musser, *Emergence of Cinema*; Whissel, "Uncle Tom." See also Whissel's "Placing the Spectator on the Scene."

34. Whissel, "Gender of Empire," 155. The quotation to which Whissel refers continues: "from the moment of his enlistment until his mustering out four months later, Roosevelt self-consciously publicized himself as a model of strenuous, imperialistic manhood. . . . As he explained to the *New York Sun*, it would be unmanly—hypocritical—to allow other men to take his place on the front lines after he had agitated so strongly for war." Bederman, *Manliness*, 190–191.

35. Sarah Watts, *Rough Rider in the White House: Theodore Roosevelt and the Politics of Desire* (Chicago: University of Chicago Press, 2003), 238. In a section relevant to material to be covered later, Watts observes that "Roosevelt's descriptions of the beauty and strength of these healthy men in their thirties [the Rough Riders] was not out of keeping in an age that

approved physically intimate, though not necessarily sexual, and intimately expressed same-sex friendships. . . . His descriptions rendered the men physically attractive and transformed the training ground and the battlefield into an erotic ground where a purified sexuality could be elicited and indulged in by the participants" (212–213). See also John F. Kasson, *Houdini, Tarzan, and the Perfect Man* (New York: Hill and Wang, 2001), for commentary on the appeal of Roosevelt as a physical being for contemporaries such as Houdini, Eugene Sandow, and Edgar Rice Burroughs: "The spectacle of the male body mounted by these three figures built on values embodied in men such as Theodore Roosevelt. In fact, at various points in their careers, all three sought to associate themselves with Roosevelt" (8).

36. *Love and War* came out late in 1899, well after the conclusion of the Spanish-American War, which lasted from April to September 1898. A formal treaty ending the extension of the war into the Philippines was signed in September 1899.

37. The scene draws attention to the role of nurses and their contribution to the Spanish-American War. See Mercedes Graf, "Band of Angels: Sister Nurses in the Spanish-American War," *Journal of the National Archives* 34.3 (2002): 197–202. Nurses had already been depicted in an earlier, very brief (forty-one seconds) re-enactment produced by James H. White, *U.S. Troops and Red Cross in the Trenches before Caloocan* (Edison Manufacturing Co., 1899). The main action of that film consists of a battle followed by the appearance of nurses who minister to the fallen men. According to the Edison catalog, "Stretchers are quickly brought out and the nurses tenderly care for the fallen and carry them to the rear." In another re-enactment about Caloocan, White shows the battle without any depiction of nurses. In *Advance of Kansas Volunteers at Caloocan* (Edison Manufacturing Co., 1899), we see Americans from behind. When the flag bearer is shot and falls, a soldier immediately picks up the flag and continues carrying it. No attention is given to the fallen soldier.

38. This is the film constructed from the paper print and viewable on the Library of Congress Web site: Library of Congress, American Memory, *The Spanish-American War in Motion Pictures*: http://memory.loc.gov/cgi_bin/query/D?papr:30:./temp/~ ammen_ 67CT8:: (accessed 3 November 2006). The *Edison Films Catalog* describes the film as having a somewhat different narrative: "An illustrated song telling the story of a hero who leaves for the war as a private, is promoted to the rank of captain for bravery in service, meets the girl of his choice, who is a Red Cross nurse on the field, and finally returns home triumphantly as an officer to the father and mother to whom he bade good bye as a private. The film presents this beautiful song picture in six scenes, each of which has a separate song, making the entire series a complete and effective novelty. PARTING.—'Our hero boy has gone.' Words and music. CAMPING.—'What! A letter from home.' Words and music. FIGHTING.—The battle prayer. 'Father, on Thee I Call.' Words and music. CONVALESCING.—'Weeping, Sad and Lonely.' Words and music. SORROWING.—The mother's lament, 'Come back, my dear boy, to me.' Words and music. RETURNING.—When our hero boy comes back again. Hurrah! Hurrah! 'Star Spangled Banner.' Words and music. The above scene can be illustrated either by a soloist, quartet or with an orchestra, and with or without stereopticon slides. This series of animated pictures, when properly illustrated or announced by the stereopticon reading matter, should make a great success." Charles Musser, *Before the Nickelodeon: Edwin S. Porter and the Edison Manufacturing Company* (Berkeley: University of California Press, 1991), 150–151; and *American Film Institute Catalog of Motion Pictures . . . 1893–1910*, 1:1129. Kemp R. Niver, *Motion Pictures from the Library of Congress Paper Print Collection, 1894–1912*, ed. Bebe Bergsten (Berkeley: University of California Press, 1967), describes it in this way: "The first scene shows the dramatic departure for the battlefield of

the only son of a closely knit family. The second shows the battlefield action between American troops and insurrectionists during the Spanish-American War. The third shows the arrival of the wounded hero at a hospital tent and his subsequent release. The fourth and final scene takes place as the hero returns home to his joyful family" (201). The Library of Congress Web site indicates: "Only four of the scenes described in the Edison catalog were submitted for copyright under the title Love and war and thus survive in the Library's paper print copy; two other scenes were likely produced and, perhaps, copyrighted as separate films but then added to the Love and war picture song when sold to fill out the description."

39. Whissel, "Uncle Tom," 389.

40. For earlier discussions of male friendship during war, see Jay Grossman, "Brothers in Arms: Masculinity in Whitman's Civil War," a wide-ranging account focusing on gender and male relationships, http://www.classroomelectric.org/volume2/grossman/gdw.html (accessed 4 November 2006).

ONE. PARADIGMS IN THE SILENT ERA

1. Altman, *Film/Genre*, 219.

2. The penultimate scene of D. W. Griffith's *The Birth of a Nation* (1915) presents a double union of two couples whose romances have figured in the narrative. The last moments of the film are devoted to Griffith's religious-mythic vision of peace.

3. All three of the major silent war films were created in part by filmmakers who had fought in World War I. Laurence Stallings, who lost a leg in combat, wrote the story "Plume" on which his adaptation of *The Big Parade* is based. Along with Maxwell Anderson, he wrote the immensely successful play *What Price Glory?* and assisted Anderson and others in the film adaptation. *Wings'* director William Wellman and author John Monk Saunders had both been fliers in the war.

4. In addition to the positive reviews in *Variety* and the *New York Times*, cited below, Anthony Slide includes two rave reviews from *Photoplay* and an earlier publication form of *Life*. Anthony Slide, *Selected Film Criticism 1921–1930* (Metuchen, N.J.: Scarecrow, 1982), 37–38.

5. See Michael T. Isenberg, "The Great War Viewed from the Twenties: *The Big Parade*," in *Hollywood's World War I: Motion Picture Images*, ed. Peter C. Rollins and John E. O'Connor (Bowling Green, Ohio: Bowling Green State University Popular Press, 1997), 39–58. For other useful material on the films of World War I, see the other essays in this anthology; Leslie Midkiff DeBauche, *Reel Patriotism: The Movies and World War I* (Madison: University of Wisconsin Press, 1997); Michael T. Isenberg, *War on Film: The American Cinema and World War I* (East Brunswick, N.J.: Fairleigh Dickinson University Press, 1981); Andrew Kelly, *All Quiet on the Western Front: The Story of a Film* (London: I. B. Tauris, 1998); and Michael Paris, ed., *The First World War and Popular Cinema: 1914 to the Present* (New Brunswick, N.J.: Rutgers University Press, 2000).

6. Laura Mulvey, "Visual Pleasure and Narrative Cinema," in *Visual and Other Pleasures* (Bloomington: Indiana University Press, 1989), 20–21.

7. Review of *The Big Parade*, 11 November 1925. Similar respect for the film's authenticity appears in a review in the *New York Times*, 20 November 1925: "There are incidents in the film which obviously come from experience, as they are totally different from the usual jumble of war scenes in films. It is because of the realism that the details ring true and it grips the spectator."

8. To this point in the history of the war film, there is only one scene comparable to this in terms of pathos of which I'm aware. In contrast to the anonymous deaths of characters we know nothing about in *Love and War* and the battles in Thomas Ince's Civil War films *The Drummer of the 8th* (1913) and *Granddad* (1913), we know a great deal about two characters who die in D. W. Griffith's *The Birth of a Nation* (1915). Tod Stoneman (Robert Herron) and Wade Cameron (George Beranger), cousins and friends, literally die in each other's arms, united in death although the Civil War has divided their families and the nation. Earlier scenes before the war have demonstrated affection between them, as we see their youthful antics and horseplay. Intertitles describing them as "chums" underscore their close ties and affectionate bonding. Now, at a climactic point in a battle, as Tod prepares to bayonet his "enemy," Griffith shows us Tod's surprise and horror as he discovers that the man about to be attacked is Wade, who is already dead. At that moment Tod is shot and falls onto his cousin, and then dies in a poignant embrace. Griffith's camera dwells on the faces of the dead and dying men as the buddies are reunited in death.

9. The film is not easily available. My commentary is based on a viewing of a print at the UCLA Library. The most recent discussion of the film is by Lea Jacobs, "Men without Women: The Avatars of *What Price Glory*," *Film History: An International Journal* 17.2/3 (2005): 307–333. See Jeanine Basinger's commentary on the film and the way it establishes some of the conventions of the genre in *World War II Combat Film*, especially 84–87.

10. Maxwell Anderson and Laurence Stallings, *What Price Glory?* in *Famous American Plays of the 1920s*, ed. Kenneth MacGowan (New York: Dell, 1959), 61.

11. Santanu Das, "'Kiss Me, Hardy': Intimacy, Gender, and Gesture in World War I Trench Literature," *Modernism/Modernity* 9.1 (2002): 56.

12. Connell, *Masculinities*, 71.

13. Mordaunt Hall, review of *What Price Glory*, *New York Times*, 24 November 1926.

14. Joan Mellen, *Big Bad Wolves: Masculinity in the American Film* (New York: Pantheon, 1977), 43.

15. Ibid.

16. Ibid., 44.

17. Spoto, *Camarado*, 210.

18. Bristow, *Sexuality*, 1.

19. Parker Tyler, *Screening the Sexes: Homosexuality in the Movies* (New York: Da Capo, 1993), 72.

20. Ibid., 73.

21. Kevin Brownlow, *The Parade's Gone By* (Berkeley: University of California Press, 1968), 149.

22. Barry Paris, commentary in chapter 22 of *Flesh and the Devil*, in *The Garbo Silents Collection*, Turner Classic Movie Archives (Turner Entertainment, 2005).

23. Vito Russo, *The Celluloid Closet: Homosexuality in the Movies*, rev. ed. (New York: Harper and Row, 1987), 70. Russo does not identify a source for this quotation. In *Garbo* (Minneapolis: University of Minnesota Press, 1994), Barry Paris presents a similar version of the quotation: "'The hardest thing about that story was the ending,' Brown told writer Scott Eyman. 'How do you have the woman die and the men embrace without making them look like a couple of fairies?'" (119).

24. Mordaunt Hall, review of *Flesh and the Devil*, *New York Times*, 10 January 1927.

25. Tamar Lane, review of *Flesh and the Devil*, *Film Mercury* 5.4 (December 1926), in Slide, *Selected Film Criticism*, 98.

26. Review of *The Big Parade*, *New York Times*, 20 November 1925.

27. Fred., review of *Behind the Front*, *Variety*, 10 February 1926.

28. Mordaunt Hall, review of *Wings*, *New York Times*, 13 August 1927.

29. As far as I know, the first time the song itself appears in a film is in the now-forgotten *My Buddy* (Steve Sekely, 1944), which is about the problems faced by a veteran returning from World War I.

30. Glenn Watkins, *Proof through the Night: Music and the Great War* (Berkeley: University of California Press, 2003), 369.

31. Ibid., 370.

32. Carl Scheele, commentary on band 8, "My Dream of the Big Parade," in *Praise the Lord and Pass the Ammunition: Songs of World Wars I and II* (New York: New World Records, 1977), 3 [inside cover]; "My Dream of the Big Parade" 1926, Mills Music, Inc. Kathryn Kalinac points out that since *The Big Parade* uses lyrics from "You're in the Army, Now" in some of its intertitles, the absence of any lyrics from "My Buddy" implies that it wasn't part of the background music. The score for *The Big Parade* is by William Axt and David Mendoza. "They specialized in exploiting existent musical literature for big orchestral scores, so it's possible they used 'My Buddy.' On the other hand, if Vidor was willing to put the song lyrics into the intertitles for 'You're in the Army, Now,' why didn't he do the same for 'My Buddy' "? E-mail, 21 June 2006. See her invaluable work *Settling the Score: Music and the Classical Hollywood Film* (Madison: University of Wisconsin Press, 1992).

33. *The Celluloid Closet* (Rob Epstein and Jeffrey Friedman, 1996). Anger's commentary on *Wings* appears in chapter 15 of the supplemental material in "Rescued from the Closet," a collection of outtakes added in the special edition of *The Celluloid Closet*. The reviewer for *Variety* comments in a way that confirms her report: "The story? An average tale. And yet it was human enough Friday to make 90 per cent. of the women in the house cry. The director, Wellman, can take credit for that, as the tale is laid out but for one situation: that of the American flyer, John [*sic*], unknowingly shooting down his pal, David, after the latter has escaped from behind the enemy lines in a German plane." Sid., Review of *Wings*, 17 August 1927.

34. Mellen, *Big Bad Wolves*, 86.

35. Ibid., 15.

36. Russo, *Celluloid Closet*, 71–72.

37. Anthony Slide, "The Silent Closet—Homosexuality in Silent Films," *Film Quarterly* (Summer 1999): 25.

38. Sarah Cole, "Modernism, Male Intimacy, and the Great War," *ELH* 68.2 (2001): 470.

39. Ibid., 472.

40. George Chauncey Jr., "Christian Brother or Sexual Perversion? Homosexual Identities and the Construction of Sexual Boundaries in the World War I Era," in *Hidden from History: Reclaiming the Gay and Lesbian Past*, ed. Martin Bauml Duberman, Martha Vicinus, and George Chauncey Jr. (New York: New American Library, 1989), 294–317; John Loughery, *The Other Side of Silence: Men's Lives and Gay Identities: A Twentieth-Century History* (New York: Henry Holt, 1998), 3–16.

41. Chauncey, "Christian Brother," 313.

42. Ibid., 316.

43. Kevin White, *The First Sexual Revolution: The Emergence of Male Heterosexuality in Modern America* (New York: New York University Press, 1993), 65.

44. Both Sigmund Freud's *Three Essays on the Theory of Sexuality* (1905) and Havelock Ellis's *Sexual Inversion* were available in the 1920s. One section of the latter's work is titled

"Sexual Inversion in Men." *Sexual Inversion*, 3rd ed., in *Studies in the Psychology of Sex Complete in Two Volumes* (New York: Random House, 1942).

45. On shell shock and psychiatric treatments, see Elaine Showalter, *The Female Malady: Women, Madness, and English Culture, 1830–1980* (New York: Pantheon, 1985).

TWO. BEYOND TRIANGLES

1. Eve Kosofsky Sedgwick, *Between Men: English Literature and Male Homosocial Desire* (New York: Columbia University Press, 1985).

2. Robin Wood, *Hollywood from Vietnam to Reagan* (New York: Columbia University Press, 1986), 291.

3. Ibid., 293.

4. Ibid.

5. Henry Benshoff, "Reviews of *Mars Attacks!* [Tim Burton, 1996] and *ID4-Independence Day* [Roland Emmerich, 1996]," http:///www.nottingham.ac.uk/film/journal/filmrev/id4-and-mars-attacks.htm (accessed 8 April 2005).

6. Sedgwick, *Between Men*, 21. See also Sedgwick, *Epistemology of the Closet*.

7. Todd Ramlow, "Review of *Ride with the Devil*," http//www.popmatters.com/film/reviews/r/ride/ride-with-the-devi12.shtml (accessed 4 November 2006)

8. John Belton, *American Cinema/American Culture*, 2nd ed. (Boston: McGraw-Hill, 2005), 205.

9. Mark Simpson, *Male Impersonators: Men Performing Masculinity* (New York: Routledge, 1994), 225.

10. Ibid., 226.

11. Ibid., 228.

12. Das, " 'Kiss Me, Hardy,' " 55.

13. Information from chapter 22 on the DVD, conversation between Gordon and Hawke.

14. Das, " 'Kiss Me, Hardy,' " 56. See also Sarah Cole, "Modernism, Male Intimacy, and the Great War," *ELH* 68.2 (2001): 47–72.

15. Das, " 'Kiss Me, Hardy,' " 72.

16. Anthony Easthope, *What a Man's Gotta Do: The Masculine Myth in Popular Culture* (Boston: Unwin Hymen, 1990), 66.

17. Simpson, *Male Impersonators*, 214–215.

18. Easthope, *What a Man's Gotta Do*, 63.

19. Simpson, *Male Impersonators*, 212.

20. Abel., "Review of *Air Force*," *Variety*, 3 February 1943.

21. Bernard Dick, *The Star-Spangled Screen: The American World War II Film*, new ed. (Lexington: University of Kentucky Press, 1985), 141.

22. Clayton R. Koppes and Gregory D. Black, *Hollywood Goes to War: How Politics, Profits, and Propaganda Shaped World War II Movies* (Berkeley: University of California Press, 1987), 304–305.

23. Richard Dyer, "*Papillon*," in *The Matter of Images: Essays on Representation* (New York: Routledge, 1993), 127. The essay originally appeared in *Movie* 27/28 (1980/81).

24. Ibid.

25. Ibid., 128.

26. Ibid.

27. Parker Tyler argues that *The Great Escape* (John Sturges, 1963), possibly the most famous prison camp film set during wartime, is readable as really about "buddy-buddy

homosexuality." But his argument is vitiated by his claim that none of the men refers to any woman or family. In fact, Bartlett (Richard Attenborough) specifically mentions the desire of the men to return to "families and children." Tyler, *Screening the Sexes*, 83.

28. I am grateful to my student James Pettinato for pointing out to me that in the novel by Erich Maria Remarque on which the film is based, their contacts are described in much more sexually evocative terms.

29. The only element in the film that could be read in terms of homosexuality involves the map that leads the men to the gold. Hidden in the anus of one of the Iraqi prisoners, it connects with the various jokes at the time of the Gulf War that conflate "Saddam" and "sodom." See Jonathan Goldberg, *Sodometries: Renaissance Texts, Modern Sexualities* (Palo Alto, Calif.: Stanford University Press, 1992), 1–3.

30. As far as I know, the first such scene in which two soldiers are shown having sex simultaneously with prostitutes occurs in the documentary *Hearts and Minds* (Peter Davis, 1974). The real soldiers there appear to be in adjoining rooms but converse during their sexual activities. *Hamburger Hill* (John Irvin, 1987, which is a fiction film, contains a scene in which two American soldiers are naked with two Vietnamese women in the same hot tub.

31. Dennis Lim concludes his review of the film in the *Village Voice* by remarking on the article that appeared in the October issue of *Interview* at the time of the film's release. Colin Farrell is on the cover, shirtless, poised to throw a football. The inside photographs feature members of the cast, many also shirtless. Lim refers to the film as "a casting director's triumph—a point reinforced in the current *Interview*, where the film is successful reimagined as a homoerotic fashion spread." *Village Voice*, 4–10 October 2000, http://www.villagevoice.com/issues/0040/lim.php (accessed 4 November 2006). How a magazine hypes a film and its stars is one thing; the film itself strenuously rejects any homosexual suggestions.

32. J. Glenn Gray, *The Warriors: Reflections on Men in Battle* (Lincoln: University of Nebraska Pres, 1998), 83.

33. Ibid., 64.

34. Ibid., 90.

35. Ibid., 94.

36. Arthur Miller, *Situation Normal* (New York: Reynal and Hitchcock, 1944), 145. The quotation in Linderman's text is slightly abbreviated: Gerald F. Linderman, *The World within War: American's Combat Experience in World War II* (New York: Free Press, 1997), 282. Miller's initial script for the film was ultimately rejected in favor of a combined script by other writers.

37. Linderman, *World within War*, 279. For treatment of bonding among British soldiers, see Bourke, *Dismembering the Male*, 124–170; Cole, "Modernism"; Das, " 'Kiss Me Hardy' "; and Fussell, *Great War and Modern Memory*, 270–309.

38. Philip Caputo, *A Rumor of War* (New York: Henry Holt, 1996), xvii.

39. Ibid., 103.

40. William Broyles Jr., *Brothers in Arms: A Journey from War to Peace* (Austin: University of Texas Press, 1986), 199–200. See also psychiatrist Robert Jay Lifton's accounts of the intimacy he observed in treating Vietnam War veterans whose experience of bonding helped in the healing process, *Home from the War: Vietnam Veterans: Neither Victims nor Executioners* (New York: Touchstone, 1973), 273–275.

41. Anthony Swofford, *Jarhead: A Marine's Chronicle of the Gulf War and Other Battles* (New York: Scribner, 2003), 195. William Broyles Jr. wrote the screenplay for the film of *Jarhead* (Sam Mendes, 2005), to be discussed in chapter 7.

THREE. DISAVOWING THREATS

1. Vito Russo cites examples of this kind of routine in two Harold Lloyd comedies: *Grandma's Boy* (Fred Newmeyer, 1922) and *The Kid Brother* (Ted Wilde, 1927). In the first, "two men sit on opposite sides of [a woman] on a park bench, each thinking he is holding her hand. When she rises unexpectedly, they discover they have been holding each other's hands." Russo, *Celluloid Closet*, 17.

2. As Thomas Doherty has explained, servicemen overseas were regularly afforded opportunities to watch Hollywood films. *Projections of War*, 75–78. An article in *Time* on domestic camp movie theaters indicated that the most popular films among soldiers were "musicals with girls." "Second Chain," *Time*, 5 July 1943, 96.

3. Review of *Objective, Burma! New York Times*, 27 January 1945.

4. William Menninger, *Psychiatry in a Troubled World: Yesterday's World and Today's Challenge* (New York: Macmillan, 1948), 224; Bérubé, *Coming Out Under Fire*, 37; John D'Emilio, *Sexual Politics, Sexual Communities: The Making of a Homosexual Minority in the United States, 1940–1970* (Chicago: University of Chicago Press, 1983), 25.

5. Bérubé, *Coming Out Under Fire*, 37.

6. See Robert Eberwein, " 'As a Mother Cuddles a Child,': Sexuality and Masculinity in World War II Combat Films," in *Masculinity: Bodies, Movies, Culture*, ed. Peter Lehman (New York: Routledge, 2001), 149–166.

7. National Research Council, *Psychology for the Fighting Man: What You Should Know about Yourself and Others* (Washington, D.C.: Infantry Journal, 1943).

8. Bérubé, *Coming Out Under Fire*, 51. He sees a level of tolerance in the authors' position. In *Masked Men*, Steven Cohan suggests: "The manual's cautious advice about the likelihood of homosexual encounters in the army's all-male environment is . . . quite striking, given the homophobia which erupted in periodic purges of effeminate men during the war and which, more perniciously, came to dominate military policy after the war ended" (86). For additional valuable historical treatments of gays in the military during World War II, see also Costello, *Virtue Under Fire*.

9. "Soldiers and Sex," *Newsweek*, 26 July 1943, 70. *Time's* article about the release of the report did not mention that it talked about sexual matters but stressed what it said about morale and dealing with fear. "Why Men Fight and Fear," *Time*, 11 January 1943, 48, 50.

10. *Newsweek*, "Soldiers and Sex," 72; *Newsweek's* ellipsis.

11. *Newsweek*, back cover, 7 December 1942.

12. *Newsweek*, 9 August 1943, 2.

13. *Time*, 27 July 1942, 1.

14. Butler, *Gender Trouble*, 6.

15. See Thomas Doherty's commentary on this and other relevant films in his chapter "Women without Men," in *Projections of War*, 149–179. For an important discussion of recent depictions of women soldiers, see Yvonne Tasker, "Soldiers' Stories: Women and Military Masculinities in *Courage Under Fire*," in *The War Film*, ed. Robert Eberwein (New Brunswick, N.J.: Rutgers University Press, 2004), 172–189. In her discussion of *Courage Under Fire* (Edward Zwick, 1996) and *G.I. Jane* (Ridley Scott, 1997), Tasker argues that a quality associated with masculinity, such as "a muscular physique," can be a "signifier of strength" for both sexes, not just males. She resists restricting the concept of "masculinity" strictly to men since that guarantees that female and femininity will be necessarily understood in terms of an opposition (178).

16. An earlier example of this maternal behavior occurs in *All Quiet on the Western Front* (Lewis Milestone, 1930). After Paul (Lew Ayres) returns to the front, his first move is to

search for his friend Kat (Lewis Wollheim). After Kat is wounded, Paul tries to giver water to his friend, holding him in his arms, unaware that he has died, a fact the medic conveys to the stunned comrade. This moment of attempted nurturing echoes in a way Paul's first meeting with Kat, when the resourceful scrounger brings food in the form of a pilfered pig to the young men in his company. Thus the maternal function introduced with Kat comes full circle now with Paul. The presence of the maternal, suggested by action or gesture, works to negate any suggestion of a sexual dimension in their relationship.

    17. *Time*, 29 May 1944, inside back cover.

    18. Eddie Rickenbacker, "Pacific Mission [Part I]," *Life*, 25 January 1943, 99–100.

    19. Connell, *Men and the Boys*, 29–30.

    20. See helpful discussions of the film in Basinger, *World War II Combat Film*, 147–154; Doherty, *Projections of War*, 272–274; and Garry Wills, *John Wayne's America: The Politics of Celebrity* (New York: Simon and Schuster, 1997), 149–157.

    21. Alfred C. Kinsey, Wardell B. Pomeroy, and Clyde E. Marx, *Sexual Behavior in the Human Male* (Philadelphia: W. B. Saunders, 1948), 650–651.

    22. The record of the Production Code Administration's approval of the film indicates no concern for the expression "Can this be love?" Part six of the evaluation form, "Sociological Factors," does not have a category for a homosexual relationship since it would have automatically rejected. *Sands of Iwo Jima* file, Margaret Herrick Library, Academy of Motion Picture Arts and Sciences (AMPAS). Reviewers of the film in 1949 commented on the effectiveness of its battle sequences, which included actual combat footage skillfully edited into the scenes shot during the film's production. Reviewers for both the *New York Times* and *Variety* remarked on the clichéd assembly of stock characters associated with the war film genre. Nothing was said about the relationship between Bass and Stryker. Reviews of *Sands of Iwo Jima*: T.M.P., *New York Times*, 31 December, 1949; Herm., *Variety*, 14 December 1949. The reviewer for *Time* was less enthusiastic about the film, calling it "fatiguing" and suggesting "the plot has no more freshness or tug than a military manual, and it is peopled by a movie-hardened cast of characters who have served too many hitches on Hollywood's back-lot battlefields." "New Picture," *Time*, 16 January 1950, 86.

    23. Following the generally negative review of the film in *Time* is a brief article about John Wayne: "[T]he film's greatest asset is leathery, lithe John Wayne. His relaxed acting of a sleepy-eyed, two-fisted he-man (6 ft. 4 in.) has made him a pillar of credibility in many an unlikely blood & thunder epic" (88). Such a comment on Wayne's masculinity is typical of the way critics had described the actor in reviews of his earlier films. The anonymous reviewer in *Time* of *Flying Tigers* (David Miller, 1942) says that Wayne and others in the film "play their parts manfully. John Wayne is a rudimentary actor, but he has the look and bearing, unusual in his trade, of a capable human male." "New Picture," *Time*, 12 October 1942, 96. Bosley Crowther calls him "magnificently robust" in his review of *They Were Expendable* (John Ford, 1945). *New York Times*, 21 December 1945, 25.

    24. "Can this be love?" evokes the use of the line "I love you too" in exchanges between Walter Neff (Fred MacMurray) and Barton Keyes (Edward G. Robinson) in *Double Indemnity* (Billy Wilder, 1944). There is a nonsexual affection between both sets of characters.

    25. See Wills on *Red River* in *John Wayne's America*, 139–149.

    26. William Wharton, *Birdy* (New York: Avon Books, 1980), 27.

    27. Edward Steichen, *The Blue Ghost* (New York: Harcourt, Brace, 1947), 54.

    28. Ibid., 58.

    29. Ibid., 59. Patricia Vettel-Becker has also discussed Steichen's photographs in "Destruction and Delight: World War II Combat Photography and the Aesthetic Inscription of

Masculine Identity," *Men and Masculinities* 5.1 (July 2002): 80–102. She remarks on how some show the men as "free to engage in open expressions of narcissism and erotic contemplation, for any homoerotic contemplations can be displaced onto the ritual framework of the heterosexist military" (84). Evan Bachner has published a collection of dozens of photos by Steichen and other World War II photographers, such as Horace Bristol, who were part of the U.S. Naval Aviation Unit in *At Ease: Navy Men of World War II* (New York: Henry N. Abrams, 2004).

30. In this regard, I am grateful to Krin Gabbard for suggesting the relevance of Roland Barthes, who discusses the concept of "anchorage" in captions. The caption delimits the potential range of meanings in the photograph: "[T]he anchorage may be ideological and indeed this is its principal function; the text *directs* the reader through the signifieds of the image, causing him to avoid some and receive others; by means of an often subtle *dispatching*, it remote-controls him towards a meaning chosen in advance. . . . Anchorage is the most frequent function of the linguistic message and is commonly found in press photographs and advertisements." *Image-Music-Text*, trans. Stephen Heath (New York: Hill and Wang, 1977), 40–41.

31. See three letters from Joseph I. Breen to J. L. Warner in the *Destination Tokyo* file, Margaret Herrick Library, AMPAS: 22 June 1943, 24 June 1943, and 17 August 1943.

32. Letter from Breen to Will Hays, 2 May 1945, Margaret Herrick Library, AMPAS.

33. Robert Plunket, "Classic War Films, Contemporary Echoes," *New York Times*, 21 March 1993. Mike Chopra-Gant discusses a scene in *Blue Skies* (Stuart Heisler, 1946) in which soldiers watch Bing Crosby singing: "One shot . . . shows several soldiers, some stripped to the waist, with their arms around each other's shoulders. While one possible reading of this image could suggest that it suggested a latent homoeroticism within the all-male group, I would argue that there are elements of this scene that function to negate such an interpretation. Although several of the men are bare-chested and the men's bodies do touch each other, the direction of all the men's gazes towards Crosby, singing on a stage in front of them, disavows any sexual element in the physical contact between the men's bodies and instead produces an impression of a masculine closeness—they 'lean on' each other for support—that lacks an erotic component." *Hollywood Genres and Postwar America: Masculinity, Family, and Nation in Popular Movies and Film Noir* (London: I. B. Tauris, 2006), 132.

34. See the file for *Guadalcanal Diary*, Margaret Herrick Library, AMPAS: Breen to Joy, 2 April 1943 and 9 April 1943. A letter of 21 May 1943 voices a similar concern about showing the men collectively "swimming naked." The PCA routinely warned the studios when the scripts seemed to suggest men might be shown nude (or could be inferred to be nude) in scenes of swimming, undergoing physicals, or taking showers. Some of the films in the AMPAS files singled out for this concern include *Bataan*, *The Fighting Seabees* (Edward Ludwig, 1944), *Wing and a Prayer*, *Flying Leathernecks* (Nicholas Ray, 1951), *American Guerrilla in the Philippines* (Fritz Lang, 1950), and *The Young Lions* (Edward Dymtryk, 1958).

35. In this regard, see Christina S. Jarvis, *The Male Body at War: American Masculinity during World War II* (De Kalb: Northern Illinois University Press, 2004), especially 56–85.

36. PCA files, Margaret Herrick Library, AMPAS: 7 July 1950 and 17 July 1951. See Frank Krutnik for examples of reviewers faulting Lewis for his "strident departures from the norms of heterosexual masculinity." *Inventing Jerry Lewis* (Washington, D.C.: Smithsonian Institution Press, 2000), 46. See also Ed Sikov, "Jerry Lewis: Gay Icon from Hell," in *Laughing Hysterically: American Screen Comedy of the 1950s* (New York: Columbia University Press, 1996), 185–190.

37. I do not know the reaction of the PCA to a scene in *Jumping Jacks* (Norman Taurog, 1952) in which Lewis provides a striking example of homosexual buffoonery. Hap Smith (Lewis) has come into the barracks with Chick Allen (Dean Martin) and is getting undressed at his cot. He draws a blanket up so that no one can see him removing his clothes and, while somewhat sensuous music plays on a radio, proceeds to do a striptease. Slowly removing one garment after another, and unaware that Sergeant McClusky (Robert Strauss) is watching him from the doorway, he finally concludes his performance by coyly and quite suggestively rolling his eyes at Chick and another soldier watching from the other side of the blanket.

38. Bérubé, *Coming Out Under Fire*, 298, 341.

39. Doherty notes: "In the combat reports, GI backsides were exposed during scenes of jungle bathing." *Projections of War*, 56.

40. For important arguments about showing males naked, see Peter Lehman, *Running Scared: Masculinity and the Representation of the Male Body* (Philadelphia: Temple University Press, 1993), especially the introduction (1–36) and chapter 8 (147–168).

41. "Picture of the Week," *Life*, 8 February 1943, 24–25.

42. "Guadalcanal," *Life*, 1 March 1943, 68–71.

43. True towel ad no. 2, *Life*, 4 October 1943, inside front cover.

44. "Battle of Buna," *Life*, 15 February 1943, 17–29.

45. The drawing of naked soldiers bathing in the first "true towel" ad was repeated in a much smaller ad for Strathmore Letterhead Papers (owned by Cannon). This ad did not have the insert of the woman, although it offers the qualifying commentary that stresses the need for the refreshment offered by the water. *Time*, 17 April 1944, 93. The caption reads: "Cannon towels get a mighty hand from the boys at the front. A cooling dip . . . a brisk rubdown with a sturdy, durable Cannon towel . . . that's tops after grilling marches or hours of combat under blazing skies and in steaming jungles." D'Emilio refers to a paper by Bérubé, "Marching to a Different Drummer: Coming Out during World War II," given at the American Historical Association Meeting (Los Angeles, 1981), as the source of his information about some of the Cannon towel ads. D'Emilio refers to two in *Life* and one in the *Saturday Evening Post*. I have not seen the ad in the *Post* but assume it reproduced what was in *Life*. D'Emilio does not indicate that the Cannon towel ads include a drawing of a woman. *Sexual Politics*, 26.

46. George H. Roeder Jr., *The Censored War: American Visual Experience of World War Two* (New Haven, Conn.: Yale University Press, 1993), 4–5.

47. Costello, *Virtue Under Fire*, 119.

FOUR. WOUNDS

1. Both Showalter and Bourke describe the effects of "shell shock," the term used to describe the condition identified during World War I. Showalter, *Female Malady*; Bourke, *Intimate History of Killing*. *Regeneration* (Gillies MacKinnon, 1997), based on Pat Barker's novel of the same name, offers a moving treatment of Dr. William Rivers (Jonathan Pryce) and his use of psychotherapy on World War I soldiers.

2. Sonya Michel, "Danger on the Home Front: Manhood, Sexuality, and Disabled Veterans in American Postwar Films," *Journal of the History of Sexuality* 3.1 (July 1992): 109–128; Tania Modleski, "Do We Get to Lose This Time?: Revising the Vietnam War Film," in Eberwein, *War Film*, 155–171; Martin F. Norden, *The Cinema of Isolation: A History*

of Physical Disability in the Movies (New Brunswick, N.J.: Rutgers University Press, 1994); Kaja Silverman, *Male Subjectivity at the Margins* (New York: Routledge, 1992), 52–90.

3. "Spit It Out, Soldier," *Time*, 13 September 1943, 60, 62. Filmic treatment of the effects of shell shock on veterans even extended to Lassie. In *Courage of Lassie* (Fred M. Wilcox, 1946), after Lassie (renamed "Bill" in this film) gets lost from his owner, Kathie (Elizabeth Taylor), he ends up in the army working in the Aleutian Islands. An extended sequence shows him responding to Sergeant Smitty (Tom Drake) in an especially noisy rescue sequence. The traumatized shell-shocked dog is sent back to the United States and eventually finds his way home to Kathie. But his antisocial behavior (raiding chicken coops) leads to a trial over whether he should be put to sleep. A chance discovery of his dog tags (literally—here a number printed within his ear) verifies his status as a soldier, and he is exonerated and returns home to a tearful Kathie. Like any other film made during the war about the service, this, too, has an acknowledgment of gratitude to the armed services: "We tender our appreciation to the office of the Quartermaster General, Army of the United States, for cooperation in parts of this production." *American Film Institute Catalogue of Motion Pictures Produced in the United States, Feature Films 1941–1950*, ed. Patricia King Hanson (Berkeley: University of California Press, 1999), 484.

4. The film, which was released more than one year before *From Here to Eternity* (Fred Zinnemann, 1953), has an extended beach scene in which the director presents the sexual attraction of Stella and Burt for each other. Although not as dramatically staged as that in the later film, nonetheless, for its time, the characters' chaste but prolonged interaction is striking.

5. Gene Evans appeared in a second film Fuller made several months later about the war, *Fixed Bayonets* (1951). Other strong military heroes in the 1950s include Lieutenant Benson (Robert Ryan) and Sergeant Montana (Aldo Ray) in *Men in War* (Anthony Mann, 1957) and Lieutenant Joe Clemens (Gregory Peck) in *Pork Chop Hill* (Lewis Milestone, 1959), based on S. L. A. Marshall's account of the famous battle to take the hill. Some of the most notable box office winners (in millions) in the 1950s include *Mr. Roberts* (John Ford, Mervyn LeRoy, 1955—$8.5), *Battle Cry* (Raoul Walsh, 1955—$8.1), and *To Hell and Back* (Jesse Hibbs, 1955—$6.0). Joel Finler, *The Hollywood Story* (New York: Crown, 1988). Except for the comically inept Captain Morton (James Cagney) in *Mr. Roberts*, all the other soldiers in these films are certainly not experiencing any crisis in masculinity signaled by mental problems. Mr. Roberts (Henry Fonda), who exemplifies quiet and assured leadership, spends the entire film trying to be given the command he should in fact have had in the first place. Major Sam Huxley (Van Heflin), the beloved leader of "Huxley's Harlots" in *Battle Cry*, pushes his men beyond their own conception of their limits, but not his own, and brings them to a new awareness of their own capabilities, especially when he succeeds in having them beat their own record time for a twenty-mile hike. His men are truly shocked and dismayed by his heroic death in battle. Audie Murphy, both the subject and star of *To Hell and Back*, and the most highly decorated soldier in World War II, would have served as a positive reminder to mid-decade audiences of the untroubled power of masculinity, all the more impressive given Murphy's boyish appearance.

6. Norden, *Cinema of Isolation*, 157.

7. Martin F. Norden, "Resexualization of the Disabled War Hero in *Thirty Seconds Over Tokyo*," *Journal of Popular Film and Television* 23.2 (Summer 1995): 53.

8. Ibid., 54.

9. Ibid., 55. This is a domesticated version of the assumption of a paternal role, in contrast to the militarized actions seen in *So Proudly We Hail!* (Mark Sandrich, 1943), described in chapter 3. In *Battle Cry*, Andy Hookens (Aldo Ray) also loses a leg and initially does not want to return to his wife and newborn son because he thinks he'll spend his life as a cripple performing worthless jobs. But he is encouraged by reading his wife's letter describing the baby.

10. See Dana Polan's essay on the role of sexual difference in this film, "Blind Insights and Dark Passages: The Problem of Placement in Forties Film," *Velvet Light Trap* 20 (Summer 1983): 27–33.

11. David A. Gerber, "Heroes and Misfits: The Troubled Social Reintegration of Disabled Veterans in *The Best Years of Our Lives*," *American Quarterly* 46.4 (December 1994): 562.

12. I am grateful to my colleague Andrea Eis for her sharp-eyed observations on this scene.

13. Letter of 27 October 1949 in the file for *The Men*, Margaret Herrick Library, AMPAS. See Christina Jarvis's discussion of the film in *Male Body at War*, 107–112.

14. See Michael Anderegg, "Hollywood and Vietnam: John Wayne and Jane Fonda as Discourse," in *Inventing Vietnam: The War in Film and Television* (Philadelphia: Temple University Press, 1991), 15–32; and Modleski, "Do We Get to Lose This Time?"

15. Dalton Trumbo's *Johnny Got His Gun* (1971) is an interesting variant on the issue of paraplegics and sex experiences. We meet Joe Bonham (Timothy Bottoms), the hero of this film about World War I, when he is completely immobile and totally bandaged. His sexual experience with his girlfriend at home is presented in one of the film's many flashbacks.

16. Kenneth Anger's decision to use a pietà in *Fireworks* (1947) when a sailor carries the hero seems less transgressive now, compared to how it must have been perceived at the time of the film's release.

17. Michael Rogin, *Blackface, White Noise: Jewish Immigrants in the Hollywood Melting Pot* (Berkeley: University of California Press, 1996), 239.

18. Ibid., 241. He notes that "Stanley Kramer [the producer] loved the image so much he used it again a decade later at the climax of *The Defiant Ones*" (239).

19. Ibid., 239. Harry S. Truman banned segregation in the service in 1948.

20. Ibid., 242.

21. E. Ann Kaplan, "Darkness Within: Or, the Dark Continent of Film Noir," in *Looking for the Other: Feminism, Film, and the Imperial Gaze* (New York: Routledge, 1997), 106.

FIVE. DRAG

1. "Shells and Petticoats," *New York Times*, 14 June 1927. The most recent example of drag in a military context appears in *All the Queen's Men* (Stefan Rusowitzky, 2001), in which soldiers pretend to be women in order to find out what secrets the Germans have about an upcoming military operation.

2. Roger Baker, *Drag: A History of Female Impersonation in the Performing Arts* (New York: New York University Press, 1994); Rebecca Bell-Meterau, *Hollywood Androgyny*, 2nd ed. (New York: Columbia University Press, 1993); Bérubé, *Coming Out Under Fire*; David A. Boxwell, "The Follies of War: Cross-Dressing and Popular Theater on the British Front Lines, 1914–18," *Modernism/Modernity* 9.1 (2002): 1–20; Marjorie Garber, *Vested Interests: Cross-Dressing and Cultural Anxiety* (New York: Harper Perennial, 1993); Russo, *Celluloid Closet*; Simpson, *Male Impersonators*; Chris Straayer, *Deviant Eyes, Deviant*

Bodies: Sexual Re-orientation in Film and Video (New York: Columbia University Press, 1996); Tyler, *Screening the Sexes*.

3. Boxwell, "Follies of War," 16–17.

4. Ibid., 17.

5. Steve Neale, "Masculinity as Spectacle: Reflections on Men and Mainstream Cinema," *Screen* 24.6 (1983): 2–17.

6. Butler, *Gender Trouble*, 137.

7. *Soldier's Girl* (Frank Pierson, 2003), discussed in chapter 6, is relevant in this regard. The transvestite drag act put on by Calpurnia Addams is a function of the character's transgendered condition, and not there to produce laughter in the viewers of the film. The act does, of course, produce a different kind of response from most of the loutish soldiers there to indulge in the cross-dressing.

8. The film grossed $8.5 million. Warner Bros. turned back all profits after actual costs to the Army Emergency Relief Fund. All contract players from Warners also donated their salaries to this. *New York Times*, 29 July 1943. It was Warner Bros.' most successful film of the decade and the fourth highest grossing film of all the studios in the 1940s, succeeded only by *The Best Years of Our Lives* (William Wyler, 1946), *Duel in the Sun* (King Vidor, 1946), and *Samson and Delilah* (Cecil B. DeMille, 1949). Finler, *Hollywood Story*, 240. Significantly, it was the highest-grossing film having World War II as its focus of any film actually made and shown during the war. All the reviews I could find of the film were laudatory. For a comprehensive discussion of the film, see David Culbert, "*This Is the Army*," *History Today* 50.4 (April 2000), http://www.historytoday.com/dm_getArticle.asp?gid=13964 (accessed 5 November 2006); Dan Caban, "*This Is the Army* (1943): The Show Musical Goes to War," *Film and History* 27.1–4 (1997): 54–60; and Laurence Bergren, "Irving Berlin *This Is the Army*," *Prologue: Quarterly of the National Archives and Records Administration* 28.2 (Summer 1996), http://www.archives.gov/publications/prologue/1996/summer/irving-berlin-2.html (accessed 5 November 2006).

9. The documentary *The Negro Soldier* (Stuart Heisler, 1944), released in April 1944, some nine months after *This Is the Army*, focuses exclusively on the African American soldier as a fighting man. It begins in a church with a mother reading a letter from her son describing his experiences in basic training and in adjusting to military life. Although African Americans and whites are together in the early stages of the induction process, the men are soon segregated into different racial divisions. *Stormy Weather* (Andrew Stone, 1943), which opened eight days before *This Is the Army*, acknowledges the contributions of African American soldiers in both World War I and World War II by beginning with the return of Bill Williamson (Bill Robinson) from the service in 1918 and concluding with the departure of a young man for duty in 1943.

10. Bérubé, *Coming Out Under Fire*, 80.

11. "New Picture," *Time*, 16 August 1943, 93–94.

12. *Life* ran an article on the stage version on 20 July 1942 (73–75). The same year *Life* had published an article in its "Speaking of Pictures" section with photographs of an all-male GI drag production at Camp Lee, Virginia, of Clare Boothe's *The Women*. *Life*, 2 December 1942, 14–16.

13. Bérubé, *Coming Out Under Fire*, 88

14. Ibid.

15. Marjorie Garber suggests that hitting Luther with a dart is a "joking version of anal penetration" that "remains, on the surface, as unthreatening as does the whole representation of switched gender roles." *Vested Interests*, 58.

16. In an earlier scene, two marines (one shirtless) dance to "Chattanooga Choo-Choo," which is being played on a harmonica. They are clearly presented as entertaining their fellow troops, who are watching appreciatively. Taxi Potts enters (holding the group's mascot dog) and talks about a conversation he had with a woman who was rejecting his advances. The dance continues, off camera, and then is seen again as Malone (Lloyd Nolan) announces lights out and "quit your skylarking." The dance concludes as the shirtless man jumps into the arms of his partner. A number of other films made during World War II show soldiers dancing with each other. These scenes appear in documentaries, such as *The Story of a Transport* (1944), which presents information about the *Wakefield*, a Coast Guard ship used as a transport vehicle for the army; *V.D. Control: The Story of D.E. 733*, a training film on venereal disease made by Paramount for the navy (1945); and *Since You Went Away* (John Cromwell, 1944), the well-known film about the home front.

17. On the importance of Betty Grable during World War II, see Robert B. Westbrook, " 'I Want a Girl Just Like the Girl That Married Harry James': American Women and the Problem of Obligation in World War II," *American Quarterly* 42.4 (December 1990): 587–614.

18. Letter from Breen in the *Stalag 17* file, Margaret Herrick Library, AMPAS, 10 March 1952.

19. Stacy Peebles Power, "The Other World of War: Terrence Malick's Adaptation of *The Thin Red Line*," in *The Cinema of Terrence Malick: Poetic Visions of America*, ed. Hannah Patterson (London: Wallflower Press, 2004), 151.

20. Stanley Kauffmann, "Thanks Anyway," *New Republic*, 13 June 1964, 33. The scene isn't mentioned in the PCA file on the film at the Margaret Herrick Library, AMPAS.

21. Although different in kind, the melancholy negative aspects of the scene in *La Grande Illusion* (Jean Renoir, 1936) come to mind. No comparable scene appears in Terrence Malick's 1998 version.

22. Straayer, *Deviant Eyes*, 43–44.

23. Ibid., 52.

24. Peter Wollen only mentions the film briefly in terms of "sex-reversal and role-reversal" in his well-known commentary on Hawks in "The *Auteur* Theory," in *Movies and Methods: An Anthology*, ed. Bill Nichols (Berkeley: University of California Press, 1976), 535. Catherine is actually one of Hawks's strongest heroines in that she directs the action.

25. Bell-Metereau, *Hollywood Androgyny*, 49–50.

SIX. "DON'T ASK, DON'T TELL"

1. See Frank Walsh, *Sin and Censorship: The Catholic Church and the Motion Picture Industry* (New Haven, Conn.: Yale University Press, 1996); Leonard J. Leff and Jerold L. Simmons, *The Dame in the Kimono: Hollywood, Censorship, and the Production Code*, rev. ed. (Lexington: University of Kentucky Press, 2001).

2. Bérubé, *Coming Out Under Fire*; in particular, see chapter 4, " 'The Gang's All Here': The Gay Life and Vice Control," 98–127, and chapter 7, "Comrades in Arms," 175–200. See also Costello, *Virtue Under Fire*; D'Emilio, *Sexual Politics*; D'Emilio and Freedman, *Intimate Matters*; Loughery, *Other Side of Silence*; George Chauncey, *Gay New York, Urban Culture, and the Makings of the Gay World 1890–1940* (New York: Basic Books, 1994); Cohan, *Masked Men*; and Fussell, *Wartime*.

3. Bérubé, *Coming Out Under Fire*, 186.

4. Studs Terkel, *The Good War: An Oral History of World War Two* (New York: Pantheon, 1984), 178–185.

5. Fred Rochlin, *Old Man in a Baseball Cap: A Memoir of World War II* (New York: Harper Collins, 1999). Thanks to Tim Moran for drawing my attention to this work.

6. C. Tyler Carpenter and Edward H. Yeatts, *Stars without Garters: The Memoirs of Two Gay GIs in WWII* (San Francisco: Alamo Square Press, 1996). I am grateful to Steven Cohan for introducing me to this book. See also Robert Peters's account of his military and sexual experiences in *For You, Lili Marlene: A Memoir of World War II* (Madison: University of Wisconsin Press, 1995).

7. See also Colin J. Martin and Martin S. Weinberg, *Homosexuals and the Military* (New York: Harper and Row, 1971).

8. With one exception, discussed below, I am excluding made-for-television films. Three recount historical events. *Sergeant Matlovich vs. the U.S. Air Force* (Paul Lief, 1978) is about Leonard Matlovich (Brad Dourif), whose admission of homosexuality prompted legal battles and drew public attention to the presence of gays in the military. Matlovich was on the cover of *Time*, 8 September 1975. *Serving in Silence: The Margarethe Cammermayer Story* (Jeff Bleckner, 1995) concerns Cammermayer (Glenn Close), a colonel in the army who falls in love with Diane (Judy Davis), an artist. Cammermayer successfully challenges the army's move to dismiss her. *A Glimpse of Hell* (Mikael Salomon, 2001) recounts the story of an explosion on the USS *Iowa* in 1989 and how a subsequent investigation clears a gay man who was suspected of having caused it. The others are not drawn from history. *Fifth of July* (Kirk Burney and Marshall W. Mason, 1982) is an adaptation of Langford Wilson's play about a gay Vietnam veteran (Richard Thomas) and his lover (Jeff Daniels). *Dress Gray* (Glenn Jordan, 1986; script by Gore Vidal and Lucien Truscott) is not about war but takes place at the "U.S. Grant Military Academy" and involves investigation of a gay cadet's murder by another cadet on the base. Alec Baldwin is falsely accused of the crime but successfully identifies the killer. *A Friend of Dorothy* is one of three stories in *Common Ground* (Donna Deitch, 2000); it concerns the exposure of a lesbian (Brittany Murphy) in the navy and her gay sailor friend (Jason Priestly).

9. This intense valorization of the rigors and advantages of military life proceeding from a closeted gay man evokes the kinds of attitudes described by Klaus Theweleit. In particular, see "Homosexuality and the White Terror," in *Male Fantasies*, Vol. 2, *Male Bodies: Psychoanalyzing the White Terror*, trans. Erica Carter and Chris Turner (Minneapolis: University of Minnesota Press, 1989), 306–346. This and *Male Fantasies*, Vol. 1, *Women, Floods, Bodies, History*, trans. Stephen Conway (Minneapolis: University of Minnesota Press, 1987), provide an interesting background against which to position Penderton's attitudes.

10. Allen Conan and Harry Lawton, *John Huston: A Guide to References and Resources* (New York: McGraw Hill, 1997), suggest: "The action takes place in an army camp just after World War II, and the theme is repressed homosexuality in the military; but in 1967 any ironical reference to the behavior of those thrust into close proximity in a military environment evoked the then-current turmoil over Vietnam" (15–16). See Stephen Cooper, "Political *Reflections in a Golden Eye*," in *Reflections in a Male Eye: John Huston and the American Experience*, ed. Gaylyn Studlar and David Desser (Washington, D.C.: Smithsonian Institution Press, 1993), 97–116. He is primarily interested in positioning the film in relation to the political and military tensions of the day in Vietnam rather than the film's treatment of sexuality.

11. Pauline Kael, "Making Lawrence More Lawrentian," in *Going Steady* (Boston: Little, Brown, 1970), 40. See the commentary of Tyler, *Screening the Sexes*, 259–261; and Russo, *Celluloid Closet*, 166.

12. I have been unable to see *The Sergeant*. According to Jennifer Ormson of the Library of Congress, the "reference copy . . . is in an advanced state of decomposition. The film cannot be rewound or viewed on a flatbed without seriously damaging the copy. In order to prevent further harm to the print, I'm withdrawing it from researcher access." E-mail, 22 December 2005. The American Film Institute's plot summary indicates that, like Penderton, the hero is a closeted military leader: "M. Sgt. Albert Callan [Rod Steiger], who distinguished himself in World War II by strangling a German soldier with his bare hands, is assigned to a petroleum supply depot in France. Upon discovering that the camp lacks discipline under the leadership . . . Callan seizes command and imposes his own strict military standards on the resentful men. At the same time he is attracted, almost subconsciously, to handsome young Pfc. Tom Swanson [John Phillip Law]. After forcing the hardworking Swanson to become his orderly room clerk, Callan tries to monopolize the private's time and even refuses to issue him passes to date his French girl friend, Solange. Mistaking the sergeant's attentions for loneliness, Swanson begins to spend more time with Callan, but after the sergeant succeeds in driving away Solange, Swanson realizes the truth and openly defies his superior. Driven to excessive drinking, Callan desperately attempts to make love to Swanson and is violently rejected. . . . Callan takes a rifle from the company armory, goes to a nearby woods, and kills himself." *The American Film Institute Catalog of Motion Pictures Produced in the United States, Feature Films 1961–1970*, ed. Richard Krafsur (Berkeley: University of California Press, 1976), 961. According to Tyler, "all that Callan does . . . is to clutch Swanson and place a full-throated smack on his lips when he can control himself no longer." *Screening the Sexes*, 258. Russo thinks that "neither *The Sergeant* nor *Reflections in a Golden Eye* offers the possibility of homosexual relationships; they deal only in sexually motivated manipulations, spitefulness and petty jealousy, most of it unconscious and unexplored. The result is caricature." *Celluloid Closet*, 167. In *The Big Red One* (Sam Fuller, 1980; reconstructed, 1984), as the sergeant (Lee Marvin) lies helplessly in a Tunisian hospital, a gay German orderly kisses him twice, the second time quite forcefully on the mouth. The sergeant responds by extending his arm and seriously choking the man.

13. Katherine Kinney, speaking of the script of the play, observes: "In expressing his desire for Billy, Richie continually suggests that Billy is denying his own homoerotic feelings." *Friendly Fire*, 132.

14. Vincent Canby's negative review pointed out that "Mitchell Lichtenstein plays Richie, the homosexual soldier, so broadly that the question of whether or not Richie 'is' or 'isn't,' which is supposed to be the trigger for the melodrama, doesn't exist in the movie." "*Streamers* Adapted by Altman: Film Festival," *New York Times*, 9 October 1983.

15. See Gary L. Lehring, *Officially Gay: The Political Construction of Sexuality by the U.S. Military* (Philadelphia: Temple University Press, 2003). In "Gays in the Military," he notes that beginning in 1982, "most service members discharged for homosexuality have received honorable discharges, but this was not the case in the past" (107).

16. For a thorough survey of the policy and its place in American culture, see Lehring, *Officially Gay*; and the collection of essays edited by Gregory M. Herek, Jared B. Jobe, and Ralph M. Carney, *Out in Force: Sexual Orientation and the Military* (Chicago: University of Chicago Press, 1996). Janet E. Halley offers a penetrating critique of the policy in *Don't: A Reader's Guide to the Military's Anti-Gay Policy* (Durham, N.C.: Duke University Press, 1999): "Every moving part of the new policy is designed to *look like* conduct regulation in order to *hide* the fact that it turns decisively on status. At least the old policy was as bad as it looked; problems of deceptive appearance, ruse, tautology, and outright misrepresentation make the new

policy a regulatory Trojan Horse" (2). The Center for the Study of Sexual Minorities in the Military maintains a Web site that monitors and updates relevant incidents in connection with the implementation of the policy and the treatment of gays in general: http://www. gaymilitary.ucsb.edu (accessed 5 November 2006). The Robert Crown Law Library at Stanford Law School, where Janet Halley is a professor, has created the "Don't Ask, Don't Tell, Don't Pursue" database: http://www.stanford.edu (accessed 5 November 2006). See "About Don't Ask, Don't Tell" on the Web site maintained by the Servicemembers Legal Defense Network:http://www.sldn.org/templates/dont/record.html?section=42&record=749 (accessed 5 November 2006).

17. James Keller and William Glass, "*In & Out*: Self-Referentiality and Hollywood's 'Queer' Politics," *Journal of Popular Film and Television* 26.3 (Fall 1998): 137.

18. The makeup evokes the later moments of *Death in Venice* (Luchino Visconti, 1971), when Aschenbach (Dirk Bogarde) begins applying cosmetics to make himself more appealing to Tadziu (Bjorn Andresen).

19. The film was shown at both the Sundance and the Tribeca film festivals in 2003 but not released in theaters.

20. See Roger Ebert, "*Basic*," 28 March 2003, www.rogerebert.com (accessed 5 November 2006); Elvis Mitchell, "And Then There Were Two (Plus a Mystery)," *New York Times*, 28 March 2003; Peter Travers "*Basic*," *Rolling Stone*, 17 April 2003, 110. Ebert puts the film in "a genre that we could call the Jerk-Around Movie, because what it does is jerk you around. It sets up a situation and then does a bait and switch. You never know which walnut the truth is under. You invest your trust and are betrayed."

21. The Israeli film *Yossi & Jagger* (Eytan Fox, 2002) presents a much more sympathetic treatment of gay soldiers.

SEVEN. BODIES, WEAPONS

1. *The 20th Anniversary Collector's Edition* (2006) contains a deleted scene that occurs outdoors in which King introduces Chris to pot.

2. John Newsinger, "'Do You Walk the Walk?' Aspects of Masculinity in Some Vietnam War Films," in *You Tarzan: Movies and Men*, ed. Pat Kirkham and Janet Thumim (New York: St. Martin's Press, 1993), refers to Chris's visit to the lair as "a remarkable 'bordello' scene. . . . The scene is charged with sexuality and homoeroticism" (129). Margaret O'Brien suggests that Elias's "attractiveness to Taylor alternates between the paternal (when the new recruit collapses from heat exhaustion en route through the jungle, Elias in a protective gesture takes his pack) and the homoerotic (when he is initiated into the world of off-duty hedonism Elias offers Taylor his 'smoke' through the barrel of a rifle suggestively cocked into his mouth)." "Changing Places: Men and Women in Oliver Stone's Vietnam," in *Me Jane: Masculinity, Movies and Women*, ed. Pat Kirkham and Janet Thumim (New York: St. Martin's Press, 1995), 264–265.

3. The published script contains an extended description by Elias of his encounter with a prostitute on the beach while on leave. Oliver Stone and Richard Boyle, *Oliver Stone's Platoon and Salvador: The Original Screenplays* (New York: Vintage Books, 1987), 48–50.

4. Mikhail Bakhtin, introduction to *Rabelais and His World*, trans. Hélène Iswolsky (Bloomington: Indiana University Press, 1984), 10.

5. Ibid., 75.

6. Gilbert Adair, *Hollywood's Vietnam* (London: Heinemann, 1989), 157.

7. Gustav Hasford, *The Short-Timers* (New York: Harper and Row, 1979).

8. The first example I am aware of in fiction occurs in Leon Uris's *Battle Cry*, which appeared the same year as *Take the High Ground*. Although the raunchier version occurs in the novel, the 1955 film of *Battle Cry* (Raoul Walsh) didn't include any version of it. Leon Uris, *Battle Cry* (New York: G. P. Putnam's Sons, 1953), 58.

9. Bourke, *Intimate History of Killing*, 132.

10. Stephen E. Ambrose, *Band of Brothers: E Company, 506th Regiment, 101st Airborne from Normandy to Hitler's Eagle's Nest* (New York: Touchstone, 1992), 20. This instruction does not appear in the HBO series produced by Steven Spielberg, Tom Hanks, and Ambrose (David Frankel, Tom Hanks, and others, 2001).

11. William T. Paull, *The Memoirs of William T. Paull: From Butte to Iwo Jima*, chapter 5, http://www.sihope.com/~tipi/marine.html (accessed 13 July 2004); Leonard E. Skinner, *One Man's View: The Book*, chapter 2, http://www.peak.org/~skinncr/oneman/chapter2.html (accessed 9 November 2006). E. B. Sledge describes another version of the punishment that occurred at the camp in San Diego in 1943 when a recruit used the wrong word: "The DI muttered some instructions to him, and the recruit blushed. He began trotting up and down in front of the huts holding his rifle in one hand and his penis in the other, chanting, 'This is my rifle,' as he held up his M1, 'and this is my gun,' as he moved his other arm. 'This is for Japs,' he again held up his M1; 'and this is for fun,' he held up his other arm." *With the Old Breed at Peleliu and Okinawa* (New York: Oxford University Press, 1990), 10. In *The Short-Timers*, even though the men do not appear to have used the wrong terminology, "Sergeant Gerheim orders us to doubletime around the squad bay with our penises in our left hands and our weapons in our right hands, singing: *This is my rifle, this is my gun; one is for fighting and one is for fun.* And: *I don't want no teen-aged queen; all I want is my M-14*" (11). Amos Williams, who served in Vietnam, learned the chant during basic training as: "This is my rifle, this is my gun. This is for killing, this is for fun." See also Richard Allen Burns, " 'This Is My Rifle, This Is My Gun . . .': Gunlore in the Military," *New Directions in Folklore* 7.7 (2003), http://www.temple.edu/lsllc/newfolk/journal_archive.html (accessed 6 November 2006).

12. Mark Baker, *Nam: The Vietnam War in the Words of the Men and Women Who Fought There* (New York: Quill, 1982): 206.

13. David Grossman, *On Killing: The Psychological Cost of Learning to Kill in War and Society* (Boston: Little, Brown, 1995): 350.

14. Ibid., 136. Joshua S. Goldstein, *War and Gender: How Gender Shapes the War System and Vice Versa* (Cambridge: Cambridge University Press, 2001), 349, also refers to this passage.

15. Bourke, *Intimate History of Killing*, 132.

16. Cynthia J. Fuchs, " 'Vietnam and Sexual Violence': The Movie," in *America Rediscovered: Critical Essays on Literature and Film of the Vietnam War*, ed. Owen W. Gilman Jr. and Lorrie Smith (New York: Garland, 1990), 126.

17. Ibid., 127. Anthony Swofford, who served as a marine in the first Iraq war, offers another perspective on the relationship: "Too much time and energy are expended during boot camp and subsequent rifle-training sessions convincing the marine that he must covet his weapons system as he does his girl back home, his girl back home a beautiful and noble creature, and so too his weapons system a beautiful and noble creature, capable of both saving the marine's life and jeopardizing the marine's life, causing him either joy or grief. The paradoxes of love are the paradoxes, the lesson goes, the thing you love most deeply might someday fail you." *Jarhead*, 57.

18. Adrienne Rich, "Caryatid: Two Columns," in *On Lies, Secrets, and Silence: Selected Prose 1966–1978* (New York: Norton, 1991), 114–115.

19. Grossman, *On Killing*, 137.

20. Carol Burke, "Marching to Vietnam," *Journal of American Folklore* 102.406 (October–December 1989): 427.

21. R. Wayne Eisenhart, "You Can't Hack It Little Girl: A Discussion of the Covert Psychological Agenda of Modern Combat Training," *Journal of Social Issues* 31.4 (1975): 15.

22. James McBride, *War, Battering, and Other Sports: The Gulf between Men and Women* (Atlantic Highlands, N.J.: Humanities Press, 1995), 55.

23. I am grateful to Dennis Peterson for having introduced me to this expression.

24. See Ross E. Milloy, "Survey on Gays Rings True to Some in Military," *New York Times*, 26 March 2000. Milloy interviews Dennis Dunn, who is speaking about his army experiences in the 1980s and 1990s. "Sometimes, said Mr. Dunn, who was a staff sergeant, the penalty for being identified as a homosexual took an uglier turn. 'If someone was gay and got left in the unit for a while there would be a "blanket party," ' he said, 'where they'd grab the guy during the middle of the night, wrap him in a blanket, and pound on him with socks stuffed with bars of soap.' " See also Kevin Heldeman, "On the Town with the U.S. Military in Korea," *Z Magazine* (February 1997), http://www.zmag.org/zmag/articles/feb97army.html (accessed 9 November 2006).

25. Paula Willoquet-Maricondi sees the attack on Pyle as a means of bringing the recruits together: "This is the film's—and the Marine Corps'—version of male bonding." "Full-Metal-Jacketing, or Masculinity in the Making," *Cinema Journal* 33.2 (1994): 17.

26. Susan White, "Male Bonding, Hollywood Orientalism, and the Repression of the Feminine in Kubrick's *Full Metal Jacket*," in *Inventing Vietnam: The War in Film and Television*, ed. Michael Anderegg (Philadelphia: Temple University Press, 1991), 212.

27. Stephanie Howse, E-mail, 17 April 2002.

28. Fuchs, "Vietnam and Sexual Violence," 129.

29. Tania Modleski argues: "For these men, whose transformation in boot camp came when they graduated from being a bunch of 'ladies,' as the gunnery sergeant calls them, to a platoon of hardened marines, the moral of the encounter might be summarized, 'We have met the enemy and she is us.' In this way Kubrick's film shows that an important objective of war is to subjugate femininity and keep it at a distance." Modleski connects the killing of the sniper with the records of soldiers used by Klaus Theweleit in his account of the Freikorps: "The ending of the film thus corroborates Theweleit's finding that the war fantasies he studied invariably build to a climax in which the woman/enemy is rendered a bloody mass." "A Father Is Being Beaten," in *Feminism without Women: Culture and Criticism in a "Postfeminist" Age* (New York: Routledge, 1991), 62.

30. Baker, *Nam*, 321. See Susan Brownmiller, *Against Our Will: Men, Women, and Rape* (New York: Fawcett Columbine, 1993), 86–113, for a detailed discussion of reports on rape during the Vietnam War, including rape-murders.

31. Gavin Smith, "Body Count: Rabe and De Palma's Wargasm," *Film Comment* 25.4 (July-August 1989): 50.

32. Ruth Seifert, "War and Rape: Analytical Approaches," Women's International League for Peace and Freedom, http://www.wilpf.int.ch/publications/1992ruthseifert.htm (accessed 6 November 2006). See also Susan Gubar, " 'This Is My Rifle, This Is My Gun': World War II and the Blitz on Women," in *Behind the Lines: Gender and the Two World Wars*, ed. Margaret Randolph Higonet, Jane Jenson, Sonya Michel, and Margaret Collins

Weitz (New Haven, Conn.: Yale University Press, 1987): "In the effort to differentiate . . . homosocial eroticism from homosexuality, both the absent woman and the whore play crucial roles, for—as the imagined object of male desire and as the body that links men to men—they ratify men as male" (254).

33. Goldstein, *War and Gender*, 359.

34. Jeremy M. Devine, *Vietnam at 24 Frames a Second* (Austin: University of Texas Press, 1999), 300.

35. Earl G. Ingersoll, "The Construction of Masculinity in Brian De Palma's Film *Casualties of War*," *Journal of Men's Studies* 4.1 (August 1995): 32.

36. Ibid., 36.

37. Jeffords, *Remasculinization of America*, 69.

38. Peter Ehrenhaus, "Why We Fought: Holocaust Memory in Spielberg's *Saving Private Ryan*," *Critical Studies in Media Communication* 18.3 (September 2001): 327–328.

39. Karen Jaehne, "*Saving Private Ryan*," *Film Quarterly* 53.1 (Fall 1999): 39.

40. Amy Taubin, review of *Saving Private Ryan*, *Village Voice*, 28 July 1998, 113.

41. Ehrenhaus, "Why We Fought," 325.

42. Ibid., 328.

43. Ibid.

44. Doherty, *Projections of War*, 307.

45. Christopher Caldwell, "Spielberg at War," *Commentary* 106.4 (October 1998): 49. Spielberg made this comment in an interview with Richard Grenier, *Washington Times*, 8 August 1998.

46. Stephen J. Dubner, "Inside the Dream Factory," *Guardian Unlimited*, 21 March 1999, http://film.guardian.co.uk/The_Oscars_1999/Story/0,4135,36555,00.html (accessed 6 November 2006). Richard T. Jameson accepts Spielberg's assertion about Upham: "we have Spielberg's own word that Upham is 'me,' the character untried by combat and hence a natural surrogate for an audience that is thrown into the thick of battle and forced somehow to get with the program." "History's Eyes: *Saving Private Ryan*," *Film Comment* (September–October 1998): 23.

47. Grossman, *On Killing*, 137.

48. Goldstein, *War and Gender*, 359.

EIGHT. FATHERS AND SONS

1. Tom Brokaw, *The Greatest Generation* (New York: Delta, 1998); Tom Brokaw, *The Greatest Generation Speaks: Letters and Reflections* (New York: Delta, 1999); Tom Brokaw, *An Album of Memories: Personal Histories from the Greatest Generation* (New York: Random House, 2001). Two videos complement the books: *The Greatest Generation* (1999) and *The Greatest Generation Speaks Father's Day: Now and Forever* (2001). The latter was originally shown on NBC's *Dateline* and released in July 2001. Terkel, *Good War*. Both Brokaw and Terkel include reminiscences from women in their books.

2. Catherine Kodat, "Saving Private Property: Steven Spielberg's American Dreamworks," *Representations* 71 (Summer 2000): 78.

3. Basinger, *World War II Combat Film*, 261. See also Krin Gabbard and William Luhr, who explore more skeptically the ideological implications of valorizing earlier generations. Gabbard sees *Saving Private Ryan* supporting "conservative retrenchment through nostalgia for the war years." "Saving Private Ryan Too Late," in *The End of Cinema As We Know It: American Cinema in the Nineties*, ed. Jon Lewis (New York: New York University Press, 2001), 132. Luhr thinks *Saving Private Ryan*, *Pearl Harbor*, *Braveheart* (Mel Gibson, 1995), *Gladiator*

(Ridley Scott, 2000), and *The Patriot* (Roland Emmerich, 2000) "associate national continuity with the survival of the nuclear family and place the futures of both nation and family in the hands of a patriarchal hero, one who embodies multiple forms of masculine potency.... This assertion of male dominance as an historical imperative can be seen as triggered by widespread anxieties ... about loss of cultural privilege to various 'others,' such as women, people of color, and gays and lesbians." "Pearl Harbor: Surprise Attack or SOS?" Paper presented at the 2002 Florida State University Conference on Film and Literature.

4. Doherty, *Projections of War*, 301.

5. Albert Auster, "*Saving Private Ryan* and American Triumphalism," in Eberwein, *War Film*, 212. See also Richard Goldstein, "World War II Chic," *Village Voice*, 13–19 January 1999, 42, 44, 47. Speaking of *Saving Private Ryan* and *The Thin Red Line* (Terrence Malick, 1998), he argues: "Fathers and sons: this is the heart of the modern combat film, and the real issue it addresses. This explains why the new generation of war movies leaves so little room for romance. The real passion is the bond between men, and the closet thing to a fervent embrace occurs when the living nurse the dying. ... [F]or guys, honoring the father also means reclaiming a world where (white) men were men and everyone else stayed out of sight" (47).

6. Linda Hutcheon, "Irony, Nostaliga, and the Postmodern," 1998, http://www.library.utoronto.ca/utel/criticism/hutchinp.html (accessed 7 November 2006).

7. A particularly transgressive parody of *Saving Private Ryan* appeared as a streaming video on the Web in 1998, *Saving Ryan's Privates* (Craig Moss). Instead of searching for the man to bring him home, soldiers have to find his genitals, which have been shot off. At various points the parody is quite clever, such as its imitation of the sonorous voice of the secretary of war, who orders the search, and the music, which shamelessly evokes the compositional style of John Williams. At times the over-the-top excess is sophomoric, such as one scene in which the soldiers sift through genitals looking for Ryan's. The ending reveals that Ryan (who has been identified earlier as married) is gay. The parody ends with Ryan standing by a gravesite accompanied by his young male lover. Ryan says, "Tell me I used it well," The young man touches the front of Ryan's pants, which cover a clearly outlined penis, and says yes.

8. The HBO series *Band of Brothers* (Steven Spielberg, Tom Hanks, and Stephen Ambrose, executive producers, 2001) is certainly relevant in this regard. Ambrose was a consultant for *Saving Private Ryan*. His book *Band of Brothers* is the basis for the eleven-part series that follows E Company, 506th Regiment, 101st Airborne, from its training in Georgia through D-Day, the campaign in Europe, the Battle of the Bulge, the liberation of one concentration camp, and the occupation of Hitler's lair. The series ends with a powerfully moving reunion in which we see the survivors, who have served as introducers to individual shows, and their children. See Thomas Schatz, "Old War/New War: *Band of Brothers* and the Revival of the World War II War Film," *Film and History* 32.1 (2002): 74–78.

9. The love triangle appears to invite the kind of analysis employed by critics using Eve Kosofsky Sedgwick's model, discussed in chapter 2. Although they do not mention Sedgwick's theoretical position, at least two reviewers have talked about the love between Danny and Rafe. Carl Cortez observes: "Knowing mass destruction wouldn't cut it for a movie like this–even though it worked in *Armageddon*—director Michael Bay and screenwriter Randall Wallace pay even more attention to the two love stories in the film which *Pearl Harbor* is really about. The first is the one between two close friends Rafe ... and Danny. ... Their friendship and undying brotherly love for each other is [*sic*] put to the test when they both fall for the same woman." *IF Magazine*, 25 May 2001,

Martha Vicinus, and George Chauncey Jr., 294–317. New York: New American Library, 1989.

Cohan, Steven. *Masked Men: Masculinity and Movies in the Fifties*. Bloomington: Indiana University Press, 1997.

Cole, Sarah. "Modernism, Male Intimacy, and the Great War." *ELH* 68.2 (2001): 469–500.

Connell, R. W. *Masculinities*. Berkeley: University of California Press, 1995.

_____. *The Men and the Boys*. Berkeley: University of California Press, 2000.

Costello, John. *Virtue Under Fire: How World War II Changed Our Social and Sexual Attitudes*. Boston: Little, Brown, 1985.

Cuordileone, K. A. "Politics in the Age of Anxiety: Cold War Political Culture and the Crisis in American Masculinity, 1949–1960." *Journal of American History* 87.2 (September 2000): 1–25.

Das, Santanu. " 'Kiss Me, Hardy': Intimacy, Gender, and Gesture in World War I Trench Literature." *Modernism/Modernity* 9.1 (2002): 51–74.

D'Emilio, John. *Sexual Politics, Sexual Communities: The Making of a Homosexual Minority in the United States, 1940–1970*. Chicago: University of Chicago Press, 1983.

D'Emilio, John, and Estelle B. Freedman. *Intimate Matters: A History of Sexuality in America*. 2nd ed. Chicago: University of Chicago Press, 1997.

Devine, Jeremy M. *Vietnam at 24 Frames a Second*. Austin: University of Texas Press, 1999.

Dick, Bernard. *The Star-Spangled Screen: The American World War II Film*. New ed. Lexington: University of Kentucky Press, 1985.

Doherty, Thomas. *Projections of War: Hollywood, American Culture, and World War II*. Rev. ed. New York: Columbia University Press, 1999.

Dyer, Richard. "*Papillon*." In *The Matter of Images: Essays on Representation*, 126–132. New York: Routledge, 1993.

Easthope, Anthony. *What a Man's Gotta Do: The Masculine Myth in Popular Culture*. Boston: Unwin Hymen, 1990.

Eberwein, Robert, ed. *The War Film*. New Brunswick, N.J.: Rutgers University Press, 2004.

Ehrenreich, Barbara. *Blood Rites: Origins and History of the Passions of War*. New York: Henry Holt, 1997.

Fuchs, Cynthia J. " 'Vietnam and Sexual Violence': The Movie." In *America Rediscovered: Critical Essays on Literature and Film of the Vietnam War*, ed. Owen W. Gilman Jr. and Lorrie Smith, 120–133. New York: Garland, 1990.

Fussell, Paul. *The Great War and Modern Memory*. New York: Oxford University Press, 2002.

_____. *Wartime: Understanding and Behavior in the Second World War*. New York: Oxford University Press, 1989.

Garber, Marjorie. *Vested Interests: Cross-Dressing and Cultural Anxiety*. New York: Harper Perennial, 1993.

Goldstein, Joshua. *War and Gender: How Gender Shapes the War System and Vice Versa*. Cambridge: Cambridge University Press, 2001.

Gray, J. Glenn. *The Warriors: Reflections on Men in Battle*. Lincoln: University of Nebraska Press, 1998.

Grossman, David. *On Killing: The Psychological Cost of Learning to Kill in War and Society*. Boston: Little, Brown, 1995.

Gubar, Susan. " 'This Is My Rifle, This Is My Gun': World War II and the Blitz on Women." In *Behind the Lines: Gender and the Two World Wars*, ed. Margaret Randolph Higonet, Jane Jenson, Sonya Michel, and Margaret Collins Weitz, 226–259. New Haven, Conn.: Yale University Press, 1987.

Halley, Janet E. *Don't: A Reader's Guide to the Military's Anti-Gay Policy*. Durham, N.C.: Duke University Press, 1999.

Herek, Gregory M., Jared B. Jobe, and Ralph M. Carney. *Out in Force: Sexual Orientation and the Military*. Chicago: University of Chicago Press, 1996.

Hoganson, Kristen L. *Fighting for American Manhood: How Gender Politics Provoked the Spanish-American and Philippine-American Wars*. New Haven, Conn.: Yale University Press, 1998.

Isenberg, Michael T. *War on Film: The American Cinema and World War I*. East Brunswick, N.J.: Fairleigh Dickinson University Press, 1981.

Jackson, Stevi, and Sue Scott. "Sexual Skirmishes and Feminist Factors: Twenty-five Years of Debate on Women and Sexuality." In *Feminism and Sexuality: A Reader*, ed. Stevi Jackson and Sue Scott, 1–31. New York: Columbia University Press, 1996.

Jarvis, Christina S. *The Male Body at War: American Masculinity during World War II*. De Kalb: Northern Illinois University Press, 2004.

Jeffords, Susan. *Hard Bodies: Hollywood Masculinity in the Reagan Era*. New Brunswick, N.J.: Rutgers University Press, 1994.

——. *The Remasculinization of America: Gender and the Vietnam War*. Bloomington: Indiana University Press, 1989.

Kaplan, Amy. *The Anarchy of Empire in the Making of U.S. Culture*. Cambridge, Mass.: Harvard University Press, 2002.

Kasson, John F. *Houdini, Tarzan, and the Perfect Man*. New York: Hill and Wang, 2001.

Kimmel, Michael S. *Manhood in America: A Cultural History*. 2nd ed. New York: Oxford University Press, 2006.

Kinney, Katherine. *Friendly Fire: American Images of the Vietnam War*. New York: Oxford University Press, 2000.

Koppes, Clayton, and Gregory D. Black. *Hollywood Goes to War: How Politics, Profits and Propaganda Shaped World War II Movies*. Berkeley: University of California Press, 1987.

Lehman, Peter. *Running Scared: Masculinity and the Representation of the Male Body*. Philadelphia: Temple University Press, 1993.

Lehring, Gary L. *Officially Gay: The Political Construction of Sexuality by the U.S. Military*. Philadelphia: Temple University Press, 2003.

Linderman, Gerald F. *The World within War: American's Combat Experience in World War II*. New York: Free Press, 1997.

Loughery, John. *The Other Side of Silence: Men's Lives and Gay Identities: A Twentieth-Century History*. New York: Henry Holt, 1998.

Martin, Colin J., and Martin S. Weinberg. *Homosexuals and the Military*. New York: Harper and Row, 1971.

McBride, James. *War, Battering, and Other Sports: The Gulf between Men and Women*. Atlantic Highlands, N.J.: Humanities Press, 1995.

Mellen, Joan. *Big Bad Wolves: Masculinity in the American Film*. New York: Pantheon, 1977.

Musser, Charles. *Before the Nickelodeon: Edwin S. Porter and the Edison Manufacturing Company*. Berkeley: University of California Press, 1991.

——. *The Emergence of Cinema: The American Screen to 1907*. New York: Charles Scribner's Sons, 1990.

National Research Council. *Psychology for the Fighting Man: What You Should Know about Yourself and Others*. Washington, D.C.: Infantry Journal, 1943.

Neale, Steve. *Genre and Hollywood*. London: Routledge, 2000.

_____. "Masculinity as Spectacle: Reflections on Men and Mainstream Cinema." *Screen* 24.6 (1983): 2–17.

Newsinger, John. " 'Do You Walk the Walk?' Aspects of Masculinity in Some Vietnam War Films." In *You Tarzan: Movies and Men*, ed. Pat Kirkham and Janet Thumim, 126–136. New York: St. Martin's Press, 1993.

Norden, Martin. *The Cinema of Isolation: A History of Physical Disability in the Movies*. New Brunswick, N.J.: Rutgers University Press, 1994.

Person, Ethyl Spector. *The Sexual Century*. New Haven, Conn.: Yale University Press, 1998.

Polan, Dana. *Power and Paranoia: History, Narrative, and the American Cinema, 1940–1950*. New York: Columbia University Press, 1986.

Ramlow, Todd. "Review of *Ride with the Devil*." http://www.popmatters.com/film/reviews/r/ride/ride-with-the-devil2.shtml.

Robert Crown Law Library. "Don't Ask, Don't Tell, Don't Pursue" Database. http://dont.stanford.edu.

Rogin, Michael. *Blackface, White Noise: Jewish Immigrants in the Hollywood Melting Pot*. Berkeley: University of California Press, 1996.

Rotundo, E. Anthony. *American Manhood: Transformations in Masculinity from the Revolution to the Modern Era*. New York: Basic Books, 1993.

Russo, Vito. *The Celluloid Closet: Homosexuality in the Movies*. Rev. ed. New York: Harper and Row, 1987.

Savran, David. *Taking It Like a Man: White Masculinity, Masochism, and Contemporary Culture*. Princeton, N.J.: Princeton University Press, 1998.

Schatz, Thomas. "Old War/New War: *Band of Brothers* and the Revival of the World War II Film." *Film and History* 32.1 (2002): 74–78.

Sedgwick, Eve Kosofsky. *Between Men: English Literature and Male Homosocial Desire*. New York: Columbia University Press, 1985.

Servicemembers Legal Defense Network. "About Don't Ask, Don't Tell." http://www.sldn.org/templates/dont/record.html?section=42&record=749.

Showalter, Elaine. *The Female Malady: Women, Madness, and English Culture, 1830–1980*. New York: Pantheon, 1985.

Silverman, Kaja. *Male Subjectivity at the Margins*. New York: Routledge, 1992.

Simpson, Mark. *Male Impersonators: Men Performing Masculinity*. New York: Routledge, 1994.

Spoto, Donald. *Camerado: Hollywood and the American Man*. New York: Plume, 1978.

Steichen, Edward. *The Blue Ghost*. New York: Harcourt, Brace, 1947.

Straayer, Chris. *Deviant Eyes, Deviant Bodies: Sexual Re-Orientation in Film and Video*. New York: Columbia University Press, 1996.

Suid, Lawrence. *Guts and Glory: The Making of the American Military Image in Film*. Rev. ed. Lexington: University of Kentucky Press, 2002.

Swofford, Anthony. *Jarhead: A Marine's Chronicle of the Gulf War and Other Battles*. New York: Scribner, 2003.

Terkel, Studs. *The Good War: An Oral History of World War Two*. New York: Pantheon, 1984.

Theweleit, Klaus. *Male Fantasies*. Vol. 1, *Women, Floods, Bodies, History*. Trans. Stephen Conway. Minneapolis: University of Minnesota Press, 1987.

_____. *Male Fantasies*. Vol. 2, *Male Bodies: Psychoanalyzing the White Terror*. Trans. Erica Carter and Chris Turner. Minneapolis: University of Minnesota Press, 1989.

Turner, Victor. *The Ritual Process: Structure and Anti-Structure*. Chicago: Aldine, 1969.

Tyler, Parker. *Screening the Sexes: Homosexuality in the Movies*. New York: Da Capo, 1993.

Walsh, Frank. *Sin and Censorship: The Catholic Church and the Motion Picture Industry.* New Haven, Conn.: Yale University Press, 1996.

Watts, Sarah. *Rough Rider in the White House: Theodore Roosevelt and the Politics of Desire.* Chicago: University of Chicago Press, 2003.

Whissel, Kristen. "The Gender of Empire: American Modernity, Masculinity, and Edison's War Actualities." In *A Feminist Reader in Early Cinema*, ed. Jennifer M. Bean and Diane Negra, 141–165. Durham, N.C.: Duke University Press, 2002.

White, Kevin. *The First Sexual Revolution: The Emergence of Male Heterosexuality in Modern America.* New York: New York University Press, 1993.

Wills, Garry. *John Wayne's America: The Politics of Celebrity.* New York: Simon and Schuster, 1997.

INDEX

Page numbers in italics indicate illustrations.

ABOUT THE AUTHOR

Robert Eberwein is Distinguished Professor of English at Oakland University, Rochester, Michigan. He is the author of *Sex Ed: Film, Video, and the Framework of Desire* and the editor of *The War Film.*